UNEMPLOYMENT: A DISEQUILIBRIUM APPROACH

UNEMPLOYMENT: A DISEQUILIBRIUM APPROACH

Mark Casson

A HALSTED PRESS BOOK
John Wiley & Sons · New York

Published in the United States of America
by Halsted Press, a Division of
John Wiley & Sons, Inc., New York

Library of Congress Cataloging in Publication Data

Casson, Mark, 1945—
    Unemployment, a disequilibrium approach.

    "A Halsted Press book."
    Bibliography: p.
    Includes index.
    1. Macroeconomics. 2. Unemployment.
3. Equilibrium (Economics) 4. Full employment
policies. I. Title
HB172.5.C38   1981   339.5'0973   81-4442
ISBN 0-470-27179-5   AACR2

Printed in Great Britain

CONTENTS

PREFACE   ix

NOTATION AND ABBREVIATIONS   xi

LIST OF FIGURES   xv

CHAPTER 1   UNEMPLOYMENT: CONCEPTS AND
            DEFINITIONS   1
            1.1   Scope of the study   1
            1.2   The central issues   2
            1.3   The dimension of unemployment   6
            1.4   Definition of unemployment   9
            1.5   Voluntary and involuntary unemployment   12
            1.6   Plan of the book   14

CHAPTER 2   THE MULTI-MARKET ECONOMY   16
            2.1   Two schemes of macroeconomic thought   16
            2.2   Methodology of macro-modelling   18
            2.3   Generalized Walras' Law   20
            2.4   General equilibrium   22
            2.5   The Mark I production model   24
            2.6   The addi-log case*   29

CHAPTER 3   ELEMENTS OF DISEQUILIBRIUM THEORY   33
            3.1   The disequilibrium principle   33
            3.2   Walras and Edgeworth on competitive
                  adjustment   35
            3.3   Two aspects of price adjustment   37
            3.4   Realized excess demand as a market signal   38
            3.5   Competitive disequilibrium   40

3.6   Disequilibrium and classical unemployment
      − a comparative static analysis   43
3.7   Dynamics of disequilibrium   48
3.8   Investment, liquidity and bankruptcy   51

CHAPTER 4   MONEY   54
      4.1   Definition of money   54
      4.2   Money as a medium of exchange   55
      4.3   Bank deposits   57
      4.4   A critique of the parable of barter   59
      4.5   Reasons for bilateral and sequential trading   62
      4.6   Transactions costs, disequilibrium trading,
            and the entrepreneurial demand for money   64
      4.7   Money as a store of value   66
      4.8   Two concepts of liquidity   67
      4.9   Money and real assets   70
      4.10 Money as a unit of account and unit of
            denomination   72
      4.11 Summary   74

CHAPTER 5   DEMAND-DEFICIENCY IN A MONETARY
            ECONOMY   76
      5.1   The Mark II monetary model   76
      5.2   Disequilibrium in a monetary economy   82
      5.3   The perception of quantity constraints 87
      5.4   Repressed inflation*   88
      5.5   The dynamics of adjustment*   91

CHAPTER 6   THE ROLE OF INTEREST RATES   96
      6.1   Introduction   96
      6.2   The Mark III model of intertemporal choice   99
      6.3   Constrained equilibrium: an IS/LM analysis   105
      6.4   Keynes and IS/LM theory: a comparison   108
      6.5   Full employment equilibrium in the addi-log
            case*   112
      6.6   Unemployment equilibrium in the addi-log
            case*   117

CHAPTER 7   INVESTMENT*   123
      7.1   The Mark IV model   123

7.2 The motives for investment 125
7.3 Investment policy 127
7.4 Macroeconomic implications 133
7.5 The compatibility of expectations 136
7.6 Unemployment due to investment deficiency 138

CHAPTER 8 QUANTITY ADJUSTMENT VERSUS PRICE
ADJUSTMENT 141
8.1 Limitations of the non-recontracting approach 141
8.2 Quantity adjustment as an optimizing policy 142
8.3 Oligopoly 144
8.4 Goodwill theory I: Price stability as insurance 147
8.5 Goodwill theory II: Price stability as a
quit-deterrent 149
8.6 Goodwill theory III: Price stability as an adjunct
to advertising 152
8.7 Quantity determination in the goodwill model 153

CHAPTER 9 WAGE RIGIDITY 156
9.1 Limitations of the goodwill theory 156
9.2 The role of trade unions 157
9.3 The living wage 159
9.4 Wage differentials and the occupational
hierarchy 160
9.5 Downward money wage rigidity 162
9.6 The Mark V model of a dichotomized labour
market* 164
9.7 Unemployment and its incidence in the Mark V
model 166

CHAPTER 10 PROFIT EXPECTATIONS 170
10.1 Introduction 170
10.2 The unpredictability of planned profit 171
10.3 Profit expectations in a non-monetary
economy 174
10.4 Evaluation of the profit expectations model 177
10.5 Profit expectations in a monetary economy 180
10.6 Relevance of profit expectations 183
10.7 Summary 185

CHAPTER 11 DYNAMICS OF EMPLOYMENT AND OUTPUT*   188
    11.1 Introduction   188
    11.2 Household expectations of income   189
    11.3 Firm's output and investment policy   190
    11.4 Inventory investment   192
    11.5 The multiplier-accelerator model   195
    11.6 A theory of inventory fluctuation   198
    11.7 Dynamics of administered prices   200
    11.8 Expectations and information networks   202

CHAPTER 12 SUMMARY AND POLICY IMPLICATIONS   205
    12.1 Summary   205
    12.2 Alternative explanations of registered
          unemployment   209
    12.3 Curing unemployment   215
    12.4 Curing stagflation: prices and incomes policies 217
    12.5 Curing stagflation through higher productivity   222
    12.6 Limitations of demand management   224
    12.7 Implications for future policy   227
    12.8 Implications for future research   228

BIBLIOGRAPHICAL REVIEW by Eleanor Moses   231

NOTES   236

REFERENCES   245

INDEX   259

PREFACE

This book has three main objects: to introduce the reader to disequilibrium theory, which is a new and very important branch of macroeconomics; to present original developments of disequilibrium theory, based on a synthesis of the theory with the theory of implicit contracts, the theory of industrial market structure and the theory of inventory behaviour; and finally to put forward policy recommendations for reducing unemployment under conditions of stagflation – conditions which currently prevail in most Western market economies.

The early part of the book is based on lectures given at Reading University to single-subject economics students in their second year. The book assumes a knowledge of basic microeconomic theory (supply and demand, the determinants of household consumption etc.) and of elementary macroeconomic theory (the Keynesian 45°-line diagram and IS/LM analysis). Only very limited use is made of mathematics: the most that is required is an understanding of partial derivatives, and a knowledge of the rank conditions for the solution of simultaneous equations (that is the relation between the number of equations and unknowns).

As its title suggests, this book is concerned with a particular aspect of macroeconomics, namely the determinants of the aggregate level of employment. Although the relation between employment and inflation is discussed, inflation itself does not have a central role in the analysis. Perhaps the most important omission is a consideration of the international dimension of unemployment. This is not because the international aspect is held to be unimportant, but rather because it is so important that it warrants separate treatment in its own right. The days are past when the international aspects of macroeconomics could be dealt with simply by appending a chapter to analysis of a closed economy. Important work has already been done on the international aspects of macroeconomic disequilibrium, and full justice could not be done to this literature within the scope of the present volume.

The core of the analysis is contained in Chapters 1, 3, 5 and 8–12. Chapters 2 and 4 are for readers who require an introduction to general equilibrium theory and monetary theory respectively, while Chapters 6 and 7 elaborate upon the basic macroeconomic model presented in Chapter 5. There are some sections which are relatively technical, and which could be omitted on a first reading without serious loss of continuity; these sections are indicated by an asterisk.

In writing this book I have benefitted greatly from discussions with Henri Lorie during his visit to Reading. He has debunked many of the ideas that were to have appeared in the book, and I am not sure that he entirely agrees with the ideas that have actually been included. Without his stimulus and help, however, this book could not have been written.

A number of people have been kind enough to read the manuscript, and I am grateful to them for their comments; in particular I wish to thank Paul Cheshire, John Creedy, Frances Dakers, Peter Hart, Geoffrey Maynard, Eleanor Moses, Ralph Musgrave and Colin Wimsett. Once again, I am grateful to my wife, Janet, for vetting the manuscript in the interests of the general reader. Finally, thanks are due to Joan Horton and Nicole Collis for typing the two drafts so accurately and efficiently.

NOTATION AND ABBREVIATIONS

The numbers in bold face indicate the section in which the symbol is first introduced. Superscripts and subscripts are listed separately at the end.

a physical depreciation of the capital stock, **9.1**;
also autonomous household consumption, **11.5**

b real value of bonds, **6.2**

c real consumption, **2.5**; also the marginal propensity to consume, **11.5**

d real dividend payment, **7.1**; also the price-sensitivity of final demand, **11.7**

e exogenous change in households' expectation of wage income, **11.2**

f exogenous change in households' expectation of non-wage income, **11.2**

g real government expenditure, **5.1**

h maximum number of hours that can be worked, **2.6**

i firms' real gross investment, **7.1**

j ratio of households' nominal money balances to nominal consumption expenditure, **5.1**

k firms' real capital stock, **7.1**

m real money balances, **5.1**

$\dot{m}$ increment in real money balances, **5.1**

n employment (man hours), **1.5**

q household real wealth, including the imputed value of leisure, **6.5**

q' household real wealth, excluding the imputed value of leisure, **6.6**

r money rate of interest, **6.2**

r' $= r/(1 + r)$, **6.6**

s real saving, exclusive of retained profit, **6.2**

s' real saving, inclusive of retained profit, **7.4**

t	real tax payment from household to government, **5.1**
u	utility of the representative household, **2.5**
u_1	unemployment (relative to full employment norm), **1.5**
u_2	unemployment (relative to realized excess supply of labour), **1.5**
v	capital–output ratio, **11.2**
w	real wage, **1.5**
x	real value of household wealth inherited at the beginning of period 1, **6.2**
y	output, **2.3**
z	net excess demand, **2.3**
B	nominal value of bonds, **6.2**
D	nominal dividend payment, **7.1**
G	nominal government expenditure, **5.1**
M	nominal money balances, **5.1**
$\dot{M}$	increment in nominal money balances, **5.1**
P	money price, **2.3**
$\dot{P}$	rate of price inflation between period 0 and period 1, **6.2**
T	nominal tax payment from household to government, **5.1**
U	money price of bonds, **6.2**
V	nominal equity valuation of the firm, **7.3**
W	money wage, **2.3**
X	household nominal wealth, **6.5**
α	parameter associated with the consumer good in the household utility function, **2.6**; also the intercept of the firm's competitive supply curve, **11.7**
β	parameter associated with leisure in the household utility function, **2.6**; also the slope of the firm's competitive supply curve, **11.7**
γ	parameter associated with j in the household utility function, **6.5**
δ	parameter associated with x in the household utility function, **6.5**; also the firm's estimate of the price-sensitivity of final demand, **11.7**
ϵ	$= \alpha + \delta$, **6.6**
ζ	$= (\alpha - \gamma)/(\gamma + \delta)$, **6.6**
η	$= \epsilon/\gamma$, **6.6**
θ	post-tax discrepancy between constrained profit income and constrained consumption under repressed inflation, **5.4**
θ_1	$= \tfrac{1}{2}(c + v + \tau)$, **11.5**
θ_2	$= \tfrac{1}{2}(c + v - \tau)$, **11.5**

ι	exogenous change in household expectation of total income, **11.5**
χ	proportional differential in the basic wage of skilled and unskilled work, **9.7**
λ	partial adjustment coefficient for household income expectations, **11.2**
μ	partial adjustment coefficient for firms' sales expectations, **11.3**
ξ	partial adjustment coefficient for firms' expectations of final demand, **11.4**
π	real profit, **2.5**
ρ	implicit real rate of interest, **6.2**
σ	exogenous change in government expenditure, **11.5**
τ	$= \sqrt{[(c + v)^2 - 4v]}$, **11.5**
ν	parameter of returns to labour in the production function, **2.6**
ϕ	exogenous change in firms' expectation of final demand, **11.4**
ψ	exogenous change in firms' target capital stock, **11.4**
ω	exogenous change in consumer demand, **11.5**
Σ	summation, **2.3**
Π	money profit, **2.3**

Subscripts

b	bond market, **6.2**
m	money market, **5.1**
n	labour market, **5.1**
q	qualified labour, **9.6**
s	skilled labour, **9.6**
t	time period, **11.2**
uq	unqualified labour, **9.6**
us	unskilled labour, **9.6**
y	product market, **5.1**

Superscripts

d	nominal demand, **1.5**
e	full employment equilibrium, **1.5**
f	planned or expected by the firm, **2.3**
g	guaranteed level, **9.6**
h	planned or expected by the household, **2.3**
s	nominal supply, **1.5**
D	effective demand, **5.2**

E   constrained equilibrium, **5.2**
F   constrained quantity planned or expected by the firm, **5.2**
H   constrained quantity expected by the household, **5.2**
K   Keynesian equilibrium, **6.6**
S   effective supply, **5.2**

Abbreviations
GE   general equilibrium, **2.3**
GWL generalized Walras' law, **2.3**
SWL   simple Walras' law, **2.3**

LIST OF FIGURES

1.1 Concept and measurement of unemployment 10
2.1 Simultaneous equilibrium in product and factor markets 27
2.2 Output, employment and income distribution in general equilibrium 28
2.3 Properties of the addi-log utility function 31
3.1 Trading at the 'short end' of the market: partial analysis 42
3.2 Unemployment due to an excessive real wage 44
3.3 Underemployment due to a too-low real wage 46
5.1 Equilibrium conditions for a monetary economy 80
5.2 Demand-deficiency unemployment due to a too-high money price level 86
5.3 The supply multiplier 90
5.4 Taxonomy of equilibrium states 92
6.1 Money interest rate and money price level in full employment equilibrium 103
6.2 IS/LM analysis, showing the effect of a reduction in expected profit 106
6.3 Reduced form of the Keynesian model 110
6.4 Full employment equilibrium in the addi-log case 114
6.5 Unemployment equilibrium with fixed money wage and fixed money price in the addi-log case 119
6.6 Keynesian unemployment equilibrium in the addi-log case 121
7.1 Intertemporal equilibrium of the firm 130
8.1 Oligopolistic equilibrium: the 'kinked' demand curve 145
8.2 The goodwill model: partial analysis of the product market 154
8.3 The goodwill model: partial analysis of the labour market 155
10.1 Unemployment due to pessimistic profit expectations 175
10.2 Effect of a real wage cut on unemployment 179
12.1 The neoclassical approach to unemployment 211

CHAPTER 1

UNEMPLOYMENT: CONCEPTS AND DEFINITIONS

1.1 SCOPE OF THE STUDY

This book is concerned with aggregate unemployment. It is not concerned with the distribution of unemployment by region or industry, nor with the personal characteristics of the unemployed.

The approach is essentially macroeconomic. The object is to explain unemployment in terms of economy-wide changes in variables such as the general level of money wages, changes in the prevailing state of expectation, and so on. There is no attempt to explain unemployment in terms of factors specific to some individuals and not to others. Thus there is no discussion of variations in aggregate unemployment which are attributable to the changing fortunes of minority groups of workers with special employment problems.

The analysis involves a number of simplifying assumptions, the most important of which is that individual households (and individual firms too, for that matter) are similar to each other. This assumption makes it easy to derive macroeconomic relations from an analysis of individual behaviour, something which is essential if the logical consistency of macroeconomic relations is to be established rigorously. Unfortunately this same assumption makes it impossible to analyse properly unemployment which stems from the heterogeneity of workers or their jobs. In practice not all workers are equally suitable for the same job, nor are all jobs equally suitable for a given worker. For example, young workers are not always suitable for very responsible jobs, nor are older workers suitable for strenuous manual work. Even in an economy with a stationary population, job changing will occur as young people who have gained experience take more responsible jobs, aging manual workers move to lighter work, and so on. If there are delays between leaving one job and starting another then some of these workers will become

1

frictionally unemployed. Although our analysis considers certain macro-economic aspects of frictional unemployment, a comprehensive analysis of this aspect of unemployment is outside the scope of the book.

The focus of the analysis is a representative market economy. We are not concerned with centrally planned economies, nor with economies in which tradition or social hierarchy exert a predominant influence on the allocation of resources. This means that our formal models are not applicable to socialist economies, nor to the typical agrarian or less-developed economy. Notwithstanding this, the analysis affords a number of insights into the way that differences in economic and social organization determine the prevalence of unemployment under alternative economic systems.

1.2 THE CENTRAL ISSUES

The main issues addressed are the following:

1. Is unemployment purely the result of frictions and other problems peculiar to the labour market? Or is it the result of a more general kind of market failure which pervades the entire economy?
2. If the latter, then what are the precise causes of unemployment? Is unemployment endemic to certain types of economy, for example economies with divorce of ownership and control of production, monetary economies, etc.?
3. Can unemployment in market economies be avoided, and if so what are the appropriate policies? How sensitive is the success of a policy to the correct diagnosis of the cause of unemployment?

The first issue has been the centre of controversy between three leading schools of thought: the classical, neoclassical and Keynesian schools.

Classical economics was a term used by Keynes to denote the views of leading pre-Keynesian writers such as W. S. Jevons, A. Marshall and A. C. Pigou.[1] Classical economists believe that, with the possible exception of the labour market, the economy is basically competitive. While they admit that competition applies in a literal sense to few if any markets, classical economists argue that because 'every commodity has a substitute', competition is still a useful working hypothesis in the analysis of a market economy.

The second important element in the classical model is that in the long run the real and monetary sectors of the economy are effectively dichotomized. Employment and output are determined in the labour and product markets, which constitute a closed system in which equilibrium in one market implies equilibrium in the other. A change in the money supply changes the level of money prices but leaves output and employment unaffected. There is a possible connection between the real and money sectors *via* the capital market but it is only a very weak one. Changes in the money rate of interest may affect the real rate of interest, which in the classical model equilibrates saving and investment in the capital market. This may alter the composition of output as between consumption and investment goods, but so long as money prices are flexible, total output, and hence total employment, will remain virtually unchanged.

Neoclassical economics maintains the tradition of the classical school, but makes even stricter assumptions about the labour market.[2] Classical writers in the 1930s did not believe that the real wage was flexible and competitively determined. They favoured the view that workers, or the trade unions representing them, stipulated for a real wage above the equilibrium level, and they regarded this as the basic cause of unemployment. For this reason unemployment due to a too-high real wage is often referred to as 'classical unemployment'.

Neoclassical economists do not accept that rigidities in the real wage can persist in the long run. They argue that in the long-run competitive forces will adjust the real wage to a level which equates the demand and supply for labour, thereby eliminating any unemployment. Long-run deviations from equilibrium are to be explained principally by unemployment benefit payments. Unemployment benefit subsidizes leisure and encourages registration for benefit by those who are not seriously seeking work. Unemployment may also result from frictions encountered by workers when they seek to change jobs. Workers become frictionally unemployed because of the advantage of searching full time when seeking a higher paid job. Job search contributes to efficiency in the allocation of labour, and is associated with a 'natural rate' of unemployment. Fluctuations about the natural rate occur because of changes in workers' expectations of the money wage. Over optimistic expectations encourage job search, and thereby cause unemployment to rise above its natural rate; conversely pessimistic expectations cause unemployment to fall below its natural rate.

Despite this difference of emphasis in the analysis of the labour market, the classical and neoclassical approaches are basically similar. In particular, both classical and neoclassical theories are partial in their approach. They seek explanations of unemployment in factors peculiar to the labour market. The repercussions of these factors on other parts of the economic system, and consequent feedbacks on the labour market, are assumed to be negligible.

This partial approach was rejected by Keynes. He focused his criticism on the classical view that a cut in the money wage would be sufficient to restore full employment. A cut in the money wage will only increase employment in so far as it reduces the real wage. The real wage will fall only if money prices remain fixed, or do not fall by as much as the money wage. But, Keynes argued, other things being equal prices will fall in proportion to the money wage. For in the short run labour is the only variable factor of production. Thus labour cost accounts for the entire marginal cost of production, and so in a competitive economy it is labour cost that governs the supply price of each product. If money wages were cut product prices would fall unless there were a simultaneous increase in product demand. If no additional demand were forthcoming, product prices would fall in the same proportion as the money wage, and the real wage would remain unchanged. Keynes inferred that because the wage is denominated in money terms, the real wage can be reduced only by an increase in product demand, which raises product prices relative to the money wage. Thus only if product demand is stimulated will the real wage fall and employment increase.

According to Keynes, a deficiency of product demand is due to a lack of business confidence. Lack of confidence encourages transactors to hold money instead of real assets. This depresses the money valuation of the existing stock of real assets, and discourages the demand for real investment. At the same time it encourages transactors to accumulate money balances, which they attempt to do by the simple expedient of spending less than they earn. Thus the demand for additional money balances increases while the demand for real investment is reduced. Additional demand for money balances does not call forth additional production of money in the same way that additional investment demand calls forth additional production in the capital goods industries; consequently aggregate product demand is depressed.[3]

While many people would accept that the Keynesian model provides a better account of short-run unemployment than do either the classical or neoclassical theories, very few people find the Keynesian account of unemployment entirely satisfactory. The model embodies a number of quite different strands of thought which it fails to integrate properly. It is difficult to disentangle these strands to find where the 'ultimate cause' of unemployment lies. The interpretation above has stressed the role of business confidence, and its impact on the relative valuation of assets. Other interpretations emphasise liquidity preference, the consumption function or the downward rigidity of the money wage.

The question of ultimate causes introduces the second of the issues mentioned above. One school of thought regards the existence of money as the ultimate cause of unemployment because, it is argued, unemployment could not arise in a barter economy. A related idea is that unemployment is a consequence of market failure. It is argued that in a changing economic environment the maintenance of full employment calls for forward contracts in labour, and perhaps in other commodities as well. It is through negotiations over such contracts that producers and consumers signal their intentions to each other. But because of defects in the law it is prohibitively expensive to organise and enforce such contracts. Thus negotiations do not take place, the information is not transmitted, and the result is unemployment.

Another long-standing tradition, from which professional economists have remained aloof, is that unemployment is a consequence of specializing the ownership and/or management of production. It is argued that while corporate organization may be necessary to exploit economies of large scale production, it weakens the link between the household as supplier of labour and the household as consumer of goods. The intermediation of the firm disrupts the flow of wealth, and leads to unemployment. We shall argue in later chapters that while previous formulations of these ideas are unsatisfactory, there is a germ of truth in them which is capable of rigorous expression.

The final issue is very much in the domain of political economy. In broad terms the issue is whether unemployment is best avoided by strengthening competitive forces through improvements in market efficiency, or by constraining or modifying market forces through interventionist policies. The first strategy represents a move toward pure economic liberalism, the second is closely identified with the 'regulated' or 'controlled' economy.

There is a broad consensus among liberals on the policies required to improve market efficiency. They call for legal reforms to eliminate potential 'externalities' by widening the scope of property rights, institutional reforms to reduce transaction costs by improving the monitoring and enforcement of contracts, organizational reforms to increase the extent and quality of information available to transactors, and so on. The main area of disagreement concerns the need for an active competition policy: should the state intervene to break up monopolies (in particular trade unions and cartels) or can long-run competitive forces be relied upon to prevent the sustained exercise of monopoly power?

In the early post-war period interventionist thinking dominated the policy field. Impatience with long-run competitive forces was apparent in the popularity of the Keynesian maxim that 'in the long-run we are all dead'. Consequently various interventionist instruments were developed: monetary policy, fiscal policy (involving both expenditure and taxation), prices and incomes policies, and planning agreements. The liberal attitude to monetary policy was somewhat ambivalent; on the whole liberals were content if monetary policy were the only form of intervention used – particularly if the policy were to hold the money supply constant, or merely adjust it to accommodate the growth of output. The most intense debate has therefore centred on whether such 'orthodox' monetary policies are sufficient to maintain the economy close to full employment.

This book does not attempt to reach any general conclusions about the superiority of any one policy. Rather it is concerned to establish that the type of policy that is appropriate depends crucially on the type of unemployment that is to be dealt with. It is suggested, however, that the current stagflation afflicting Western economies contains elements of both Keynesian and classical unemployment. In the light of this a long-term policy is proposed which involves two instruments: one to increase employment and the other to suppress inflation. Employment would be stabilized by making the government employer of last resort; the effect of this would be to make demand management automatic, rather than discretionary as at present. Inflation would be controlled by a wages policy, designed not to freeze money wages, but to adjust real wages and occupational wage differentials in accordance with criteria established through a political process.

1.3 THE DIMENSION OF UNEMPLOYMENT

Unemployment may be measured either by the number of workers wholly unemployed, or by the number of man-hours normally worked which are spent idle. Unemployment statistics are usually based on the numbers of wholly unemployed, though statistics of short-time working are also published.[4]

The macroeconomic effects of short-time working and full-time unemployment differ in at least two respects. Suppose we compare a 10 per cent reduction in working hours with a situation in which 10 per cent of the workforce is wholly unemployed and the remainder work normal hours. To begin with, the inequality of personal incomes is likely to be greater in the second case than in the first, and this will have implications for aggregate consumption and labour supply. Taking the first case as the norm, the wholly unemployed in the second case constitute a very poor minority, while the fully employed are a relatively wealthy majority. When aggregated, the product demands and labour supplies of the very poor and the relatively rich may be quite different from the scaled up demands and supplies of the medium-income short-time workers. This applies even if all households have identical preferences; the results in the two cases are the same only if the preferences common to the households satisfy very stringent conditions.[5]

A second consideration stems from imperfections in capital markets.[6] In a perfect capital market any household can borrow or lend unlimited amounts of money at the same market-determined interest rate. Thus the unemployed worker can finance his consumption by borrowing against future wage income. But in practice lenders are exposed to a risk of default, and so to cover themselves they set a margin between borrowing and lending rates. Also since the risk of default increases with the amount borrowed by any one individual, the borrower is faced with a rate which increases with respect to the amount borrowed. The borrowing needs of the wholly unemployed are much greater than the needs of those on short-time working, but just because their needs are greater the borrowing rate they must pay is likely to be almost prohibitive. It follows that the wholly unemployed are unable to finance as much consumption as they would like to, given their employment prospects. They may be able to finance consumption for a while by running down their cash balances and other financial asset holdings, but eventually these will be exhausted. Being unable to borrow they are forced to reduce their consumption to a level which can be sustained on state benefits. Thus borrowing constraints are likely to be much more important when a proportion of workers is wholly unemployed than when there is general short-time working. Normally product demand will be lower when some workers are wholly unemployed, than when everyone works short-time.

In practice aggregate unemployment usually involves a mixture of people wholly unemployed and people working short-time. In a recession employers face a trade-off between making a proportion of the workforce redundant or introducing short-time working. Similarly workers face a trade-off between short-time working and full-time unemployment. In some segments of the labour market workers and employers may find it mutually beneficial to instigate short-time working, while in other segments employers may prefer to make workers redundant, or workers may prefer to quit.[7]

For both employers and workers the choice between short-time working and full-time unemployment involves trading off the recurrent fixed costs of employment against the costs of turnover. The lower is the recurrent fixed cost, and the higher the cost of turnover, the greater is the incentive for short-time working.

A recurrent fixed cost is a weekly or monthly charge which is independent of the number of hours worked. For the employer, it comprises personnel administration costs and the cost of non-wage benefits such as paid holidays, pension rights, and so on. These costs continue to be incurred by short-time working, but are avoided by redundancy.

Labour turnover imposes two non-recurrent costs on the employer: the cost of redundancy payments, and the cost of hiring and training a replacement (when business recovers). Costs of hiring are related to the responsibility of the job, while the training costs borne by the firm normally depend on the degree of firm-specific skill involved. It is usually assumed that turnover is reduced by substituting short-time working for redundancy; in other words if short-time working is introduced the number of workers who quit is less than the number who would otherwise have been made redundant. If this is so then it is advantageous for the firm to offer short-time working first to those workers with the greatest degree of firm-specific skill.

For the worker the recurrent fixed cost of employment includes the cost of the journey to work, and his inability to take up alternative full-time pursuits (whether leisure activities, or other employment). The cost of job turnover is basically the cost of searching for another job. These costs are likely to increase with the frequency of job changing. Although a frequent job changer may become experienced in methods of search, his chances of re-employment will tend to diminish because rational employers will discriminate against job applicants who seem unable to 'hold down' a job. If the cost of commuting to work is low, and the penalties faced by persistent job changers are high, a worker will prefer short-time working; otherwise he may prefer to quit. Thus depending on their personal circumstances some workers will go onto short-time while others will, at least temporarily, become wholly unemployed.

In subsequent chapters it is assumed that the incidence of unemployment is the same for all workers. This assumption is made for analytical simplicity — to avoid having to distinguish two separate groups of workers, the fully employed and the wholly unemployed. Under this assumption it is only in the extreme case where aggregate employment is zero that anyone becomes wholly unemployed; consequently the appropriate dimension of unemployment is man-hours rather than the number of wholly unemployed. Given the assumed similarity of individual households (p. 1) the man-hours of unemployment for the economy as a whole is directly proportional to the hours of unemployment experienced by the representative household. This is the measure of unemployment which will be used in this book.

1.4 DEFINITION OF UNEMPLOYMENT

There are two aspects to unemployment. The first is that actual employment is below full employment. The second is that there is a realized excess supply of labour.

The concepts of 'full employment' and 'realized excess supply' are usually defined in the context of a competitive labour market. Let us anticipate the analysis of the next chapter, and postulate competitive demand and supply schedules for labour (DD' and SS' in Figure 1.1). Full employment is defined as the level of employment, n^e, at which demand and supply are equal. The first condition for unemployment is therefore that actual employment is $n < n^e$.

The realized excess supply of labour at a given real wage, say w_1, is equal to the excess of supply n^s over actual employment, n (*realised* excess supply is different from excess supply; the latter is the excess of supply, n^s, over demand, n^d — see Chapter 2). The second condition for unemployment is thus that $n < n^s$. The set of wage-employment combinations satisfying both these conditions is illustrated in the figure by the shaded area wSEJ (excluding the right hand boundary, the solid line SEJ).

If the economy is at less than full employment, but there is no realized excess supply of labour, then there is said to be underemployment. The wage-employment combinations associated with underemployment are represented in Figure 1.1 by the area OSEn^e (excluding the right hand boundary En^e).

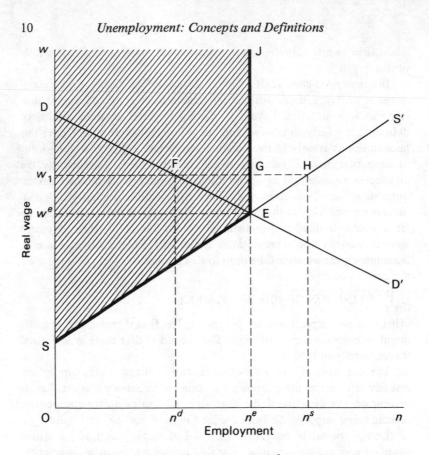

Figure 1.1 Concept and measurement of unemployment

It is also useful to distinguish two situations in which employment exceeds the full employment level. In the first case, known as excess employment, there is a realized excess supply of labour; this is represented in the figure by the interior of the area JES′. The second case, known as overemployment, has no excess supply of labour, and is represented by the area S′E$n^e$$n$ (excluding the left hand boundary En^e).

It should also be noted that the existence of full employment does not necessarily mean that the economy is in equilibrium. Any point on the line Jn^e represents full employment, but only E is a full employment equilibrium. The other points represent disequilibrium states of full employment.

It can be seen that unemployment is a relative concept, based on comparing actual employment with a norm such as full employment or the supply of labour. Each of these norms affords a different measure of unemployment.

The most useful measure of the opportunity cost of unemployment is the short-fall with respect to full employment, $u_1 = n^e - n$. For reasons explained in Chapter 2, the competitive equilibrium which defines full employment is under certain conditions the only efficient level of employment for the economy as a whole. Thus u_1 measures the under-utilization of labour, and hence the loss of output, relative to the efficiency norm. The loss of output is only an approximate measure of opportunity cost, however. Workers benefit from unemployment to the extent that they value the increase in leisure it provides; they lose from it to the extent that they become demoralised, or feel stigmatized by it. Different workers will be affected in different ways, and it is impossible to assess whether the loss of output understates or overstates the cost of unemployment.

In general, workers themselves will not perceive unemployment from the point of view of the efficiency norm. They will measure unemployment in terms of the difference between actual hours worked and the number of hours they would like to work at the prevailing wage. Thus the unemployment perceived by workers is based on the realized excess supply of labour, $u_2 = n^s - n$. This approach is implicit in statistical measures of unemployment based on counts of respondents to household surveys who describe themselves as unemployed because they are actively seeking work at the prevailing wage.

If unemployment is associated with a real wage above the equilibrium value then $n^s > n^e$ and the second measure of unemployment exceeds the first. Thus in Figure 1.1 at $w_1 > w^e$ the supply of labour n^s exceeds demand n^d, and so only n^d workers will actually be employed; thus the wage — employment outcome is represented by F. The shortfall with respect to full employment, u_1, is measured by the length FG, while the realized excess supply, u_2, is measured by the length FH > FG. Statistical counts of the unemployed will overstate the efficiency losses because the high wage will encourage workers to seek work who would not do so at the equilibrium wage. Thus workers who would not wish to work at the equilibrium wage will report themselves as unemployed. Conversely if the real wage is below the equilibrium value the statistical measure of unemployment will understate the efficiency losses because the low wage will deter workers from seeking employment who would do so at the equilibrium wage. It should be noted however that these results will be reversed if the labour supply curve bends backwards at the equilibrium real wage.

Both measures of unemployment will be used in this book. The first measure — the shortfall with respect to full employment — is most useful when discussing fluctuations in the level of employment, for since the full employment norm is fixed in the short run, fluctuations in unemployment are simply mirror images of fluctuations in aggregate employment. It is also the appropriate measure of unemployment when considering welfare implications as a guide to policy. The second measure of unemployment — the realized excess supply of labour — is appropriate when the theory is used to predict statistical counts of the unemployed.

1.5 VOLUNTARY AND INVOLUNTARY UNEMPLOYMENT

The distinction between voluntary and involuntary unemployment has a strong political, and perhaps even moral, aspect. Intuitively, voluntary unemployment is unemployment for which the worker himself is responsible, whereas responsibility for involuntary unemployment lies either with the impersonal forces of the economic system as a whole, or more specifically with those who control the system.

It is perhaps not surprising that attempts to translate the distinction into analytic terms, and to discriminate empirically between the two types of unemployment, have been singularly unsuccessful. It appears that the distinction belongs more to the realm of normative economics than to positive economics.

Keynes defined unemployment as involuntary when the unemployed, though resistant to a cut in money wages, would accept a reduction in the real wage if it were brought about by a general rise in prices.[8] On this view, involuntary unemployment can always be cured by an inflationary policy.

The use of the term 'involuntary', however, to describe a situation in which workers refuse to accept money wage cuts seems rather anomalous. It certainly calls for a close examination of their motives in refusing a cut.

One possibility is that workers suffer from money illusion, and so do not perceive changes in money prices. Hence they stipulate for a money wage when they should be stipulating for a real wage. Another possibility is that workers are concerned with wage relativities; if money wages are fixed in annual rounds, with settlements staggered at different times throughout the year, then anyone who accepts a wage cut is accepting a reduction in his wage relative to others, at least until the others have had their wages reduced too.

Although these are both plausible explanations of why workers may be reluctant to accept a cut in money wages, they do not imply that the individual worker is incapable of recognizing that a reduction in his money wage (particularly a reduction relative to others' wages) might well improve his employment prospects. Of course, the individual worker may not be an entirely free agent. The context of Keynes' analysis suggests that workers stipulate for a minimum money wage negotiated by a trade union. Although individual union members are bound by collective agreements, however, it is possible, in principle, for members to quit the union, if they wish, in order to undercut the negotiated wage. This argument suggests that unemployment as defined by Keynes is involuntary only in so far as workers are bound by social or economic obligations to insist upon the money wages negotiated for them by trade unions.

Another possible interpretation of Keynes is that unemployment is involuntary if a cut in the money wage would fail to restore full employment. Since reducing his money wage is the main weapon by which a worker can improve his job prospects in a competitive labour market, the failure of money-wage cuts to increase employment would indeed make unemployment involuntary. In some passages Keynes suggests that a general reduction in money wages would not increase aggregate employment, and indeed might reduce it.[9] One of his reasons is that a reduction in money wages may lead to an expectation of a further fall in money wages, which would damage business confidence and encourage entrepreneurs to defer investment. He appears to have in mind a statutory wage cut initiated by the government, which carries with it the prospect of further cuts should the first prove insufficient. It is not obvious, however, why the same expectations should be created by competitive wage cuts initiated by individual workers. In any case Keynes' analysis ignores the 'real balance effect' of a cut in wages and prices, which would stimulate aggregate demand. For these reasons little interest now attaches to the concept of involuntary unemployment described above. It is argued later, however, that using a model somewhat different to Keynes', it may be possible to rehabilitate this concept of unemployment.

Another widely held interpretation of involuntary unemployment is that it is unemployment resulting from lay-offs and redundancies. Workers who quit jobs without having another job to go to are assumed to be voluntarily unemployed. This distinction accords with the practice in many countries of paying unemployment benefit immediately to those who have been laid off, but deferring benefits to those who quit.

The distinction is not quite so sharp as it may at first seem, however. An important feature of labour contracts is that they generally allow separations (that is quits or redundancies) to occur at short notice from either side. In many cases the notice required is much shorter than the time that would be required if the adjustment costs of either party were to be minimized. This is a consequence of imperfections in the law of labour contract, which damage the interests of both employer and employee. A worker can impose considerable costs on his employer by quitting at short notice. Equally an employer can impose considerable costs on a worker by firing him at short notice. It follows that if either party believes that the other party has a separation in mind then it may be to that party's advantage to precipitate the separation at a time convenient to themselves. Thus workers who expect to be fired may quit, while employers may fire workers who they expect will quit. A worker who quits may therefore argue that he is involuntarily unemployed because if he had not quit he would have been made redundant. Equally a worker may be made redundant because he was thought likely to quit.

Nowadays the widespread practice of redundancy payments makes the tactical aspect of separation even more complex. For example it encourages workers who wish to quit to behave inefficiently or disruptively, and so to precipitate their own redundancy. This strategy is rational whenever the cost of uncertainty about the date of the separation is outweighed by the expected gain from the redundancy payment. But these complications only reinforce the basic argument, which is that the distinction between quits and redundancies has little to do with the voluntary nature of unemployment because the form of separation is very often determined by purely tactical considerations.

1.6 PLAN OF THE BOOK

The remainder of the book falls naturally into three main parts. The next three chapters present preliminary material on three crucial topics: general equilibrium theory, disequilibrium theory and monetary theory. These chapters introduce concepts and definitions which are crucial to the modelling of a monetary economy.

The following chapters, 5–7, develop a model of a monetary economy and examine its behaviour in equilibrium, and in various types of disequilibrium. Chapter 5 presents a simplified version of the Barro and Grossman model, in which households and firms take decisions over a one-period time horizon. Chapter 6 extends the model to allow for intertemporal choice by households, but not by firms. Households have a choice between money and bonds; when money wages and money prices are fixed the model reduces to an IS/LM analysis of income and the rate of interest. Chapter 7 introduces intertemporal choice by firms, in which the focus is on inventory investment rather than investment in illiquid producer durables. The basic properties of the model remain unchanged but the range of possible disturbances to equilibrium is increased. In particular it becomes possible to examine the impact of changes in business confidence on the level of employment and output.

Chapters 8–11 present some original theoretical developments. Chapter 8 develops a theory of market adjustment, whose aim is to synthesize disequilibrium theory with the theory of implicit contracts and the theory of industrial organization. Chapter 9 considers the role of social and cultural constraints in wage bargaining, and assesses their impact on the level of unemployment.

Chapter 10 develops a point which is hinted at in the earlier analysis. This concerns the possibility that household profit expectations may not agree with the profit levels implied by firms' production plans. Information costs which inhibit market adjustment may also prevent households from recognizing the profit implications of changes in firms' production plans. Equally households may revise their expectations of profit income even though firms have not changed their production plans. Although mistaken expectations may be revised quite quickly, their destabilizing effect may be so great that in the meantime realized profit, and income and employment, alter quite substantially.

Chapter 11 combines the analysis of the two preceding chapters to develop a dynamic analysis of output and employment. The model has a number of variants, the simplest of which turns out to be the multiplier – accelerator theory. The shortcomings of this model are well-known, and other variants are discussed which offer a much more sophisticated explanation of fluctuations in income and employment. The key to the alternative models is a theory of the firm which integrates decisions on administered prices and on inventory adjustment.

Chapter 12 returns to the issues raised in the present chapter, and evaluates the classical, neoclassical and Keynesian theories in the light of the current unemployment situation. It is argued that the neoclassical model can explain only a very limited aspect of the current situation, and that there are many aspects which are completely contrary to its predictions. It is suggested that the Keynesian model is correct in all but its assumptions about trade-union behaviour, and that in this respect the classical model is correct.

CHAPTER 2

THE MULTI-MARKET ECONOMY

2.1 TWO SCHEMES OF MACROECONOMIC THOUGHT

Macroeconomics is concerned with modelling the prices and aggregate volumes of the different types of transaction in a market economy. There have been two main approaches to macroeconomics; they may be characterized as the pure and the applied. The pure approach is closely identified with the classical and neoclassical models, the applied approach with the Keynesian one.

The pure approach deduces macroeconomic relations from a small number of fundamental postulates about individual behaviour. Individuals are supposed to be rational egotists: they have consistent preferences, defined over their own consumption, which they optimize by transacting in competitive markets. Markets offer individuals an opportunity for co-ordinating their activities to mutual advantage; at the same time they are a focus of conflict between individuals over the distribution of the gains from co-ordination. The competitive forces create a constant tendency to equilibrium in each market; the simultaneous equilibrium of the interdependent market then determines the price and aggregate volume of transactions in each market.

The applied approach views macroeconomics as a problem-oriented subject, with unemployment the main focus of attention. In particular the postwar interpreters of Keynes – notably Hansen and Klein – have sought to make macroeconomic theory 'relevant', in the sense of giving it immediate practical policy implications.[1] Unfortunately this relevance has been achieved at a certain cost.

Simplified versions of the Keynesian model have been developed on the basis of what appear to be quite *ad hoc* behavioural assumptions. The models are usually presented in terms of a few key functional relations: the consumption function, the liquidity preference function, the marginal efficiency of capital schedule, and so on. These relations are all specified as macroeconomic relations, but each of them obviously has implications for behaviour at the individual, or micro level. It is unfortunate that the assumptions about individual behaviour which underlie these macro-relations have rarely been made explicit. Keynes himself was careful to distinguish between micro- and macro-relations, but until recently his interpreters have given very little consideration to the micro-foundations of the Keynesian model.

If we take the market scheme suggested by the pure theory then the Keynesian functional relations must be interpreted as aggregate demand and supply functions. But if so, then some of them have very peculiar properties. The pure theory of household behaviour assumes that households pursue an integrated plan of consumption, saving and labour supply. In this case each household's demands and supplies should all be functions of the same set of price variables.[2] This means for example that consumer demand should depend on the same variables as labour supply and the demand for money. In Keynesian theory labour supply depends on the wage (both real and monetary) while the demand for money depends on money prices and the money rate of interest. Thus wages, prices and interest rates should also influence consumer demand. But in the naive formulation of the consumption function none of these variables appears – not even the price of consumer goods. Moreover the main variable that does appear – total household income – cannot be regarded as truly exogenous to the household since it depends in part on labour supply, which is one of the variables supposedly determined simultaneously with consumption. It is therefore difficult to see how in the Keynesian model consumption decisions can be regarded as part of an integrated household plan, and in particular how they can be rendered consistent with labour-supply decisions.

Another problem with Keynesian theory is an apparent conflict with Walras' Law. This law is fundamental to all multi-market systems in which households and firms are subject to binding budget constraints. One of the implications of this law (see section 2.3) is that an excess supply in one market will always be associated with an excess demand in another market. Unemployment represents an excess supply of labour and so in the Keynesian model this should imply an excess demand for either goods or money. Keynes suggests instead that unemployment can coexist with equilibrium in all other markets.

The attitude of the more doctrinaire Keynesians toward these criticisms has been rather cavalier. In part this may reflect their overriding concern with the policy implications of the theory. But another, more powerful factor may be that Keynesian economics was believed to offer an alternative to the market-oriented view of the economy.

This alternative was based on the mechanistic concepts of injections and leakages to and from the circular flow of income. Just as Marshall illustrated market adjustment by biological analogy, so Keynesians sought an analogy with physical systems. The rigidity of the physical system, relative to its biological counterpart, parallelled the relegation of market forces to a minor role. The Keynesian model was presented as a system in which aggregate quantities were determined by feedback mechanisms. Price adjustments were recognized as complicating the laws of motion of the system, but were not believed to have any significant influence on its fundamental properties.

It is clear that there is a considerable gulf between the two approaches. Recently the movement to bridge this gulf has gathered momentum. While the classics and the Keynesians have continued their debates in the policy field, theorists have been working out the steps needed to make the transition between the two models. They have worked out a path from 'general equilibrium' to *The General Theory* and back again.

The natural approach when synthesizing two models is to seek a more general model still – one that contains both theories as a special case. Keynes argued that the classical theory was a special case of his own General Theory. If correct, this suggests that progress can only be made by generalizing the General Theory. But in fact the opposite strategy has proved most successful. The classical model, with its market-oriented view of the economy, is used as the basis of the new theory, but with modifications to meet the legitimate criticisms of Keynes. Constraints on the efficiency of markets are then imposed to generate results similar to those obtained by Keynes. It is this approach which is followed up in the present work.

2.2 METHODOLOGY OF MACRO-MODELLING

A major feature of macroeconomics is that it analyses a closed interdependent system. Partial analysis of such a system can be very misleading. It is unusual for a change in one part of the system to leave other parts of the system unaffected; this occurs only when the change is a small one and the rest of the system is sufficiently large to absorb its repercussions with little or no effect. In general, other parts of the system will react and their effects will feedback to modify the original disturbance. Partial analysis is therefore inadequate as a technique of macroeconomic theory; general analysis is called for.

General analysis tends to be complex, and so for analytical purposes it is important to simplify the structure of the system as much as possible. In a market system the degree of complexity is related to the number of markets and the number of transactors. Introducing additional markets naturally increases the dimensions of the model. But the complexity actually increases by more each time a new market is introduced. This is because the structure of the model is determined by the interdependencies between the markets; if the interdependency between any pair of markets is represented by the coefficient of a matrix then it is apparent that the number of coefficients increases not in proportion to, but as the square of the dimensions of the matrix. There are thus considerable economies to be achieved by keeping the number of markets to an absolute minimum.

The introduction of additional transactors does not introduce additional dimensions provided that the additional transactors are identical to those already in the system. The important parameter is the number of different types of transactor, and not the number of transactors of each type.

Most production models distinguish two types of transactors: households and firms. Households delegate all production decisions to firms. Firms are owned by households, but are controlled on a day to day basis by managers employed by the firm.

Enormous simplification can be achieved by assuming that all households are identical and all firms are identical. If in addition it is assumed that there are the same number of firms and households then it is possible to conduct the entire analysis in terms of a representative firm and a representative household. Macroeconomic relations can be derived consistently simply by scaling up the microeconomic relations of the representative firm and the representative household. It is unnecessary to introduce special variables to represent macroeconomic aggregates.

Of course, in deriving the microeconomic relations it must be recognized that the representative unit, whether firm or household, does not know that it is representative, and so it does not anticipate the macroeconomic effects which ensue when its own actions are replicated many times over elsewhere.

2.3 GENERALIZED WALRAS' LAW

Some of the most important properties of multi-market systems depend on very weak assumptions. This section considers properties that depend solely on the relation between the budget constraints of households and firms.

Consider an economy in which a single variable factor of production, labour, is used to produce $n - 1$ different products, indexed $i = 1, \ldots,$ $n - 1$. Labour, and each of the products, is available in non-negative infinitely divisible amounts; they constitute the n commodities traded in the economy. Each commodity has a non-negative uniform price. There are two aspects to price uniformity: the same price is quoted to both buyer and seller, so there is no margin between buying price and selling price, and there is no discrimination in the prices quoted to different buyers or different sellers. Money functions solely as a unit of account.

Let W be the money wage, n^d the demand for labour, and n^s the labour supply. Let P_i be the money price of the ith product, y_i^d the amount demanded, and y_i^s the amount supplied. Let Π^f be the profit planned by the firm and Π^h the profit anticipated by the household.

The household's budget constraint asserts that it cannot spend more than it earns. Under certain conditions, explained in the following section, the household will always wish to spend up to the limit of its income. Consequently planned household expenditure will equal planned household income:

$$\sum_{i=1}^{n-1} P_i y_i^d = Wn^s + \Pi^h \tag{2.1}$$

The firm's budget constraint is an identity, since profit is defined as a residual, namely the excess of sales receipts over wage payments. The profit implied by the firm's production plan is

$$\Pi^f = \sum_{i=1}^{n-1} P_i y_i^s - Wn^d \tag{2.2}$$

Let us define the net excess demand for a commodity as the excess of demand over supply:

$$\begin{aligned} z_n &= n^d - n^s \\ z_i &= y_i^d - y_i^s \qquad (i = 1, \ldots, n-1) \end{aligned} \tag{2.3}$$

The term net is used to indicate that there is no presumption that this quantity will be positive; if the net excess demand is negative then we say that there is excess supply. A net excess demand of zero defines a market equilibrium. If all net excess demands are zero then there is general equilibrium.

Summing equations (2.1) and (2.2) and rearranging terms gives the Generalised Walras' Law (GWL):

$$Wz_n + \sum_{i=1}^{n-1} P_i z_i + (\Pi^f - \Pi^h) = 0 \tag{2.4}$$

Suppose to begin with that the household's profit expectation is equal to the profit generated by the firm's production plan; then GWL implies that:

1. the total value of all net excess demands in the economy is zero; this is known as Simple Walras' Law (SWL). It follows from SWL that
2. if there is excess demand in one market than there must be excess supply in another market, and *vice versa*; from which it follows that
3. it is impossible for one market alone to be in disequilibrium; from which it follows that
4. if all markets but one are in equilibrium then the final market is in equilibrium too.

These results are fundamental to the structure of multimarket systems. They depend only one the existence of uniform prices in each market, and the fact that the household's consumption exhausts its income. No other behavioural assumptions are required.

In the case where the household's expectation of profit differs from the firm's planned profit very different results are obtained:

1. the total value of all net excess demands is equal to household's over-estimate of firm's planned profits; from which it follows that
2. general equilibrium is impossible; if the household over-estimates profit there is bound to be excess demand in some market, while if the household underestimates profit there is bound to be an excess supply; and
3. generalized excess demand — that is excess demand in all markets — is quite possible if the household over-estimates profit, while generalized excess supply is possible if the household underestimates it.

The case in which household profit expectations differ from firms' planned profit has not been considered explicitly in the literature. However we shall argue (in Chapters 10 and 11) that because of information costs such differences can easily emerge, and that when they do emerge they have important macroeconomic implications.

2.4 GENERAL EQUILIBRIUM

The preceding remarks have been of a very general nature. In constructing a specific model it is necessary to introduce additional postulates from which behavioural relations can be derived. These postulates form the basis for an intuitive understanding of system behaviour.

The pure approach is normally based on postulates of the following kind: (a) individual rationality, (b) suitable household preferences, (c) suitable production technology, (d) perfect information, (e) profit maximization, (f) uniform prices, (g) parametric prices, that is prices which cannot be influenced by an individual transactor, and (h) price flexibility, that is prices can adjust freely to equilibrate markets.

The significance of these postulates will become apparent as the analysis proceeds. We are concerned here only with their application to the economy outlined in the previous section.

Let the representative household have consistent preferences defined over the amounts of the products consumed and the amount of leisure enjoyed. Leisure is measured by the time in each period which is not devoted to work. Products and leisure are all 'goods'; the household always prefers more of each and no point of satiation is ever reached. Preferences are smooth and strictly convex, which means that the marginal rate of substitution between any two goods diminishes continuously as the consumption of one good is increased and the consumption of the other is reduced.

The representative firm is a multiproduct firm.[3] It has a single variable factor of production, labour, and fixed endowments of various other factors. Each product is produced quite separately: units of the fixed factors are allocated specifically to the production of particular products. It is only labour that can be used in different ways. All products require labour for their production. The marginal product of labour in each use is finite and non-negative, and diminishes continuously as the labour used increases.

The household consumption plan is determined by maximizing welfare subject to a budget constraint. This determines the product demands and labour supply as functions of prices and profit income. The firm's production plan is determined by maximizing profit subject to technological constraints. This determines labour demand and product supplies as functions of prices. It also determines planned profit as a function of prices.

Suppose that households correctly anticipate firms' planned profit: $\Pi^h = \Pi^f$. Using the fact that profit is a function of prices we can derive a 'reduced form' of the household demands and supplies by substituting out profit to obtain demands and supplies as function of prices alone. It can then be shown that:[4]

1. all demands and supplies in the system are homogeneous of degree zero in prices, which means that demands and supplies depend only on relative prices and not on absolute prices; this is a consequence of the fact that both consumer preferences and firms' production constraints depend only on real quantities, and not on money values;
2. each set of relative prices determines unique consumption and production plans; conversely each consumption and production plan is associated with a unique set of relative prices; this is a consequence of smoothness and convexity in consumer preferences, and of analogous properties in production technology;
3. all demands and supplies are continuous functions of prices, that is a small change in any price induces only a small change in the quantity demanded or supplied.

Using these and other results it is possible to establish the following fundamental propositions: (a) price adjustment can bring about a general equilibrium of the economy; (b) the general equilibrium is unique, and (c) it is socially efficient.

These propositions may be elucidated as follows.

Suppose that at the outset there is an arbitrary set of prices, which is then adjusted by the following procedure: if there is excess demand for a good its price is raised, if there is excess supply its price is lowered, while if supply is equal to demand its price is left unchanged. This adjustment procedure transforms the initial set of prices into a modified set of prices, the modification being determined by the pattern of net excess demands. The net excess demands are continuous functions of prices, so that the transformation is a continuous one, that is transforming two very similar sets of prices yields two new sets of prices which are also similar to each other. It is a property of continuous transformations of this kind that there exists a fixed point, that is a point which is transformed into itself. In terms of the model this means that there is at least one set of prices which remains unchanged by the transformation. It follows from the specifications of the adjustment procedure that at this set of prices there are no excess demands or supplies, that is that the economy is in equilibrium. Hence there exists at least one equilibrium set of prices.

In an economy where individuals differ in their behaviour the uniqueness of equilibrium is guaranteed only under certain quite restrictive conditions. The main complication is that price changes redistribute income between individuals; thus a rise in the price of a commodity redistributes income towards those who specialize in its production. This may lead to difficulties with uniqueness if, for example, the producers have a high income elasticity of demand for their own product. In this case a rise in price redistributes income in favour of those who prefer the commodity, and so actually increases rather than reduces the demand for it. When all individuals are identical, however, income redistribution does not occur, and it can be shown that the equilibrium is unique. The proof is quite straightforward, but is outside the scope of this book.

Social efficiency is defined in terms of the Pareto criterion: an allocation of resources is efficient if no-one can be made better off without making someone else worse off. In general there are many efficient allocations, and the market equilibrium is but one of them.

When all households are identical Pareto efficiency implies that it is impossible to make the representative household better off. Since the household is maximizing its welfare subject to a budget constraint with equilibrium prices, the only way it can increase its welfare is by violating its budget constraint. Any such violation is equivalent to an increase in the value of production at equilibrium prices. But since profits are already being maximized at equilibrium this could only be achieved by violating technological constraints. Hence the improvement is not feasible, and so the equilibrium is Pareto-efficient.

2.5 THE MARK I PRODUCTION MODEL

In subsequent chapters we shall be concerned with a number of specific examples of multi-market models. Each model will be examined under a variety of different market structures. The Mark I model, presented below, is the simplest of all possible models of a production economy.

A Mark II model is introduced in Chapter 5; it has a similar production structure, but contains financial assets as well.

The Mark I model is a simplified version of the model presented in the preceding section. There is a single variable factor of production, labour, and a single product, a consumer good. There is no saving or investment, and money functions solely as a unit of account. Labour receives a uniform money wage W and the product is sold at a uniform money price P. Real values are indicated by the use of small letters, for example the real wage is $w = W/P$ and real profit is $\pi = \Pi/P$.

Households plan consumption c^d to be financed by a labour supply n^s, while firms demand labour n^d to produce a planned output y^s. The general equilibrium of the system may be derived as follows.

Households maximize smooth convex preferences represented by the utility function $u = u(c^d, n^s)$ subject to the real budget constraint

$$c^d \leqslant wn^s + \pi^h \tag{2.5}$$

where π^h is anticipated real profit. Because both consumption and leisure are 'goods' and no point of satiation is ever reached, the household always consumes all it earns. Consequently the constraint (2.5) is always binding, *viz*:

$$c^d = wn^s + \pi^h \tag{2.6}$$

When prices are parametric the first order condition for a maximum of u is

$$dc^d/dn^s = w \tag{2.7}$$

where the derivative on the left-hand side is evaluated assuming a constant level of utility. This condition equates the marginal rate of substitution between consumption and work to the real wage. Solving equations (2.6) and (2.7) simultaneously determines the consumer demand and labour supply functions

$$c^d = c^d(w, \pi^h) \tag{2.8a}$$

$$n^s = n^s(w, \pi^h) \tag{2.8b}$$

Since consumption is a 'good' while work is a 'bad', $\partial c^d/\partial \pi^h > 0$, $\partial n^s/\partial \pi^h < 0$.[5] When the real wage changes, the income and substitution effects normally reinforce one another on consumption and oppose each other on work; hence $\partial c^d/\partial w > 0$, while $\partial n^s/\partial w$ is indeterminate. In fact it is usually assumed that the income effect of a wage change on the supply of labour increases relative to the substitution effect as the wage increases, so that $\partial n^s/\partial w > 0$ at low wages, and $\partial n^s/\partial w < 0$ at higher wages.

Firms maximize real profit subject to a production technology

$$y^s \leqslant y(n^d) \tag{2.9}$$

which exhibits positive but continuously diminishing marginal returns, $dy/dn^d > 0$, $d^2y/dn^{d2} < 0$. Maximizing profit implies minimizing the cost of producing any given output, and this in turn means that the firm will always produce on the production frontier, so that the constraint (2.9) is always binding:

$$y^s = y(n^d) \tag{2.10}$$

Planned real profit is by definition the excess of planned output over the real wage bill:

$$\pi^f = y^s - wn^d \tag{2.11}$$

With parametric prices the first order condition for a maximum of (2.11) is

$$dy^s/dn^d = w \tag{2.12}$$

which equates the marginal product of labour to the real wage. Solving equations (2.10) and (2.12) simultaneously determines the labour demand and product supply functions

$$n^d = n^d(w) \tag{2.13a}$$

$$y^s = y^s(w) \tag{2.13b}$$

and also the profit function

$$\pi^f = \pi^f(w) \tag{2.14}$$

Because of diminishing returns $\partial n^d/\partial w < 0$, whence $\partial y^s/\partial w$, $\partial \pi^f/\partial w < 0$ too.

Combining (2.6) and (2.11) gives the GWL for the system:

$$(c^d - y^s) + w(n^d - n^s) + (\pi^f - \pi^h) = 0 \tag{2.15}$$

If households have complete information about firms' planned profit then $\pi^h = \pi^f = \pi$. Inspection of GWL shows that, with this restriction, a sufficient condition for equilibrium is that either the labour or the product market is in equilibrium; for if one market is in equilibrium then the other must be in equilibrium too. When prices are flexible the real wage can in principle adjust either market to equilibrium.

Combining either of the equilibrium conditions

$$c^d (w, \pi) = y^s (w) \tag{2.16a}$$

$$n^d (w) = n^s (w, \pi) \tag{2.16b}$$

with (2.14) determines the equilibrium values w^e, π^e, and hence equilibrium employment and output n^e, y^e. Alternatively equation (2.14) can be dropped, and equations (2.16) solved simultaneously to get the same result.

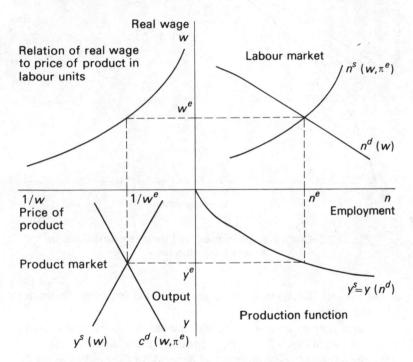

Figure 2.1. Simultaneous equilibrium in product and factor markets

The general equilibrium is illustrated geometrically in Figure 2.1. The top right-hand quadrant illustrates the labour market equilibrium at the real wage w^e and employment n^e. The bottom left-hand quadrant illustrates the product market equilibrium with the price of the product in labour units at $1/w^e$ and the output y^e. The relation between n^e and y^e is determined from the production function shown in the bottom right-hand quadrant. The relation between the real wage and the price

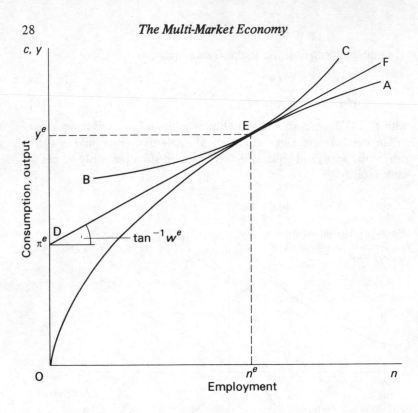

Figure 2.2. Output, employment and income distribution in
general equilibrium

of the product in labour units is shown by the hyperbola in the top
left-hand quadrant.

A much simpler, and more useful, representation of general equilibrium is shown in Figure 2.2. Supply and demand for labour are measured
along the horizontal axis, supply and demand for the product along the
vertical axis. Technology is represented by the production function OA.
Household preferences for consumption and work are illustrated by the
specimen indifference curve BC. The straight line DF has an intercept
with the vertical axis equal to real profit π^e and a slope equal to the real
w^e. It represents both the household budget constraint and an iso-profit
locus for the firm.

Simultaneous equilibrium in the product and labour markets is represented by the point of tangency E between the indifference map and
the production function. Households' plans and firms' plans are mutually

consistent because the point of tangency between the household indifference map and the household budget constraint DF coincides with the point of tangency between the production function and the firms' iso-profit line (also DF). Households receive a profit income π^e and a wage income $w^e n^e$ which just exhausts the product y^e.

Figure 2.2 illustrates very clearly how the distribution of income is determined in general equilibrium. In this model the wage represents a subjective opportunity cost — the value of leisure foregone — whilst profit is a quasi-rent, that is a reward to owners of fixed factors.

The figure also shows why the equilibrium is unique. The uniqueness of the quantities is ensured by the strict convexity of the consumption/ leisure preferences and the strict concavity of the production frontier OA. The uniqueness of the equilibrium wage is guaranteed by these properties, together with the smoothness of preferences and technology, as indicated by the continuity of the slopes of the indifference curve and the production frontier.

The efficiency of the equilibrium is obvious from the fact that BC is the highest indifference curve that can be reached from the production frontier OA.

2.6 THE ADDI-LOG CASE*

This section may be omitted on a first reading, and referred back to once Chapter 6 has been reached.

When the more complex Mark II model is introduced it will be useful to be able to derive simple algebraic formulae for the equilibrium states. Simple formulae are most easily obtained by assuming that the representative household has a logarithmically additive ('addi-log') utility function,

$$\log u = \sum_{i=1}^{n} \alpha_i \log x_i \tag{2.17}$$

where $x_i \geqslant 0$ is consumption of the ith good and $\alpha_i > 0$ is a parameter $(i = 1, \ldots, n)$. In general one of the goods, say the nth, is leisure, so that we have the supplementary equation

$$n^s = h - x_n \tag{2.18}$$

where h is the maximum number of hours that can be worked. The function (2.17) can be rewritten in the multiplicative form

$$u = x_1^{\alpha_1} x_2^{\alpha_2} \ldots x_n^{\alpha_n} \tag{2.19}$$

Since utility is only an ordinal measure of welfare any monotone increasing transformation of u has the same behavioural implications. Hence without loss of generality we can set

$$\sum_{i=1}^{n} \alpha_i = 1 \qquad (2.20)$$

Let $P_i > 0$ be the parametric price of the ith good $(i = 1, \dots, n)$. Maximizing u subject to the budget constraint

$$\sum_{i=1}^{n-1} P_i x_i \leqslant \Pi^h + Wn^s \qquad (2.21)$$

determines the demand functions

$$x_i = \alpha_i (\Pi^h + Wh)/P_i \quad (i = 1, \dots, n-1) \qquad (2.22)$$
$$x_n = \alpha_n (\Pi^h + Wh)/W$$

It follows that:[6] (a) all the cross-price elasticities of demand are zero; (b) the own-price elasticity of demand is unity; (c) the income elasticity of demand is unity; and (d) expenditure shares are constant, that is the expenditure $P_i x_i$ on the ith good is a constant proportion α_i of real income (including the notional value of leisure).

For the purposes of our model it is the properties (a) and (c) which are fundamental. Figure 2.3 illustrates these properties for the case $n = 2$.

Property (a) is a consequence of the fact that with addi-log utility the income and substitution effects of a relative price change are always equal. In the figure a fall in the price of good 2 causes the budget line to swing out from AB to AC. The income effect is represented by the move from G to H and the substitution effect by the move from H to J. The effects on the good whose price has fallen are reinforcing, but the effects on the other good are equal and opposite, and so cancel each other out. Consumption of good 1 remains at $\bar{x}_1$, although the price of good 2 has fallen.

Property (c) is a consequence of the homothetic nature of addi-log utility, namely that the marginal rate of substitution between two goods depends only on the ratio of their consumptions, and is independent of the absolute amount consumed. In the figure an increase in profit income causes the budget line to shift out in parallel fashion from AB to DE. Planned consumption changes from G to H. The homothetic property implies that the expansion path OF through G and H will be a straight line. It follows that a given proportional change in income induces an equiproportional increase in consumption of each good.

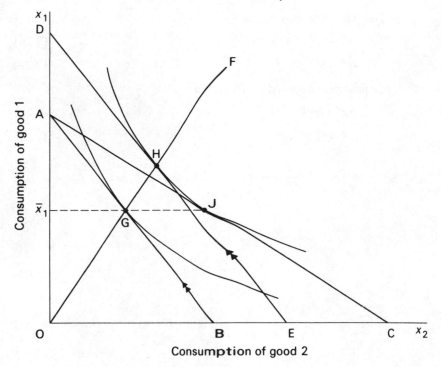

Figure 2.3. Properties of the addi-log utility function

The use of the addi-log specification in the Mark I model may be illustrated as follows. The household utility function becomes

$$U = c^{d\alpha}(h - n^s)^\beta \qquad (2.23)$$

where $\alpha > 0$ is a parameter associated with consumption of the product and $\beta > 0$ is a parameter associated with the consumption of leisure.

For the production function another logarithmic specification is used:

$$\log y^s = \nu \log n^s \qquad (2.24)$$

or equivalently

$$y^s = n^{s\nu} \qquad (2.25)$$

where $0 < \nu < 1$ is a technological parameter.

Using the methods of the previous section equilibrium employment and output can be shown to be

$$n^e = h/(1 + (\beta/\alpha v)) \tag{2.26}$$

$$y^e = n^{ev} \tag{2.27}$$

and equilibrium wage and profit to be

$$w^e = v n^{e(v - 1)} \tag{2.28}$$

$$\pi^e = (1 - v) y^e \tag{2.29}$$

CHAPTER 3

ELEMENTS OF
DISEQUILIBRIUM THEORY

3.1 THE DISEQUILIBRIUM PRINCIPLE

The disequilibrium approach, as its name suggests, is based on the view that the typical market spends more time out of equilibrium than in equilibrium. It may be true that in a world where exogenous change never occurred markets would, given sufficient time, adjust to an equilibrium in which they would remain indefinitely. This proposition has little relevance to the real world, however, in which markets are subject to continuous disturbance. The proportion of time the representative market spends in equilibrium depends upon the relation between the frequency of disturbance and the length of the adjustment lag. If disturbances are infrequent and markets adjust quickly then the representative state will be an equilibrium one. On the other hand, if the adjustment lag is long and the frequency of disturbance is high then markets will be in perpetual disequilibrium. The typical market may be continuously adjusting towards equilibrium, but the equilibrium constitutes a moving target — it changes as circumstances change — and so as soon as the market begins to approach it, it shifts to another position.

The relevance of equilibrium analysis is thus essentially a question of the speed of market adjustment. But this question is not usually considered in isolation. The view that markets adjust quickly is closely identified with the view that prices and quantities are determined competitively. The two propositions are quite distinct, but are indeed related. As we shall see, the conditions which facilitate fast adjustment also tend to create a competitive market environment.

Advocates of equilibrium theory might argue that the disequilibrium approach fails to take full account of competitive forces. This criticism can in fact be turned around, however, and used against equilibrium theory. For orthodox equilibrium theory is essentially static. It postulates

33

that certain conditions prevail, but does not explain how these conditions are set up and maintained. It assumes the existence of a market adjustment mechanism, but does not explain what it is or how it works.

This is reflected in a sleight of hand used in the previous chapter, which the discerning reader may perhaps have noticed. The assumption of price flexibility was used as though it were sufficient to ensure that markets adjust to equilibrium. Now it is apparent that price flexibility is a necessary condition for equilibrium, for if prices cannot adjust following an unforeseen change, then markets will be unable to respond fully to the new situation. But price flexibility is by no means a sufficient condition for equilibrium. It is also necessary for there to be a mechanism which adjusts price in the right direction and by the right amount.

Two possible mechanisms are examined below, neither of which is plausible as a description of market behaviour. The simplest process, proposed by Walras, involves an auctioneer; the other, proposed by Edgeworth, involves recontracting between individual transactors. The important point is that not only are these two processes implausible, but there is no other process which makes markets behave as though there were an auctioneer, or as though recontracting occurred.

Once it is recognized that markets may operate in disequilibrium it is possible to rationalize the apparent anomalies of the Keynesian model noted in section 2.1. In disequilibrium traders on one side of a market will be unable to buy or sell the exact amount they wish at the prevailing price. Such traders face not only a price constraint in the market, but also a quantity constraint. In particular when the money wage is too high households face a constraint on their labour supply. As a result of this, income becomes exogenous to the household. This means that household consumption becomes a function not only of relative prices but also of income. Thus the Keynesian consumption function is correctly specified once it is reinterpreted as a description of disequilibrium behaviour.

The disequilibrium approach also sheds light on the relevance − or in some sense, the irrelevance − of Walras' Law to Keynesian theory.[1] For given that labour supply is constrained, consumer demand is constrained, and hence so is product demand. Thus two concepts of demand must be distinguished: a notional demand which applies when equilibrium prices prevail, and an effective demand which applies when transactors are subjected to quantity constraints. Walras' Law must be reformulated in terms of effective demands before it can be applied to Keynesian theory.

3.2 WALRAS AND EDGEWORTH ON COMPETITIVE ADJUSTMENT

Adjustment to equilibrium must be explained in terms of a market *process*, that is in terms of a sequential procedure which takes the economy from an arbitrary initial state to the equilibrium. This is essentially a question of information-processing; it concerns the way in which individuals recognize net excess demands, calculate the appropriate response to them, and announce their response to other transactors. Processes of this kind cannot be analyzed using static concepts; it is necessary to enter the realms of dynamic analysis.

The adjustment mechanism mostly commonly appealed to is that of competition. This mechanism not only explains how prices adjust; it also rationalizes two important properties of price which are postulated in the static theory, namely uniformity and parametricity.

There have been two main attempts to model the dynamics of the competitive process. The first is a highly artificial model constructed by Walras. The second, more realistic model, is due to Edgeworth.[2] To simplify the discussion, the two models will be compared in the context of a partial analysis. In each case it is shown how the price of one good is adjusted relative to the prices of all other goods, assuming that the income effects of the price change are negligible and that the prices of all other goods remain constant.

Walras postulates that the market is organized by an auctioneer. The auctioneer begins by announcing a trial price. On the basis of this price transactors determine their bids for demand or supply. At this stage all the bids are provisional. The auctioneer aggregates the bids to determine the net excess demand. If net excess demand is zero he confirms the bids and transactions proceed. If it is non-zero then he announces a new trial price and a new set of bids is collected. The new price is determined by the algorithm described in section 2.4: if the excess demand is positive he raises the price, if it is negative he reduces the price. Provided that net excess demand is everywhere a decreasing function of price, and that prices do not overreact to excess demand, the process will eventually converge to equilibrium.

In this model there is no margin between buying price and selling price because the auctioneer is altruistic: he does not seek to maximize profit by setting a margin which he can appropriate for himself. There is no price discrimination because it is assumed that the auctioneer, having the authority to intermediate all transactions, decides to enforce a uniform price. The authority of the auctioneer also means that the price is parametric to each transactor. Price adjusts to equilibrium because information on provisional transactions is centralized with the auctioneer; he can therefore apply his algorithm to determine its equilibrium value.

In the Edgworth model transactors bargain directly with each other over price. In the simplest variant of this model the demanders and suppliers constitute two distinct groups; the demanders each wish to purchase one unit of the commodity while the sellers each wish to sell one unit. A transaction is set up as a two-party coalition between a buyer and a seller. To establish the coalition it is necessary for the parties to agree on the price. To bargain for the most favourable price each buyer explores possible coalitions with each of the sellers, while each seller explores possible coalitions with each of the buyers. All coalitions remain provisional until everyone is satisfied that they cannot improve on their existing coalition. Anyone who is not satisfied can recontract — that is can quit one coalition and form another.

There is no margin between buying and selling price because there is no intermediation; buyers and sellers trade directly with each other.

Uniformity of the price on each side of the market is achieved through arbitrage. So long as each buyer regards all sellers as homogeneous, a transaction with any one seller is a perfect substitute for a transaction with any other seller. Similarly if sellers are indifferent between the buyers then a transaction with one buyer is a perfect substitute for a transaction with any other buyer. It follows that if two provisional transactions have been set up at different prices then the buyer in the high-price transaction will have an incentive to switch to the seller in the low-price transaction, and *vice versa*. Once this threat has been recognized by the other parties to the transactions, the prices will be renegotiated until the threat has been eliminated, that is until the prices have become uniform.

Price is parametric if the withdrawal of any transactor from the market would exert an insignificant influence on price. In this case a threat by any transactor to withdraw from the market is of no use to him in bargaining for a higher price. Thus the price he can negotiate is independent of his own decision on what quantity to trade.

Following one transactor's withdrawal from the market, equilibrium can be restored either by inducing a compensating entry on the same side of the market or by an equivalent withdrawal on the other side of the market. If the original transactor was involved in only a small amount of trading then the adjustment need only be a marginal one. This is guaranteed in the present case because by assumption each transactor trades only one unit. A marginal adjustment will require a significant change in price only if there is a discontinuity in the reservation prices of both the marginal buyers and the marginal sellers, that is if the supply and demand schedules are both discontinuous in the region of the equilibrium quantity. The more buyers and sellers there are in the market the greater is the likelihood of continuity in the reservation prices, and so the greater is the probability that entry and exit of marginal transactors will be induced by only a very small change of price. It follows that price is likely to be parametric provided that there are many buyers and sellers in the market.

Price adjusts to equilibrium on the initiative of transactors whose plans are frustrated: buyers who cannot find sellers or sellers who cannot find buyers. The obvious strategy for these transactors is to break up existing coalitions by offering suppliers a higher price, or buyers a lower price, as appropriate. Higher prices attract new supplies and deter existing demand; lower prices have the opposite effect. Thus what begins as an attempt to bid away supplies or demands from other transactors ends by altering the aggregate quantity traded. Price adjustment ceases once the net excess demand has been eliminated.

Both the Walras and Edgeworth mechanisms can be generalized to simultaneous transactions in many markets. The generalization is quite straightforward in principle, though in practice the amount of information required to implement adjustment procedures increases considerably as additional markets are introduced.

3.3 TWO ASPECTS OF PRICE ADJUSTMENT

In presenting a critique of the competitive adjustment mechanism two separate issues must be distinguished. These issues are relevant to any market adjustment mechanism, and although they are superficially very similar they are analytically quite distinct.

1. Does the market adjust in response to notional or realized net excess demand? A notional net excess demand is a difference between planned demand and planned supply *before any transactions have actually taken place*. On the other hand a realized net excess demand arises from a discrepancy between transactors' plans and the actual amount traded. If the market responds to notional excess demand

then incompatible plans can be revised before they are ever put into effect. If they are suitably revised, the economy need never be out of equilibrium. If the market responds to realized net excess demand, however, then following an unforeseen change the market will typically lapse into disequilibrium before the need for corrective action is recognized.

2. Once a disequilibrium has been recognized, will transactors prefer to adjust price, or to maintain prices and make accommodating changes in quantities? This question is concerned with the nature of transactors' optimal response to disequilibrium (whether realized or notional). This response will be determined by the relative size of price-adjustment costs and quantity-adjustment costs.

Only the first of these issues is considered in the present chapter. Discussion of the second issue is deferred to Chapter 8. We argue below that in almost all markets transactors will prefer to respond to realized net excess demands rather than go to the trouble of computing notional net excess demands, even though in doing so they risk short-term frustrations of their quantity plans. This case is examined in the context of the Mark I production model outlined in section 2.5. It is shown how realized excess demands are determined through the principle of 'trading at the short end of the market'. The chapter concludes with an examination of the implications of disequilibrium for unemployment.

3.4 REALIZED EXCESS DEMAND AS A MARKET SIGNAL

In both the Walras and Edgeworth mechanisms prices are adjusted in response to notional net excess demands. Equilibrium is guaranteed by the fact that the market does not open for actual trading until the set of planned transactions has been 'screened' for consistency. In the Walrasian mechanism the screening is done by the auctioneer. In the Edgeworth mechanism it is effected through recontracting among individual transactors.

Screening obviously involves processing considerable amounts of information. Information processing is a costly activity. It is normally uneconomic for the processing of the same information to be replicated by different individuals. On these grounds the Walrasian mechanism, which centralizes information processing, is *prima facie* more efficient than the Edgeworth mechanism, which requires transactors to independently process very similar information as part of the negotiation process.

Few, if any, markets in free enterprise economies conform to the Walrasian model, however. Rather ironically, it is the 'internal markets' used to allocate resources within organizations which conform most closely to the model.[3] When auctioneers are used it is almost invariably to allocate resources which are already under common ownership. Socialist economies using decentralized planning techniques sometimes employ 'auctioneers' to administer allocations to independent business units within the state sector. Vertically integrated firms use auctioneers to set shadow prices for intermediate products.

When resources have to be allocated, not within an organization, but between different organizations, transactors appear unwilling to accept the authority of an auctioneer. In these 'external markets' transactions involve change of ownership. Price acts not only as an allocator, but as a distributor of rewards between the new owner and the old. It appears that in these circumstances transactors perceive considerable risk in foregoing their right to negotiate over price. It could of course be argued that since they are in a competitive situation they may as well accept the authority of the auctioneer as accept the discipline of impersonal market forces. But transactors may have doubts about the integrity of the auctioneer. The theory requires the auctioneer to be a non-profit maker. But given the usual behavioural postulates of economics, it is difficult to see why a rational individual who has a monopoly of intermediation should accept such a constraint: if he does accept the constraint then he has little incentive to perform the job efficiently, since there is no longer a link between his performance and his reward. Under these circumstances it may be rational for transactors in an external market to refuse the services of an auctioneer.

If the Walrasian mechanism is ruled out then the use of notional excess demands depends upon the viability of the Edgeworth mechanism. We have already seen that this may involve considerable renegotiation of contracts before transactions can proceed. Such renegotiation may lead to very high transactions costs.

When the need for a transaction is inadequately foreseen protracted negotiations will delay completion and thereby incur costs for the impatient transactor. In any case, the more protracted the negotiation the greater is the risk that market conditions will change and render obsolete the provisional contracts already established. But as negotiations are speeded up to avoid delays so resource costs increase as faster communication and quicker decisions are called for.

The optimal strategy for the individual transactor is to trade off the resource cost of speeding up negotiations against the costs of delaying completion of the transaction. In the typical market unexpected changes are continually occurring, so the optimal strategy is likely to involve very fast negotiation and hence relatively high resource costs. Thus even with the optimal strategy the average cost per transaction is likely to be high.

An obvious way for a transactor to economize on information costs is to respond to realized excess demand rather than notional excess demand. This eliminates altogether the calculation of notional excess demand prior to the transaction. The use of realized excess demands was explained in detail by Marshall.[4] Transactors proceed on the basis that they will trade today at yesterday's price, so long as none of yesterday's plans were frustrated; if yesterday's plans were frustrated they will announce a new price which, on a simple rule of thumb, should be just sufficient to eliminate yesterday's quantity constraint. This strategy maintains information processing costs at an absolute minimum. Its disadvantage is that in a changing environment it exposes the transactor to continual minor frustrations of his transaction plans. But given the high cost of information-processing, it seems likely that the balance of advantages will almost invariably lie with the rule of thumb adjustment using realized net excess demands.

3.5 COMPETITIVE DISEQUILIBRIUM

The competitive disequilibrium model assumes that trading takes place at arbitrary prices. These prices may be interpreted as the previous period's prices, adjusted to compensated for realized excess demands. The adjustment is *ad hoc*, however, and it is only by accident that they will produce equilibrium in the current period.

The model also assumes that the prices — even though arbitrary — are uniform and parametric. This is an important simplification for it allows the analysis to be developed in terms of conventional competitive demand and supply schedules. It is by no means obvious, however, that these simplifying assumptions are compatible with the rest of the theory. It must be recognized that the existence of information costs has implications not only for price adjustment, but for the uniformity and parametric nature of price.

To begin with, when information costs are significant the diseconomy of replicating information processing creates an opportunity for brokers. Transactors can economize on their own information costs by obtaining free price quotations from brokers; in return the brokers take a margin on each transaction they intermediate.

When the law and institutions of the market make it difficult for brokers to operate, transactors may know very little about the various options open to them. Because they are unable to monitor other transactions, different transactions may take place at different prices. Thus uniformity of price is replaced by a dispersion of prices.

Ignorance of other transactions also means that each transaction has an element of bilateral monopoly. Each party incurs a cost if he seeks out another party with whom to transact instead. Since each party suspects the other party is in the same position, each party anticipates that the other is willing to sacrifice something in order to conclude the negotiation successfully. This creates a 'zone of indeterminacy' in the price, within which the strategic aspects of bargaining govern the result. With all transactors in this position, no-one faces a parametric price.

If disequilibrium theory were to take account of all these complications it would become unmanageable as a tool of macroeconomic analysis. But while the assumptions of uniform and parametric prices may be indispensable to a simple analysis of disequilibrium, it must not be forgotten just how strong these assumptions are.

In competitive equilibrium theory, price and quantity are simultaneously determined at the intersection of the supply and demand schedules. In the product market illustrated in Figure 3.1 the equilibrium is at E, where the demand and schedules DD′ and SS′ intersect. E is the point that will be attained if adjustment is based on notional excess demand.

If realized excess demand is used instead then in the short run price will be set by rule of thumb at, say, P_1 in excess of the equilibrium price P^e. Demand is less than supply and, since trading is voluntary, sellers cannot insist on buyers taking all they have on offer. Consequently the quantity actually traded, q_1, is equal to the amount demanded, q_1^d. Similarly if the price is set at $P_2 < P^e$, so that demand exceeds supply, then demanders cannot insist that suppliers meet all their needs. Consequently quantity is set at $q_2 = q_2^s$.

In general, because transactions are voluntary, the quantity traded cannot exceed either the amount demanded or the amount supplied. And because traders will not forego opportunities for mutually beneficial transactions, the quantity traded will never be less than the minimum of the demand and the supply. It must therefore be equal to the minimum

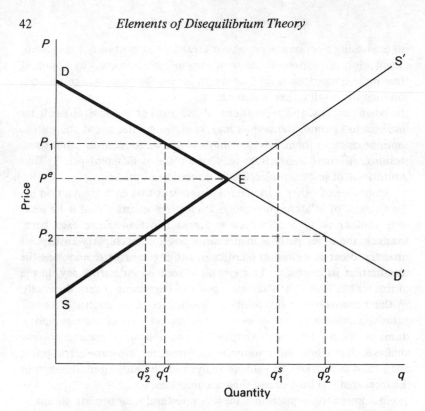

Figure 3.1. Trading at the 'short end' of the market: partial analysis

of demand and supply. This proposition is summarized by saying that 'quantity is set at the short end of the market'. A corollary of this is that transactors on both sides of the market cannot be quantity-constrained at the same time.

It should be noted that, unlike the equilibrium model, price and quantity are not uniquely determined. The disequilibrium model determines a relation between price and quantity, indicated in the figure by the frontier DES. The equilibrium state is a special case corresponding to a single point on this locus.

In a multi-market system — such as that described in section 2.4 — a quantity constraint experienced in one market will modify behaviour in the other markets. Transactors who are rationed by quantity will exhibit income and substitution effects in just the same way as they would if they had been rationed by an adverse movement of price. They will reduce their demands or supplies for complements of the quantity-constrained commodity, and increase their demands and supplies for substitutes. Demands and supplies for unconstrained commodities become functions not only of prices but also of the quantities that constrain the demands and supplies for the remaining commodities. These demands and supplies are known as effective demands and supplies, to distinguish them from the notional demands and supplies which would prevail in the absence of any quantity constraints.

3.6 DISEQUILIBRIUM AND CLASSICAL UNEMPLOYMENT – A COMPARATIVE STATIC ANALYSIS

Disequilibrium macroeconomics is concerned with the transmission of quantity constraints between markets, and between different groups of transactors. Its particular concern is to predict the cumulative effect of this interaction on aggregate employment and output.

Conventional macroeconomics is usually conducted in terms of comparative statics – that is, the comparison of different equilibrium situations. It might be thought that the comparative static method is not applicable to disequilibrium theory, since its very name suggests the absence of an equilibrium state. This is not correct, however; equilibrium is a powerful concept, indispensible to most economic theorizing. What disequilibrium theory does is to utilize a weaker concept of equilibrium, applicable to a much wider variety of situations. Equilibrium is defined simply in terms of the mutual compatibility of individual trading plans. These trading plans are assumed to be drawn up conditional on the quantity constraints perceived by the individuals concerned. The prices that prevail in individual markets may be fixed quite arbitrarily; all that is required is that the individuals who are quantity constrained perceive their constraints correctly, so that there is no need for any of them to revise their plans.

This approach permits a meaningful definition of unemployment equilibrium. There is an unemployment equilibrium when all markets – for goods as well as labour – are in equilibrium, but in the labour market suppliers are employment-constrained. The concept may be illustrated using the Mark I model of section 2.5. This model exhibits two possibilities: classical unemployment and underemployment. Because of the simplicity of the model the analysis can be presented entirely in diagrammatic terms.

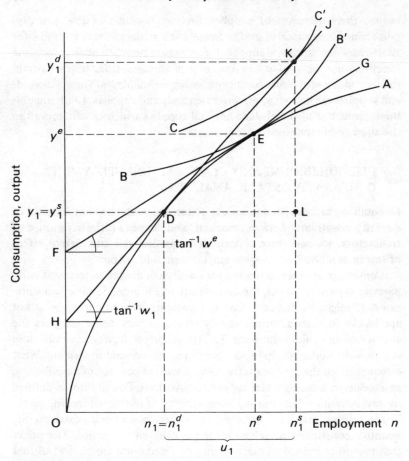

Figure 3.2. Unemployment due to an excessive real wage

Figure 3.2 is based upon Figure 2.2; the vertical axis represents output and the horizontal axis employment. Technology is represented by the production frontier OA and the household indifference map is exemplified by the indifference curves BB′ and CC′. Full employment is at E, where the indifference curve BB′ is tangent to the production frontier OA. The equilibrium real wage w^e is determined by the slope of the tangent FG at E, and real profit π^e by the intercept OF on the vertical axis.

Suppose now that the real wage is set above full employment level at

$w_1 > w^e$. The real wage w_1 is represented by the slope of the line HJ. Profit-maximizing firms plan to product at D, demanding n_1^d units of labour and supplying y_1^s units of product. The profit implied by this production plan is OH. Households face the budget constraint HJ and they optimize at K, by supplying n_1^s units of labour and demanding y_1^d units of product. The supply of labour exceeds the demand, and so with employment set at the short end of the labour market, $n_1 = n_1^d$.

Comparison with the full employment equilibrium indicates that there is less than full employment. Since the wage is above its equilibrium level the slope of the budget line HJ exceeds the slope of the budget line FG. Since the budget lines are both tangents to the curve OA, and the slope of this curve diminishes continuously, it follows that the point of tangency D must be to the left of the point of tangency E, whence $n_1 < n^e$. Since there is also a realized excess supply of labour ($n_1 < n_1^s$), n_1 corresponds to a state of unemployment, as defined in section 1.5. Since by assumption the real wage is above its equilibrium level the unemployment is classical, that is it is unemployment associated with a too-high real wage.

The diagram also illustrates one of the implications of SWL, namely that the excess supply of labour is associated with an excess demand for goods, and that the excess supply and excess demand are of the same value. The excess supply of labour, $n_1^s - n_1^d$, is measured by the horizontal distance DL. The real wage w_1 is equal to the tangent of the angle JDL subtended by the lines HJ and DL at D; hence by trigonometry the real value of the excess supply of labour, $w_1 (n_1^s - n_1^d)$, is measured by the distance KL. But translating KL to the vertical axis shows that it measures the excess demand for the product, $y_1^d - y_1^s$, which proves the proposition.

Consider now the case of a low real wage $w_2 < w^e$. According to Figure 3.3 profit-maximizing firms plan to produce at M, giving employment n_2^d and profit OP. Assuming that households correctly anticipate this profit income they face a budget constraint PQ and they optimize at R, where the indifference curve XX' is tangent to PQ. Planned labour supply is $n_2^s < n_2^d$ and so with employment set at the short end of the labour market, $n_2 = n_2^s$. Comparison with the full employment equilibrium E shows that there is less than full employment, but since there is no realized excess supply of labour, n_2 represents underemployment and not unemployment.

There is an excess demand for labour, and SWL implies that this excess demand is associated with an excess supply of the product of

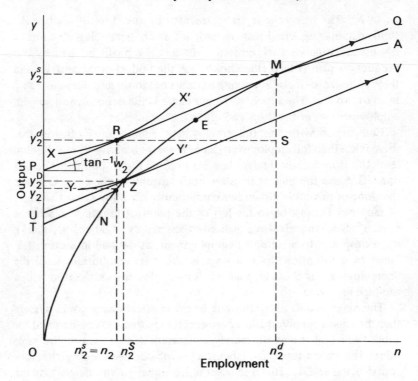

Figure 3.3. Underemployment due to a too-low real wage

exactly the same value. The excess demand for labour is measured by the distance RS and the excess supply of the product by the distance MS. The proposition follows from the fact that the right-angled triangle RMS has a hypotenuse RM whose slope is given by the real wage, w_2.

When there is underemployment, firms' production plans are constrained by the supply of labour. Their target is to employ n_2^d workers to generate output y_2^s and profit OP. But in practice they must operate at N: they can secure only $n_2 = n_2^s$ workers which, from the production function, generate an output y_2, and hence realize a profit of only OT.

The point N cannot represent an equilibrium, however, because the actual profit OT differs from the households' anticipation of profit OP. As a result households are obliged to consume much less than they had planned. The shortfall of profit PT means that household consumption is reduced from y_2^d to y_2.

Equilibrium will be achieved when the households' perception of their budget constraint is adjusted to take full account of the impact of the labour supply constraint on firms' profitability. Equilibrium is illustrated by the point Z in Figure 3.3. Because of households' more realistic profit expectations their budget constraint shifts down to UV. Its point of tangency Z with the indifference curve YY' determines labour supply n_2^S and consumer demand y_2^D. Since the point Z lies on the production frontier OA household labour supply is now consistent with household consumer demand. Although firms are labour supply-constrained, they are in equilibrium subject to this constraint because households demand exactly what firms can produce.

Comparing the cases of a too-high real wage and a too-low real wage gives a number of insights into the properties of disequilibrium in a non-monetary economy.

In each case the initial disequilibrium involves either the household or the firm being quantity-constrained, but both are not constrained at once. Whoever is constrained is constrained in both the labour and the product markets. In the case of a too-high real wage the household experiences a constraint on employment and a constraint on consumer demand: it cannot supply as much labour as it wishes, neither can it consume as much as it plans to. The firm on the other hand is unconstrained — it can obtain as much labour as it requires and sell as much output as it wants to. In the case of a too-low real wage the firm is constrained both by household unwillingness to supply the required amount of labour, and by their unwillingness to demand as much output as it plans to supply. Households on the other hand experience no constraint on either the amount of labour they can supply or the amount of product they can consume.

Consider now the transactors' response to the initial disequilibrium, and the subsequent adjustment process. There are two points to note here.

First, the quantity-constrained transactor, although constrained in both labour and product markets, will normally only perceive one of the constraints. For example in the unemployment case the household experiencing an employment constraint simply cannot afford to consume as much as it had planned to do in the absence of the constraint. Thus the employment constraint taken together with the budget constraint makes the consumption constraint appear quite irrelevant. Only if the household failed to perceive its budget constraint correctly would it perceive a consumption constraint independent of the employment constraint. Similarly in the underemployment case the firm facing a constraint on labour supply simply cannot produce as much as it would like to, and the amount it can produce is either less than, or in equilibrium equal to, the amount that households demand. Consequently the firm never actually perceives the sales constraint because given the labour supply constraint it is never possible to supply more than would be demanded anyway.

The second point is that when households are constrained, only households need to revise their plans, whereas when firms are constrained both firms and households must revise their plans. In other words, whoever is constrained, the household must always adjust in order for the economy to attain an equilibrium. The reason for this is quite simple: households' behaviour depends on their budget constraint, the budget constraint depends on firms' profits, and firms' profits depend on the quantity-constraints they experience. Thus the consequences of firms' quantity-constraints are channelled to the households through an income constraint. Equilibrium can be achieved only when household profit expectations have adjusted into line with the profit implications of the firms' quantity-constrained production plans.

3.7 DYNAMICS OF DISEQUILIBRIUM

To analyse the dynamics of disequilibrium it is necessary to specify how transactors signal their demands and supplies to each other and how, in the light of the signals received, each transactor adjusts his perception of quantity constraints.[5]

Suppose that all transactors know the levels at which prices are fixed, and are aware that prices will be maintained at this level for a short time at least. At the beginning of each period the representative transactor formulates expectations of the quantity constraints he is likely to encounter in each market. Suppose to begin with that expectations are held with complete conviction. It is reasonable to assume that the transactor formulates an integrated trading plan by optimizing subject to the expected quantity constraints, and to any other relevant constraints (a budget constraint for the household, a technological constraint for the firm). The net amounts demanded in each market according to this plan are known as the Drèze demands.

In general some of the expected constraints will be binding and others will not. When no constraints are binding the Drèze demands reduce to the notional demands of Walrasian theory. If one or more of the constraints is binding then in general the Drèze demands for *all* commodities will differ from the notional demands. In markets where the constraint binds the Drèze demand will be equal to the constraint. In markets where the constraint does not bind the Drèze demand will be a function of the binding constraints in the other markets, as well as of the prevailing prices.

The Drèze demands are the demands that the transactor will signal to other transactors in each of the markets. If all transactors correctly anticipate the quantity constraints to which they are subject then the system will be in equilibrium, in the sense that no transactor has any incentive to revise his plan next period on account of the non-fulfillment of his plan in the current period. A necessary condition for an equilibrium of this kind is that in each market the excess Drèze demand is zero.

It is highly unlikely of course that all transactors will be 'right first time'. This implies that some at least of the transactors on the short side of the market — that is on the side of the market where rationing is experienced — will be subject to constraints which are tighter than those they anticipated; precisely who is subjected to constraints, and by how much, will be determined by the rationing mechanism enforced in the market. Transactors on the long side of the market will realize, from the signals transmitted to them from the short side, that they could have increased their volume of transactions had they wished. If they did not anticipate being quantity-constrained anyway then this is a matter of little consequence to them, and merely confirms their expectations. But if they anticipated being constrained, but actually were not, then it is a cause for regret that they did not signal their desire for a larger volume of trade.

These considerations have two important implications for transactor behaviour. First they point to the need for an error-correction mechanism in the formation of expectations of quantity constraints. It is appropriate that each period the expectation of quantity constraints should be revised in the light of the quantity constraints experienced in the previous period. If a constraint was tighter than anticipated then the expected value of the constraining quantity should be reduced. If the constraint was slacker than anticipated then the expected value of the constraining quantity should be increased. If the constraint was not expected to be binding, and this prediction was correct, then there is no need to revise the expectation.

The second point is that transactors should take account of the possibility of error in their expectations when deciding what demand signals to transmit. If a transactor is fully confident of his expectations then he has no incentive to express anything other than his Drèze demands. But if he is only 99 per cent certain then, where the expected quantity constraint is binding, it may be worth his while communicating to transactors that he would be willing to trade more than he expects to be able to. How much more should he be willing to trade? The logical answer is that he should be willing to trade up to the level where he optimizes subject to all expected quantity constraints *except the expected constraint in the market under consideration*. This level defines the Clower demand.

In markets where no constraints are expected to bind the Clower demand and the Drèze demand are the same. In markets where the constraints are expected to bind the Clower demand is of greater magnitude than the Drèze demand.

It is sometimes suggested that it is illogical for a transactor to express his Clower demand in every market because collectively the Clower demands do not constitute the solution of a meaningful optimization problem. For a household, for example, the Clower demands may collectively imply the underspending of the budget — which is suboptimal — or the overspending of the budget — which is just not feasible.

This is very much beside the point, however. To begin with, Clower visualized that transactors would visit markets sequentially. Thus the Clower demand expressed in any given market would be based on different information from the other Clower demands — it would include new information on whether a quantity constraint was binding in the market that had just been visited. Because the transactor reappraises the situation after visiting each market, there is little point in requiring that demands expressed in sequence are mutually consistent.

There is another objection which is more powerful and applies whether or not trading is sequential. This is that there is no point in a transactor expressing a Clower demand unless he believes that his expectation of the quantity constraint may be wrong. If he is certain of the constraint then he may as well express his Drèze demand, since that is as much as will be satisfied. If Clower and Drèze demands are to be evaluated in conditions where expectations are incorrect, then the consistency of the Drèze demands is of no advantage at all. For it is not obviously better to be consistently wrong than inconsistently wrong.[6]

The point may be illustrated by an example from the labour market. Suppose there is an unemployment equilibrium, in which all suppliers of labour have a correct perception of the employment constraint. If the suppliers were to signal only their Drèze supplies then employers would not necessarily be aware that there were people still seeking additional work. By signalling their Clower supplies the households keep employers aware of their continual desire for work, so that if and when product demand increases employers need not hesitate in hiring more labour. There is evidence to suggest that in practice, while a minority of households signal Drèze supplies, the majority signal Clower supplies. Studies of the 'discouraged worker' show that when unemployment is high a small proportion of the unemployed cease to actively seek work, though a majority continue to register as unemployed.[7] It is reasonable to interpret the former as a Drèze strategy, the latter as a Clower strategy. Indeed it could be argued that if workers did not follow a Clower strategy, unemployment would be understated in the statistics, and in general would not be perceived as the serious problem that it is.

3.8 INVESTMENT, LIQUIDITY AND BANKRUPTCY

To complete the discussion of dynamics it is necessary to consider what happens in the current period once transactors' expectations have been proved incorrect.

One possibility is that transactors who are violating their budget constraint or their technological constraint indicate that they are unable to proceed, and recontracting occurs on the basis of modified expectations of quantity constraints. This implies a tacit recognition by transactors that quantity signals are only provisional, and require confirmation before trade. A procedure of this kind would be most unusual, for two reasons. If transactors are going to recontract in terms of quantity then they may as well recontract in terms of price as well, so that the fixprice assumption will no longer be tenable. Secondly, recontracting of any kind increases information costs, for the reasons explained in section 3.4.

It would appear that in the absence of recontracting, an individual with mutually incompatible commitments to trade is bound to renege on some of them. This ignores an important dimension to the problem, however, namely that the existence of stocks affords the individual an additional degree of freedom in adjusting to disequilibrium. By owning stocks of some or all of the commodities the transactor can allow for a margin of error in realized trades.

When a transactor holds a stock of a commodity his net demand has two components: one component is to use during the period to maintain a flow equilibrium, the other is an 'investment' demand to adjust the stock to equilibrium. By foregoing his planned investment the transactor can ensure that the flow equilibrium is maintained at the expense of the stock equilibrium. Essentially the transactor avoids reneging on others by reneging on himself instead. He makes unplanned adjustments to his stock, which he hopes to compensate for through planned adjustments the following period. Thus the consequences of disequilibrium in the current period are mitigated by thrusting the burden of adjustment forward onto the next period. Next period, presumably, further unplanned adjustments occur, and the process continues until eventually the transactor's expectations of quantity constraints are fully realized, at which stage equilibrium is achieved.

It is possible though that the transactor may hold insufficient stocks. In this case he may be unable to fully internalize his adjustments, and may have to renege on some of his contracts. In a production economy, such as that described in Chapter 2, there are two main circumstances under which transactors may have to renege. The first is where there are unforeseen constraints on the supply of inputs to production, so that insufficient output can be generated to meet the firms' sales commitments. This is a case in which the firms hold insufficient inventories of inputs to make good the shortfall of supply, and/or hold insufficient inventory of finished product to make good the shortfall of output. The second case is where there is insufficient demand for inputs to production, so that households cannot finance their product demand out of factor incomes. In a monetary economy this problem is resolved by households running down their money balances. The money is drawn out of stock and paid over to the firms in exchange for goods. Unlike the firms' inventories however there is no need for readjustment the following period. For the money received by the firms is paid back to the households in the form of factor payments and profit. Household money balances are only run down temporarily while the money circulates from the household to the firm and back again to the household. Difficulties arise only when some households have insufficient money balances to make good the initial deficit in their budget. In this case liquidity constraints may force households to renege on the purchase commitments made to firms.

It is necessary for transactors to arrive at conventions among themselves for dealing with situations in which one or more of them is forced to renege. So far as firms are concerned it is usually accepted that offers of product supply are made subject to availability; provided no payment has been made, the only penalty suffered by the firm for failing to supply is a loss of goodwill. Households on the other hand often enter into long-term purchase commitments which firms will hold them to by law. They can only escape from these commitments through bankruptcy. There is no doubt that bankruptcy can exert an important influence on the dynamics of disequilibrium, but a full treatment of it is beyond the scope of this book. It might be thought that the law of bankruptcy would be designed to minimize the repercussions of bankruptcy on those who trade with the bankrupt person, but in practice the exact opposite seems to occur. The bankruptcy of one transactor threatens the solvency of others, and what begins with a single contract being reneged upon may end with a large part of the pattern of trade being disrupted.

The relevance of these issues to unemployment should be apparent. Inventories and money balances have a crucial role in stabilizing the economy while transactors adjust their expectations. Unplanned stock adjustments allow flow equilibrium to be be maintained, and avoid contracts being reneged upon. Flow equilibrium is essential if employment is to be maintained; otherwise bankruptcies and the ensuing dislocation of trade may cause widespread redundancies. Once the dislocation has occurred it may be difficult to re-employ the workers until business enterprises have been reorganized and contracts renegotiated.

CHAPTER 4

MONEY

4.1 DEFINITION OF MONEY

Keynes regarded money as having a central role in the analysis of unemployment. He did not deny that a non-monetary economy could experience classical unemployment. But he argued that in a monetary economy unemployment was most likely to be caused by a deficiency of aggregate demand, arising from the diversion of purchasing power into the accumulation of money balances. Before examining this argument in detail it is appropriate to examine the nature and functions of money.

Money can be defined either functionally or indicatively. A functional definition is based on the maxim that 'money is what money does'. An indicative definition describes money by its observable characteristics, for example as notes and coin, bank deposits, and so on. For analytical purposes the functional approach is most appropriate as a starting point.

It is usual to distinguish three functions of money: unit of account, medium of exchange and store of value. Of the three, the medium of exchange is usually regarded as the most fundamental, in the sense that anything that performs this function should be potentially considered as money. The other functions are usually discharged by money too, but they are not exclusive to it. There are other assets which can be used both as units of account and as stores of value. Throughout this book the role of medium of exchange will be taken as definitive where money is concerned.

Most expositions of monetary theory offer only a cursory treatment of the functions of money.[1] Their discussion is centred instead on the components of the demand for money. Following Keynes, these are usually identified as the transactions demand, the precautionary demand and the speculative demand. In principle there ought to be a straightforward connection between the various functions of money and the various components of its demand. In the analysis of other markets there is usually a one-to-one relation between the various functions of the commodity and the components of its demand. This is not so in conventional analysis of the money market.

Superficially the transactions demand represents the demand for money as a medium of exchange, and the speculative demand the demand for money as a store of value. The precautionary demand does not fit easily into this scheme, however; perhaps for this reason it has come to be regarded as a kind of cross between the transactions demand and the speculative demand, and is therefore seen as being of little analytical interest. A rather similar fate has befallen the role of money as a unit of account. This role is regarded as no more significant than is the choice of a *numeraire* in a general equilibrium model.

The present chapter is intended as an antidote to this view. Its standpoint is that the 'components of demand' approach is essentially myopic. It assumes that society has already decided to use a form of money, and that a particular commodity has already been chosen for this role; it is the demand for this particular commodity that then forms the subject of study. Thus even before the analysis begins society is assumed to have reached a kind of equilibrium in the way in which transactions are organized − an institutional equilibrium centred on the use of money. It is legitimate to enquire, however, how this institutional equilibrium was attained in the first place. It is also very important to know whether the equilibrium is stable. In particular, will the commodity that currently acts as money continue to do so, or are there circumstances in which it is liable to be displaced by another?

These issues were explicitly considered by Keynes in the General Theory. Unfortunately though, they constitute the most opaque passages in the book. As with other aspects of his *General Theory*, his interpreters have developed the most clearly expressed and most readily formalized parts of his analysis and ignored the rest. The result has been not only a distortion of Keynes' views, but the neglect of some important insights into the nature of money.

4.2 MONEY AS A MEDIUM OF EXCHANGE

A medium of exchange may be described as a circulating means of payment.[2] A means of payment is a commodity which is accepted as final settlement of a transaction. Typically the means of payment is specified in the contract of exchange, and once payment has been made the payee has no further claim against the payer. A medium of exchange is a means of payment which is accepted with the specific intent, not of consuming or producing with it, but of using it in some further exchange. Thus the medium of exchange circulates, because each payee uses it to pay someone else in a subsequent transaction.

The rationale for a medium of exchange is that it economizes on transaction costs. The parable of barter explains how these costs originate. According to the parable the demand for a medium of exchange stems from the difficulty of achieving a 'coincidence of wants'. If two traders meet at random and one has something to offer which is attractive to the other there is no guarantee that the other will be able to offer something suitable in exchange. In the absence of a medium of exchange the opportunity to trade is lost.

The alternative is for a trader to accept something in exchange which is not desired by himself, but which will be acceptable to other people. He can then offer this commodity as part of his next exchange to obtain a commodity he really wants. It may be that the commodity is acceptable to others because they wish to consume or utilize it themselves, or because they in turn believe that the commodity is acceptable to yet another party in a further exchange.

The model of a barter economy suggests a number of desirable characteristics for a medium of exchange.

1. It should be a standardized and homogeneous commodity, so that it is easy for those who accept it to check the quality of the units offered.
2. It should be finely divisible, so that it can be used in any transactions however large or small the value.
3. It should be portable and easily made secure in transit. This enables traders to move around with the commodity to hand, and so reduces the administrative costs of effecting transactions.
4. It should be durable, so that it does not deteriorate or perish while being held over between one transaction and the next.
5. It should be widely acceptable. Historically, the acceptability of money has been closely linked to the taxation powers of governments. When government is willing to accept a particular commodity in exchange for tax obligations it confers wide acceptability on that commodity.

These five characteristics establish a link between the functional definition of money and the indicative definition of money. For not all commodities share these characteristics to the same degree. There will be a tendency toward functional specialization, in which some commodities are regularly used as a medium of exchange, while others are never used in this way. In particular government notes and coin are standardized, divisible, portable, durable and acceptable in payment of taxes. It is for this reason that the functional definition of money as a medium of exchange corresponds with the indicative definition of money as government notes and coin.

4.3 BANK DEPOSITS

Government notes and coin form part of the 'money base' of the banking system. The banking system increases the utilization of the money base by using it to construct a 'pyramid of credit'. The other elements in the pyramid are assets owned by the banks, such as government debt and advances to customers. The banking system serves to 'monetarize' these other assets.

In its most elementary form a bank operates on the 'cloakroom ticket' principle. An item (part of the money base) is deposited and a token of deposit is issued by the bank. The token can then be redeemed on demand for the item whenever it is required. The banking system exploits two particular features of the money base: its homogeneity and the stochastic nature of the demand for it. The homogeneity of the money base means that it is unnecessary to supply the depositor with the specific item he deposited. Since all items are indistinguishable it is only necessary to supply the same number of units, not the actual ones deposited.

The stochastic nature of demand for the money base is such that the probability that any given individual will deposit or withdraw at a given time is largely independent of whether or not he has just made a deposit or withdrawal and whether other people have just made – or are making – deposits or withdrawals. The law of large numbers[3] implies that under these conditions aggregate deposits and withdrawals will fluctuate very little over time. In particular the net withdrawal (that is withdrawals less deposits) will fluctuate so little that ample reserves are available simply by utilizing a small proportion of the total number of units deposited.

The residual assets can be lent out, or used by the bank to purchase other assets; in either case these units are put back into circulation instead of remaining idle in the bank. In this way the banking system allows the velocity of circulation of the money base to be increased. The increase in the velocity means that better use is being made of the stock of the money base.

This benefit is not obtained without cost, however. The security for the depositors' claims against the bank is no longer provided exclusively by the commodity that the claims are denominated in (that is the money base) but also by other assets in which the bank, and borrowers from the bank, have invested. There is a risk that these assets may depreciate in value relative to the money base, so that the total value of its assets becomes less than its liabilities (that is its total deposits). Once this is recognized by depositors, their confidence will diminish, withdrawals will increase and the bank may be forced to suspend payments.

These risks can be reduced by instituting a central bank controlled by the government. The central bank is the government's banker and is backed by the taxation powers of the government. A deposit with the central bank offers the same security as does ownership of government notes. The central bank is always willing to buy assets from the banks at short notice. The seller is credited with a deposit at the central bank, which he can then convert into notes and coin as required. Thus the central bank acts as a 'banker to the banks'. In this way banks can increase their holdings of notes and coin whenever there is a run of withdrawals. In extreme cases the central bank may also be willing to take over the liabilities of an insolvent bank.

At the same time the central bank must ensure that the banks do not take advantage of the insurance it offers by taking greater risks with the investment of deposits. It does this in two main ways. First, it penalizes forced sales by offering low prices for assets purchased at short notice, and secondly it regulates the banks so that deposits cannot exceed a certain multiple of the bank's holdings of the money base. In a closed economy the money base is measured by banks' holdings of notes and coin plus their deposits with the central bank.

On the whole, the banking system is successful in 'monetarizing' the non-monetary assets held by the banks and their borrowers. Such is the confidence in banks that individuals are willing to accept a deposit in their bank account as final payment for a transaction, *in lieu* of notes and coin. When two transactors both have bank accounts, payment can therefore be made simply by a transfer of deposit from one account to another, provided that both accounts are with the same bank, or that banks are willing to clear cheques drawn on other banks' accounts. The widespread use of bank accounts, and the existence of a clearing system among the major banks has allowed payment by cheque to supersede the use of notes and coin for many transactions. This gives each individual a choice of two ways of economizing on transaction costs: either by reducing the frequency of his visits to the bank, or by holding a smaller amount of notes and coin in hand. To the extent that this second strategy is used, the proportion of the money stock held in the non-bank private sector will fall and the amount held on deposit with the banks will increase. This in turn will allow the volume of bank deposits to increase, permitting a still more efficient utilization of the money base.

4.4 A CRITIQUE OF THE PARABLE OF BARTER

The parable of barter makes certain crucial assumptions about the way in which transactions are organized. It assumes that trading is bilateral and sequential, that trading needs are unforeseen, and that trades are effected spot. It is these assumptions that provide the clues to the ultimate significance of money in the macroeconomy.

These assumptions are critically examined in this section and the next. It is shown that in each case the rationale for money lies in the efforts of individual transactors to reduce the amount of information needed to set up transactions, and to effect them without risk to their property rights.[4]

It is easiest to consider the assumptions in reverse order, beginning with the assumption that trading is spot. The parable of barter assumes that when an exchange has been agreed payment must be made immediately; there can be no delay on either side. It is this immediacy of payment which characterizes the spot transaction. There are, however, alternatives to spot trading; these involve one or other (or both) of the parties accepting a claim on a commodity *in lieu* of the commodity itself. For example, individual A could pay for a commodity by offering individual B a claim on a commodity that B wants but that A does not possess. A could obtain this commodity through a subsequent transaction and pass it on to B. The use of such claims would allow a greater flexibility in achieving a coincidence of wants.

The claim could simply specify that it will be redeemed as soon as possible (a quasi-spot claim) or that it will be redeemed at a specific date (a futures claim). The claim may be non-transferable, specifying that A is under obligation to B; or it could be transferable, specifying that A is under obligation to whoever holds the claim. In the latter case B could, if he wished, sell the claim to someone else, say C, in exchange for another claim that he preferred.

There are three main difficulties associated with the use of claims to simplify trading.

First, whatever kind of claim is involved, it is unlikely to prove acceptable unless the person on whom the claim is made is known to the claimant. Although a claim may be nominally transferable, it will not be acceptable to the transferee unless he knows the person against whom the claim is made. Thus *de facto* a transferable claim is likely to be marketable only if the issuer of the claim is widely known and respected.

The reason is that any claimant is exposed to a risk of default. The risk is greater, the greater is the probability of default, and the greater are the costs associated with it. The probability of default is greatest when there are few sanctions against the defaulter. Unless the settlement of reciprocal claims is synchronized, so that payment is made at the same time the commodity is received, one party will have discharged his obligations before the other, and so will have no direct sanction against the other party. He must rely either on legal penalties or on damaging the other party's reputation (and hence increasing his future transaction costs). Legal redress is usually slow, expensive and uncertain; bad publicity may adversely affect those who have a reputation to preserve, but can do little to damage those who have no reputation to begin with.

It appears therefore that the only effective way of controlling the risk of default is to have prior knowledge of the integrity of the other party. The importance of personal knowledge of the other party means that claims are likely to be acceptable only when a regular pattern of transactions with that party has been established, or where the claim is underwritten by a reputable person. The underwriter must be someone who knows the issuer of the claim, and has confidence in him, and who is also known to the claimant, and commands the claimant's confidence. In practice the costs of organizing underwriting are likely to be high, and since the costs are largely fixed costs, they are likely to prove prohibitive for transactions of small value. Spot trading will therefore remain essential for 'one-off' or 'first-time' transactions where the value of the transaction is relatively small.

A second problem with the use of claims is the memory costs involved. Once the contract is agreed each party has to put details of the uncompleted part of the transaction onto file; the issuer of the claim has to arrange to trigger the discharge of the claim at the appropriate time, and the holder of the claim has to make arrangements to monitor him.

There is a third problem which applies to future claims but not to quasi-spot claims. It arises from the fact that economic circumstances are subject to unpredictable change. There are two aspects to this. First, the economic circumstances of the individual may change, so that he no longer requires the commodity on which he holds the claim. The greater the time that elapses between contract and completion – that is the greater the maturity of the claim – the greater is the probability that such change will occur. The individual still has the option of selling the claim to acquire another more appropriate to his current needs, but as we have seen, claims may be difficult to sell unless they are underwritten by a person of repute. The second aspect is that the change of circumstances may affect not just the claimant himself: it may be a general rather than a specific change, affecting all individuals. If the claim is marketable, then following an adverse change its market value will be diminished and the claimant will sustain a capital loss.

The difficulty does not arise from change itself, for in so far as change can be foreseen the individual trader can allow for this when deciding which kind of claim to accept. The problem is that the change cannot be foreseen – that future economic circumstances are uncertain. Nevertheless, it is possible in principle, to resolve the difficulty using contingent claims, that is claims which offer different commodities according to which state of the world prevails at the date of maturity. Contingent claims are exemplified by insurance contracts, in which the benefits received by the insured are contingent on the events which occur.

In practice though the use of contingent claims is subject to three difficulties (all of which are manifest in the high administrative costs associated with insurance contracts). First there is the complexity of defining the claim, and the consequent difficulty of explaining it to the other party. Secondly there is the cost of monitoring the state of the world; both payer and payee will wish to take precautions against misreporting of the state of the world by the other party. This can create difficulty when the relevant state is essentially a subjective one, for example the current state of the payee's consumption preferences. Finally the relevant state of the world, though objective, may be endogenous, that is it may be susceptible to influence by one or other of the parties. In this case the outcome of the transaction may depend on the strategic interaction of the two parties as each attempts to influence the state of the world so as to achieve an outcome favourable to themselves.

The problems created by unpredictable change make quasi-spot claims a more attractive proposition than future claims, for the quasi-spot claim specifically aims to minimize the lag between contract and completion. The conventions that govern quasi-spot trading are dictated mainly by the need to control the risk of default. As we have seen, this means that personal knowledge and reputation are vital in making a quasi-spot claim acceptable.

The practice of quasi-spot trading may be illustrated by an example drawn from a monetary economy. An uncleared cheque is an example of a quasi-spot claim; for payment by cheque is not completed until the cheque has been cleared and money deposited in the payee's account. In the meantime using a cheque allows a transaction to proceed on the basis that payment will be made at the earliest opportunity. Cheques are not normally acceptable unless the payer is known to the payee, or unless the cheque is underwritten. In this connection banks themselves have developed into specialist underwriters, using their privileged access to information on account-holders to screen them for credit-worthiness.

4.5 REASONS FOR BILATERAL AND SEQUENTIAL TRADING

The parable of barter assumes not only that trading is spot, but that it is bilateral and sequential, that is that each transaction involves just two parties, and that each individual carries out a succession of such transactions one at a time. Now in principle this need not be the case. Suppose for example that all transactors sat round a table together and considered the various ways in which their consumption and production activities could be co-ordinated. Their purpose would be to choose between alternative economy-wide plans of co-ordination. Each plan would specify the utilization of each resource and the distribution of the products among transactors. In this hypothetical situation each transactor bargains for the plan which benefits him most, subject to a competitive constraint. The constraint is that a plan cannot be implemented unless it is acceptable to all the resource-owners involved; and it will not be acceptable unless it offers each of them a benefit at least as great as they would expect to receive were another plan adopted instead.

Under such a regime all bargaining is multilateral, and the chosen plan can be implemented through a set of simultaneous trades. There is no necessity for a medium of exchange because the internal consistency of the chosen plan guarantees the coincidence of wants.

The impracticality of multilateral bargaining arises from the information costs involved in putting all transactors into contact with each other. In the natural course of their daily life individuals come into contact with only a small proportion of all the traders they could potentially transact with. To seek out additional traders involves search costs, and the returns to search are liable to diminish quite quickly as the field of search is widened.

Because of search costs the economy becomes segmented. In an extreme case, for example, individual A may know only one person, B, who is willing to supply a particular commodity, say bread, on reasonable terms. At the same time B knows only one person, C, who is willing to supply another commodity, say meat, on reasonable terms. But A has only clothing to offer B, and B already has plenty of clothing. However B knows that C requires clothing. B can trade with A only by accepting clothing in exchange for bread, and then using the clothing to obtain meat from C. Thus B must act as an intermediary, passing on the clothing from A to C. B is involved in two separate bilateral transactions using clothing as a medium of exchange.

If instead A, B and C had all been in direct contact with each other they would have arrived at a multilateral trading arrangement. Using a triangular pattern of trade, B would have supplied bread to A, C would have supplied meat to B, and A supplied clothing direct to C. The clothing would no longer move to C via B, and so would no longer function as a medium of exchange.

In principle the bilateral negotiations between A and B, and between B and C, could be carried on simultaneously or sequentially. In such a simple case simultaneous negotiation is unlikely to cause any difficulty. But in general, participation in a large number of simultaneous negotiations is likely to tax an individual's mental capacities. The 'bounded rationality' of the transactor means that either the quality of his decision-taking will suffer, or completion of transactions will be delayed because each set of negotiations interrupts the others. To keep negotiation costs to a minimum the transactor may prefer to sequence his negotiations. This exposes him to the risk that future transactions may not turn out as anticipated, so that in the light of future transactions the present transaction may be regretted. However this factor is outweighed by his ability to focus all his mental capabilities on the current negotiation, and so make superior decisions on the basis of admittedly more limited information.

The sequencing of transactions means that the medium of exchange must be held in stock by the transactor until it is passed on to someone else. It is this that makes finite the velocity of circulation of the medium of exchange. It also means that the medium of exchange must be accepted

on the prospect rather than the certainty of the value it will command
in a subsequent transaction. This point is fundamental for it means
that the medium of exchange acts as a short term store of value. The
consequences of this are considered in some detail in sections 4.7—4.9.

4.6 TRANSACTION COSTS, DISEQUILIBRIUM TRADING, AND THE ENTREPRENEURIAL DEMAND FOR MONEY

Transaction costs have an important time dimension to them. A seller
making a forced sale, or a buyer making a forced purchase, must accept a
less favourable price than they would expect to obtain if there were
more time to complete the transaction. The main reason for this is the
difficulty of seeking out, at short notice, the person who is in the best
position to offer favourable terms. While commodities in widespread
demand may be readily marketable under these circumstances, most
other commodities are not. Either the transactor incurs heavy search
costs in order to realize the price he expects in the time allowed, or he
must accept a less favourable price with only normal expenditure on
search. One way or another, the net proceeds of the forced seller represent a discount on the normal price, while the net purchase price of
the forced buyer is equivalent to a premium on the normal price. This
discount or premium measures the additional transaction cost on a
forced purchase or forced sale. This additional transaction cost, in
common with the normal transaction cost, is specific to the commodity
involved. Indeed the additional cost is likely to vary much more between
commodities than does the normal transaction cost.

The term 'liquidity' is often used to describe the property of having
low transaction cost on a forced sale. This is of course just one possible
definition of liquidity, and the concept is often given a much wider
connotation. Nevertheless it draws attention to the fact that a significant
proportion of transactions do indeed take place at short notice.[5]

Keynes emphasized this by isolating a special motive — the precautionary motive — for holding money in order to accomplish transactions
which must occur at short notice. The use of the word precautionary
suggests that the transactor is responding urgently to bad news, but this
does not appear to be Keynes' meaning at all. He also considers the possibility that the transactor is responding to good news, in the form of an
unforeseen trading opportunity. The need for urgency presumably arises
because the opportunity is associated with a market disequilibrium: it
is a once for all opportunity which the trader must pre-empt before
others do.

This second aspect of the precautionary motive is much more important than is usually believed. Disequilibrium theory suggests that traders are often rationed by quantity, and the most common form of rationing is undoubtedly 'first come − first served'. In such cases time is of the essence in being able to trade at the quoted price. Most market economies have a specialized class of traders who seek to profit by trading at disequilibrium prices. These are the speculators, middlemen and entrepreneurs (call them what you will) whose object is to buy now at a low price and resell at a higher price later on. These entrepreneurs are a vital element in the competitive process described in Chapter 3. The continual rivalry between them means that if someone does not pre-empt an opportunity for profit as soon as he sees it, then someone else will. An entrepreneur must always have an acceptable commodity to offer those with whom he trades; and it is imperative to his success that its transaction costs are low when it is sold at short notice.

It appears therefore that the rationing procedures which apply in disequilibrium provide transactors with a distinctive motive for holding money. This motive is closely allied to Keynes' precautionary motive, but to avoid confusion it may be given its own terminology − the entrepreneurial motive. The entrepreneurial motive describes the demand for money not only by the professional intermediator but by anyone who recognizes the need to act quickly to take advantage of a market disequilibrium.

The factors which influence the transactions demand for money, namely price and output, will also influence the entrepreneurial demand, for basically similar reasons. The entrepreneurial demand, however, also depends on another factor which does not normally appear in discussions of the transactions demand. The demand will be greater the greater the amount of unforeseeable change that is anticipated in the near future. An expectation that new profit opportunities are about to arise, or that some form of crisis is about to develop, will increase demand in the short run. Once the uncertainty has been resolved − the profit opportunities have been pre-empted or the crisis averted − demand will return to its normal level. Thus demand is sensitive to expectations that change is imminent. If these expectations themselves change frequently then the demand for money may be less stable than is sometimes assumed.

A rather similar point was made by Friedman in his restatement of the quantity theory of money.[6] However Friedman refers only to the influence of 'uncertainty' on the demand for money; he does not specify precisely to what the uncertainty relates nor does he explain how the need for a quick reaction generates a demand for liquidity.

4.7 MONEY AS A STORE OF VALUE

The fact that trading is sequential means that money must act as a store of value between one transaction and the next. When considering the role of any asset as a store of value it is important to distinguish between changes in value which arise from physical changes in the quality of the asset, and changes arising from market revaluation when quality is fixed. The former is usually referred to as depreciation, the latter as capital appreciation – a rather unfortunate terminology, but one we shall adhere to none the less.

The rate of depreciation of an asset normally depends on the environment in which it is stored. Given the storage technology relating to the asset, there is an optimal input of storage services which trades off the additional cost of storage against the saving in depreciation. The sum of storage cost and loss of value due to depreciation associated with this level of storage services will be termed the depreciation cost.

It is usual to assume that the depreciation cost of money is zero. Although this is an oversimplification, it is certainly true that the depreciation cost is much smaller for money than for other assets, and on this basis at least, money is eminently suitable as a store of value.

The capital appreciation of an asset is measured by the proportional increase in its spot price between one period and the next. Future capital appreciation is uncertain; there is always a risk that the expected appreciation will not materialize. Thus capital appreciation has two dimensions to it, not one: firstly expected appreciation, and secondly the risk associated with the rate of appreciation.

In order to achieve capital appreciation it is not necessary to hold the asset itself, but merely to hold a forward claim on the asset. Both the asset and the forward claim will necessarily have the same value at the date the claim matures, and so the risk associated with the future value will be the same in each case. The expected appreciation will normally differ, however. Although the future value is the same in each case, the value of the forward claim at present is unlikely to equal the current price of the asset. The reason is that the holder of the asset gains certain user services from holding it, and also incurs depreciation costs, neither of which apply to the holder of the forward claim. The investor will be in equilibrium, holding partly claims and partly asset, when at the margin the value of user services provided by the asset, net of depreciation cost, is equal to the expected capital appreciation foregone. The latter is in turn measured by the discount at which the price of the forward claim stands with respect to the current price of the asset.

Applying this analysis to money, the forward claim to money is represented by a one-period bond, which is a claim to a unit sum of money one period hence. The discount at which the money price of the bond stands with respect to the monetary unit defines the money rate of interest.[7] The marginal value of user services is equal to the saving in transaction costs effected by a marginal increase in the holding of money; as explained above, the depreciation cost of money is zero. Investor equilibrium therefore requires that money is held up to the margin where the saving in transaction costs is equal to the money rate of interest. At this point the user services of money are exactly offset by the capital appreciation foregone.[8]

4.8 TWO CONCEPTS OF LIQUIDITY

The one-period bond is not the only kind of forward claim available to investors, nor is money the only kind of asset. This section introduces long-term bonds into the analysis, the next introduces real assets.

Consider a very extreme form of long-term bond, which offers a fixed annual money payment in perpetuity. An important feature of a perpetual bond is that it does not change its characteristics from one period to the next – in particular it never comes closer to maturity. Suppose that the perpetual bond can be sold without cost after one period if desired. Suppose furthermore that the expected value of the bond after one period is equal to the redemption value of a one-period bond. It might be thought that, under these conditions, the perpetual bond would command the same current price as the one-period bond, since both offer the same amount of money one period hence. The one-period bond offers a certain claim on money, however, while the perpetual bond offers an uncertain claim. The money value of the perpetual bond one period hence may be influenced by new information which becomes available between now and the next period. Since by definition the content of 'new' information cannot be predicted, this creates uncertainty about the future value of the bond. Thus the long-term bond is similar to the one-period bond in all respects except this: that there is a higher risk associated with its capital appreciation. Consequently when transactors are risk-averse the price of the long-term bond will stand at a discount with respect to the price of the one-period bond.

The fact that one asset has a more certain price at a future date than does another asset constitutes a second aspect of liquidity. In fact it may be termed 'liquidity of the second kind', to distinguish it from 'liquidity of the first kind' which involves having low transaction costs on a forced sale. The two concepts are however related; liquidity of the first kind means that the expected proceeds of sale are high (relative to the price obtainable in a perfect market), while liquidity of the second kind implies that the risk associated with these proceeds is very low because the future spot price can be predicted with accuracy.

It has already been established that the opportunity cost of liquidity of the first kind is measured by the rate of interest on a one-period bond, more familiarly known as the short-term money rate of interest. The opportunity cost of liquidity of the second kind may be determined as follows.

Consider an investor who borrows money in order to buy a perpetual bond, and also makes a forward contract to sell the same bond to someone else next period. The investor receives the fixed annual payment due on the bond, and in return incurs short-term interest charges on the money borrowed while the bond is being held. If the future value of the bond were completely certain then, with competitive financial markets, the spot price of the bond would stand at a premium with respect to its forward price by an amount equal to the annual payment, net of short-term interest charges.

In practice, however, the future value of the bond is uncertain, and in this case the investor carries all the risk associated with the future value of the bond. He becomes a speculator who is speculating purely and simply on the spot price of the bond one period hence. His reward for bearing this risk is measured by the reduction in the premium that the spot price of the bond commands over its forward price. It may be deduced from above that the 'risk premium' is measured by the annual payment, less short-term interest charges, less the actual premium at which the spot price of the bond stands with respect to its forward price. It is this premium which governs the individual's substitution between the risk-free one period bond and the risky perpetual bond. We shall refer to it as the 'speculative premium'.

So far as the individual is concerned each of the three assets described above − money, the one-period bond and the perpetual bond − is a potential substitute for the others. Each of these assets may be classified three ways according to the value of its user services, its depreciation cost and its riskiness (see Table 4.1). The first point to note is that the assets only differ with respect to their user services and their riskiness; in each case depreciation cost is zero. Making pairwise comparisons, note first that the only difference between money and the one period bond is that money generates user services while the bond does not; secondly

TABLE 4.1 CLASSIFICATION OF ASSETS

Asset	*Asset characteristics*		
	User Services	*Depreciation cost*	*Risk*
Money	Yes	No	No
One-period bond	No	No	No
Perpetual bond	No	No	Yes
Real asset	Yes	Yes	Yes

the only difference between the one-period bond and the perpetual bond lies in the degree of risk: the one-period bond is risk-free, while the perpetual bond is not. The greatest difference is between money and the perpetual bond: money generates user services while the bond does not; and money is risk-free, while the bond is not.

Investors seeking to maintain portfolio equilibrium will establish a set of price relativities for the different assets. These relativities will be determined so that the expected appreciation of each asset compensates for the net disadvantage of holding that asset rather than any other.

The pairwise comparisons above indicate that portfolio choice can be broken down into two quite separate problems. The first is to determine the relationship between money and one-period bonds in the risk-free part of the portfolio, and the second to determine the relation between the risk-free component as a whole and the other component, namely perpetual bonds. The first choice is governed by the short-term rate of interest, the second by the speculative premium. Since the one-period bond is the closest substitute for money it is to be expected that the short-term money rate of interest will exert the strongest influence on the demand for money. Because money is a major constituent of the risk-free component of the portfolio, however, the demand for money will also depend on the speculative premium.

In the literature it is often asserted that the demand for money is a function not of the short-term money rate of interest and the speculative premium, but simply of the long-term money rate of interest. The long-term rate is defined as the rate of discount which when applied to the annuities yielded by the perpetual bond gives it its current market value. It is readily established that if the same annuity is payable each year then the long-term rate is measured by the value of the annuity normalized with respect to the price of the bond.

The long-term money rate of interest, so defined, measures the opportunity cost of holding money indefinitely instead of holding the perpetual bond. Although the opportunity cost is expressed as an annual charge, it involves the comparison of two strategies, both of which have an infinite time horizon. It is therefore a measure of opportunity cost over an infinite length of time. It is quite different from a short-term opportunity cost as measured, for example, by the opportunity cost of holding money for one year and then reverting to the holding of a bond. The short-term opportunity cost can only be evaluated by examining the 'yield curve' of the bond; in a world of perfect certainty the appropriate point on the yield curve would correspond to the short-term money rate of interest. In a world of uncertainty the short-term opportunity cost is measured by the sum of the short-term money rate of interest and the speculative premium.

This point has probably been neglected in the literature because the analysis of portfolio choice usually omits consideration of the one-period bond. For example the Tobin—Markovitz model[9] contains just a single risk-free asset, money. Although Tobin's analysis is conducted in a short-period framework, the model itself, by focusing on the perpetual bond, suggest that it is the long-term rate of interest rather than the short-term rate which is relevant. The omission of the one-period bond also results in the two concepts of liquidity being merged into one. As noted earlier, money differs from a perpetual bond both in its transaction costs and in its degree of risk; this distinction is apparent only when there is a one-period bond which differs from money only in its transaction costs, and differs from the perpetual bond only in its degree of risk.

4.9 MONEY AND REAL ASSETS

Consider now the introduction of a real asset such as a producer durable. To simplify the analysis it is assumed that the durable is maintained in prime condition indefinitely. The user services generated by the producer durable are measured by the value it adds in production, and its depreciation by its maintenance costs. Real assets are subject to obsolescence from a variety of causes, and this means that their future capital value is uncertain.

The real asset is unlike all of the three assets previously introduced. It is true that both the real asset and the perpetual bond last indefinitely, but here the similarity ends. The producer durable is riskier than the perpetual bond, it incurs a depreciation cost and generates user services (see the last line of Table 4.1).

One of the main themes of post-Keynesian economics[10] concerns the relation between the demand for real assets and the demand for money. Real assets, like money, generate user services, but of a different kind. Unlike money, however, they incur depreciation cost and carry a risk associated with their capital value. It is on this element of risk that most emphasis has been placed. Investors' confidence in the future value of real assets is extremely volatile. They may suddenly believe that the existing capital structure of the economy is inappropriate to future needs, without having any very clear idea of what these needs are. They become very uncertain about the valuation of individual real assets. As a result they switch into risk-free assets such as money and one-period bonds.

If the important thing is to avoid risk, rather than to hold transactions balances, then they will switch mainly into one-period bonds, and so the short-term money interest rate will fall. This is what happened in Britain in the Great Depression of 1929—33 when the short-term interest rate fell as low as 0.5 per cent. If the owners of some real assets begin to go bankrupt, however, there may develop a precautionary demand for money; equally if it is expected that the uncertainty will soon be resolved and new trading opportunities will emerge then the entrepreneurial demand for money may rise. In this case investors will switch into money rather than one-period bonds, and so the short-term interest rate will, if anything, rise.

In either case, however, the money price of real assets will fall. Any fall in the value of the existing capital stock will cause the demand for additions to the capital stock to fall too. If the existing stock is large in relation to the flow of newly produced assets then this will induce a dramatic fall in the demand for capital good production. Production can only be sustained if the prices of newly produced assets fall in line with the value of the existing stock. Since labour is the major element of variable production cost, the only way this can be achieved is by a dramatic fall in money wages. If money wages are slow to adjust then unemployment will result.

This argument, as originally presented by Keynes, did not link the demand for money directly to the demand for real assets. Instead he proceeded in two stages, linking the demand for money to the demand for perpetual bonds, and the demand for perpetual bonds to the demand for real assets. The first stage of his argument involves a liquidity trap

in which the price of perpetual bonds is prevented from rising above a
certain level by investors' worries that it may soon return to its normal
level and so involve them in heavy capital losses. The second stage of
his argument implicitly assumes that perpetual bonds and real assets
are close substitutes, because sales of the first are normally used to
finance purchases of the second. Consequently the ceiling on the price
of bonds depresses the price of real assets because it raises the cost of
financing their purchase. Because the price of existing real assets is kept
low, the production of new assets is deterred and so the economy
becomes depressed.

This suggests that in Keynes' view it is liquidity of the second kind
which is crucial in determining the demand for money relative to the
demand for real assets. Uncertainty about the future value of long-lived
assets creates a propensity to under-value them. Investors would prefer
to hold money instead. But the overvaluation of money does not lead
to increased employment in money production to absorb the workers
discharged from capital good production, and so unemployment is the
result.

4.10 MONEY AS UNIT OF ACCOUNT AND UNIT OF DENOMINATION

A unit of account is a *numeraire*, or commodity of unit value. Economies
are achieved if individuals standardize on the same unit of account, and
thereby avoid the need for conversion between different units. It is
natural in these circumstances to standardize on the medium of exchange,
since this is the most frequently exchanged commodity.

The role of a unit of account is often assumed to be of little or no
economic interest, but this is not strictly correct. For a unit of account
is usually also a unit of quotation and unit of denomination, and for
this reason its value in terms of other commodities tends to be relatively
stable, at least in the short run.

A unit of quotation is the unit in which sellers advertise their price
to buyers (and *vice versa*). For reasons explained in Chapter 8, advertisers
may be reluctant to change their prices very frequently, so that prices
tend to remain fixed for some time in terms of the unit of quotation.

A unit of denomination is the unit which is used when a contract is
drawn up by specifying the price of a purchase or sale. The unit of
denomination is particularly significant for long-term contracts, where
renegotiation occurs only at discrete intervals of time. Where long-term

contracts are common this gives the unit of denomination considerable stability in its real value.

It is by no means necessary that the medium of exchange should function as a unit of denomination. It is quite possible for prices to be denominated in one unit but payment specified in another. For example oil may be priced in SDRs but payment specified in dollars; antique dealers may denominate prices in Swiss Francs but require payment in sterling; or prices may be index-linked, so that denomination is in 1970 sterling equivalents but payment is in contemporary currency.

When the unit of denomination and the means of payment differ, however, it is necessary for transactors to convert from one to the other, and this obviously increases transaction costs. In the absence of any strong preference for denomination in a particular currency, it is therefore natural for prices to be denominated in the means of payment.

Because the medium of exchange is a natural choice as a unit of denomination, the stability of the value of the unit of denomination contributes to the stability of the value of the medium of exchange. This helps to justify one of the assumptions made in the earlier analysis of risk. In section 4.7 money was said to be a risk-free store of value simply because its future money value was certain. The certainty of the future money value of money, however, is almost a tautology; what is important for the analysis is that the future real value of money in terms of, say, consumption goods should also be certain. This certainty comes not from the role of money as a medium of exchange, but from its role as a unit of denomination.

Conversely the stability of the value of money is important in order for it to retain its role as a unit of denomination. Given the costs of continually adjusting wage and price quotations, and renegotiating contracts, it is important for transactors to select a unit of denomination whose value is stable. Thus an initial propensity to stability is necessary for a commodity to be considered as a unit of denomination. Once it has been adopted for this purpose, its use as a unit of denomination will enhance its stability.

To illustrate, Keynes assumed (often implicitly) that wages were renegotiated only at certain intervals, for example once a year. If the magnitude of wage adjustments is limited, and adjustment itself is infrequent, then the rate of change of money wages will be confined within narrow bounds, and so money wages will tend to be stable. As noted earlier, wages are a major component of short-run marginal cost and in a competitive economy the equilibrium of the firm implies that price is equal to marginal cost. It follows that the short-run stability of the money wage implies the short-run stability of money price. The stability of money prices in turn makes money a low-risk short-term store of value. It was fundamental to Keynes' argument that the denomination of wages in money terms made money attractive as a short-term store of value, and thereby underpinned its role as medium of exchange. If wages were denominated in some other unit then that unit would become attractive as a store of value, while the stability of the value of the money unit would be imparied.

The one thing most likely to make workers switch to another unit of denomination would be the introduction of a flexible money wage policy. Given the volatility of investors' expectations, noted above, wage and price flexibility would lead to considerable instability in the real value of the money unit. This would encourage workers to stipulate for wages denominated in some other unit, which might then become preferred not only as unit of denomination but also as means of payment. Thus what began as an attempt to free wages and prices in terms of one money unit might simply result in wages and prices becoming sticky in terms of some other money unit instead.

4.11 SUMMARY

Conventional monetary theory is based on a 'components of demand' approach. Three components of the demand for money are distinguished: the transactions demand, the precautionary demand, and the speculative demand. The transactions demand depends principally on the nominal value of transactions, the speculative demand on the long-term money rate of interest, while the precautionary demand depends on a mixture of the two.

A careful analysis of the functions of money, however, based on a critique of the parable of barter, shows that the demand for money is essentially a single demand of a precautionary or entrepreneurial nature. The demand originates because of the 'liquidity' that money provides. There are two kinds of liquidity. Liquidity of the first kind is represented by the saving in transaction costs that money affords, because on average money commands a good price in a 'forced sale'. Liquidity of the second kind is represented by the low risk associated with the future spot price of money. An important contribution to liquidity of the second kind is made by the role of money as a unit of denomination, particularly in denominating long-term labour contracts.

Like other commodities, the demand for money is a function of its opportunity cost in terms of various substitutes. The opportunity cost of holding money instead of a one-period bond is measured by the short-term money rate of interest; money is held up to the point where the saving in transaction costs equals the short-term rate of interest. Comparing money with other assets introduces further arguments into the demand for money function. In particular the introduction of a perpetual bond makes the demand for money a function also of the speculative premium, which itself depends upon the short-term rate of interest and the forward price of the perpetual bond. When real assets are introduced the demand for money also becomes a function of the real rate of interest – a point explained and developed in Chapter 6.

The entrepreneurial demand for money depends not only on interest rates and on the speculative premium; like the transactions demand, it depends on the nominal value of transactions, and it is also influenced by expectations of change – in particular by expectations that disequilibrium trading opportunities will emerge.

Overall, the entrepreneurial theory differs from the conventional theory of money in four main ways: (a) it emphasizes short-term rather than long-term rates of interest; (b) it identifies two different aspects of liquidity; (c) it exhibits explicitly the speculative premium which regulates demand for liquidity of the second kind; and (d) it emphasizes the instability of the relation between interest rates, the value of transactions and the demand for money, and identifies the instability with changing expectations of market disequilibrium.

CHAPTER 5

DEMAND-DEFICIENCY
IN A MONETARY ECONOMY

5.1 THE MARK II MONETARY MODEL

This chapter considers the consequences of the existence of money for unemployment. It presents a highly simplified version of the model developed by Barro and Grossman.[1] Money functions as a medium of exchange and as a unit of denomination; it is identified with notes and coin issued by the government and held by the private sector. There are no banks or bank deposits. To further simplify the analysis it is assumed that firms do not hold money balances; all money is held by households.

Households demand money purely as a medium of exchange. Money balances economize on transaction costs. It is assumed that these costs arise chiefly in connection with consumption activities. Costs are lower the greater is the nominal money balance in relation to the nominal value of consumption expenditure per period.

Households plan over a single period horizon. Consequently they hold no assets; there are no bonds, and money does not act as a store of value between one period and the next. No attempt is made to model the circulation of money during the period, and in fact the rationale for a transactions demand in the one-period model is very weak. Our only defence is that the restriction to one period simplifies the analysis and so highlights some of the most important results. These results generalize to more complex models, such as the model presented in Chapter 6, where households plan over a two-period horizon and have a choice between money and bonds as stores of value.

There are three markets − for labour, goods and money − and three types of transactor − households, firms and government. Given the three markets there are two independent relative prices, the money wage W and the money price P.

The representative household pursues an integrated plan of consump-

76

tion, saving and work. It supplies labour n^s and demands consumption c^d; it anticipates a money profit income Π^h and pays a lump sum tax T. The excess of post-tax income over consumption expenditure goes into savings, which take the form of additional holdings of money:

$$\dot{M}^d = M^d - M \tag{5.1}$$

where M^d is the nominal demand for money stock and M is the household's initial holding of it. Thus the household faces a budget constraint

$$Pc^d + \dot{M}^d = Wn^s + \Pi^h - T \tag{5.2}$$

As before, real variables are defined by normalizing monetary variables with respect to money price; they are denoted by small letters, that is $w = W/P$, $\pi = \Pi/P$, $t = T/P$, $m = M/P$ $\dot{m} = \dot{M}/P$. Thus the budget equation (5.2) becomes in real terms

$$c^d + \dot{m}^d = wn^s + \pi^h - t \tag{5.3}$$

Subject to this constraint the household maximizes utility

$$u = u(c^d, n^s, j) \tag{5.4}$$

where j is the value of nominal money balances relative to nominal consumption expenditure

$$j = M^d/Pc^d = m^d/c^d \tag{5.5}$$

The first order conditions for a maximum determine the household demand and supply functions

$$
\begin{aligned}
c^d &= c^d \ (\underset{(+)}{w}, \ \underset{(+)}{\pi^h}, \ \underset{(+)}{m}, \ \underset{(-)}{t}) \\
n^s &= n^s \ (\underset{(+)}{w}, \ \underset{(-)}{\pi^h}, \ \underset{(-)}{m}, \ \underset{(+)}{t}) \\
\dot{m}^d &= \dot{m}^d \ (\underset{(+)}{w}, \ \underset{(+)}{\pi^h}, \ \underset{(-)}{m}, \ \underset{(-)}{t})
\end{aligned}
\tag{5.6}
$$

Each function has the same arguments because each decision variable is part of the same overall household plan. The signs in brackets refer to the partial derivatives. Convexity of household preferences is not sufficient to determine all these signs; some additional restrictions need to be made. The most significant restriction in (5.6) is that the supply of labour is everywhere an increasing function of the real wage. Labour supply is also shown as an increasing function of taxation, but this is because taxation is, by assumption, administered on a lump sum basis, so that the substitution effect on labour supply is zero.

Once again the representative firm maximizes real profit

$$\pi^f = y^s - wn^d \tag{5.7}$$

where n^d is labour demand and y^s product supply. Technology exhibits diminishing marginal returns to the single variable factor:

$$y^s = y(n), \qquad dy/dn > 0, dy^2/dn^2 < 0 \tag{5.8}$$

Maximizing (5.7) subject to (5.8) determines the labour demand and product supply functions

$$n^d = n^d\ (w); \qquad y^s = y^s\ (w) \tag{5.9}$$
$$(-) \qquad\qquad (-)$$

and also the profit function

$$\pi^f = \pi^f\ (w) \tag{5.10}$$
$$(-)$$

All the partial derivatives of (5.9) and (5.10) are unambiguously signed.

Government spends on a *per capita* basis G^d, which it finances out of taxation and by increases in the money supply. Both government expenditure and taxation are set exogenously in money terms. The government budget constraint is, in real terms,

$$g^d = t + \dot{m}^s \tag{5.11}$$

where

$$\dot{m}^s = m^s - m \tag{5.12}$$

Summing the budget constraints (5.3), (5.7) and (5.11), substituting in the equation of aggregate demand

$$y^d = c^d + g^d \tag{5.13}$$

and rearranging terms gives the GWL for the economy:

$$z_y + wz_n + z_m + (\pi^f - \pi^h) = 0 \tag{5.14}$$

The first three terms on the left-hand side are the respective excess demands for goods, labour and money:

$$z_y = y^d - y^s; \quad z_n = n^d - n^s; \quad z_m = \dot{m}^d - \dot{m}^s \tag{5.15}$$

The final term is the discrepancy between firms' planned profits and households' perception of them. If household perceptions are correct,

$$\pi^h = \pi^f \tag{5.16}$$

then (5.14) reduces to

$$z_y + w z_n + z_m = 0 \tag{5.17}$$

This is SWL; it asserts that the total value of all excess demands in the economy is zero. Amongst other things this implies that if the goods and labour markets are both in equilibrium then the money market must be in equilibrium too. Conversely if the money market is in disequilibrium then either the labour market or the product market must be in disequilibrium too.

General equilibrium is achieved when all excess demands are zero:

$$z_y = z_n = z_m = 0 \tag{5.18}$$

Substituting (5.6), (5.9) and (5.13) into (5.18) determines the excess demands as functions of w, π^h, m, t, g^d and $\dot{m}^s$. Use of (5.11) and (5.16) makes it possible to eliminate respectively $\dot{m}^s$ and π^h. Separating the endogenous arguments W,P from the exogenous arguments gives

$$z_y \quad (W, \quad P; \quad M, \quad T, \quad G^d) = 0 \tag{5.19a}$$
$$\quad (+) \quad (-) \quad (+) \quad (-) \quad (+)$$

$$z_n \quad (W, \quad P; \quad M, \quad T) \quad = 0 \tag{5.19b}$$
$$\quad (-) \quad (+) \quad (+) \quad (-)$$

$$z_m \quad (W, \quad P; \quad M, \quad T) \quad = 0 \tag{5.19c}$$
$$\quad (+) \quad (+) \quad (-) \quad (-)$$

Not all of the partial derivatives can be unambiguously signed; the signs indicated here are typical of those assumed in the literature.

SWL indicates that only two of the three equations are independent. Full employment equilibrium is determined by solving any two of the equations for W^e, P^e, and then substituting into (5.9) to determine employment, n^e and output, y^e:

$$\begin{aligned}
W^e &= W^e\ (M, T, G^d) \\
P^e &= P^e\ (M, T, G^d) \\
n^e &= n^e\ (M, T, G^d) \\
y^e &= y^e\ (M, T, G^d)
\end{aligned} \tag{5.20}$$

The equilibrium is illustrated graphically in Figure 5.1. To assist in the economic interpretation the axes represent not the money wage and

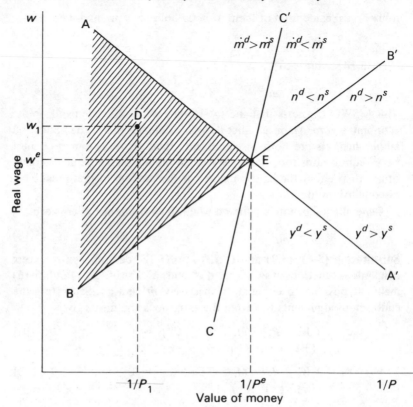

Figure 5.1. Equilibrium conditions for a monetary economy

money price but the real wage and the reciprocal of the money price. The significance of the real wage is obvious: if monetary factors are held constant then it is the real wage which governs equilibrium on the real side of the economy.

The reciprocal of the money price measures the value of money in terms of goods. When money price is low the real value of households' initial endowments of money is high and this encourages them to spend more on all 'normal goods', which include consumption. This is the wealth effect — analogous to the income effect in consumer theory.

Equilibrium in the product market is represented by the locus AA', derived from equation (5.19a). It is downward sloping from left to right because when the value of money is increased the wealth effect stimulates consumption, and so to maintain product market equilibrium, supply must be increased by a reduction in the real wage. A lower real wage also helps to restore equilibrium by reducing household planned wage income, thereby discouraging consumption.

Equilibrium in the labour market is represented by the locus BB', derived from equation (5.19b). It is upward sloping from left to right because when the value of money is increased the wealth effect encourages increased consumption of leisure, and hence a lower labour supply. To maintain equilibrium the demand for labour must be reduced by an increase in the real wage. The increase in the real wage may also encourage households to substitute work for leisure, and so help to counteract the reduction in labour supply.

Equilibrium in the money market is represented by the locus CC', derived from equation (5.19c). Because of SWL, the locus CC' passes through the intersection E of the loci AA' and BB'. The upward slope of the locus CC' may be deduced as follows. When the value of money increases the value of initial household money balances increases. At the same time the wealth effect increases household demand for real money balances. There are two separate wealth effects. The first encourages households to increase the ratio j of money balances to consumption expenditure in order to reduce transaction costs. The second arises because the planned level of consumption expenditure increases too, so that money balances must be increased merely to keep j constant.

Unless the demand for real money balances is highly wealth-elastic, however, the increase in real demand will be less than the increase in the real endowment. It follows that households will wish to decumulate nominal money balances. Since by assumption the supply of nominal money balances is exogenous, equilibrium must be maintained by further stimulation of nominal demand. This calls for an increase in the real wage which will increase the nominal demand through an income effect. Thus to maintain equilibrium in the money market an increase in the value of money must be associated with an increase in the real wage, and so the locus CC' is upward-sloping, as shown in Figure 5.1.

Using Figure 5.1 it is possible to distinguish various regimes according to the excess demand situation in each market. Suppose for example that the real wage is fixed at w_1 and the money price level at P_1, as illustrated by the point D in the figure. Point D lies to the left of AA' which means that, given w_1, the value of money is too low for equilibrium in the product market. Because of the low real value of money balances consumer demand is low and so there is excess supply in the product market. Point D also lies to the left of BB', which means that the value of money is too low for equilibrium in the labour market as well. The low real value of money balances encourages households to top up their income by increasing their labour supply. Consequently there is an excess supply in the labour market. D also lies to the left of CC': the low real value of initial money balances encourages households to accumulate nominal balances, creating a demand for new nominal money balances in excess of their supply.

It can be seen that the point D represents a state of generalized excess supply on the real side of the economy – that is excess supply in both product and labour markets. As predicted by SWL, this is associated with an excess demand for money balances.

A similar analysis can be applied to any wage/price combination. All points to the left of AA' are associated with excess supply in the product market, and all points to the right of it with an excess demand. All points to the left of BB' are associated with excess supply in the labour market, and all points to the right of it with an excess demand. All points to the left of CC' are associated with an excess demand for new money balances and all points to the right of it with an excess supply. Thus for example, the shaded area in the figure, containing all points to the left of both AA' and BB', represents the set of wage/price combinations which are associated with generalized excess supply on the real side of the economy. This case will be the focus of attention later on.

In a perfectly competitive economy money price will be bid up when there is an excess demand for the product, and bid down when there is excess supply. Likewise the money wage will be bid up when there is an excess demand for labour and bid down when there is an excess supply. Thus wage and price adjustments will tend to eliminate excess demands in labour and product markets.

General equilibrium is represented by the intersection E of the loci AA', BB', CC'. Because there are just two dimensions to the diagram, any two of the three loci can be used to determine full employment; SWL guarantees that if any two of the markets are in equilibrium then the third will be in equilibrium too.

5.2 DISEQUILIBRIUM IN A MONETARY ECONOMY

In a monetary economy disequilibrium can lead to unemployment even though the real wage is at or below its full employment level. If money price is fixed too high – so that the real value of households' initial stock of money balances is unacceptably low — then there may be an excess demand for new money balances. This generates excess supply in both labour and product markets, setting off a downward spiral of output and employment adjustments, which ends only when the impoverishing effect of lower incomes has reduced the demand for money balances into equality with the exogenous supply.

This case of 'generalized excess supply' on the real side of the market was first systematically discussed by Barro and Grossman. Both households and firms experience quantity constraints (unlike classical unemployment in which only the households are constrained). Households cannot supply as much labour as they would wish at the prevailing money wage, while firms cannot sell as much output as they would wish at the prevailing money price. These two constraints had been considered separately, by Clower and Patinkin respectively; the present model analyses their interaction.[2]

It is appropriate at this stage to introduce some special notation for effective demands and supplies. They will be denoted respectively by the capital superscripts D, S, to distinguish them from notional demands and supplies, which continue to be denoted by the small superscripts d, s. The objective functions and budget constraints which were specified in terms of notional demands and supplies still apply to effective demands and supplies. An equation first specified in terms of notional quantities and rewritten in terms of effective quantities is indicated by a prime following the equation number.

To simplify the analysis it is now assumed that household preferences between current consumption and money balances are based on an exogenous estimate of constrained employment, n^h, independent of actual employment, n.

When there is notional excess supply in the labour market, households maximize

$$u = u(c^D, n^h, j) \tag{5.21}$$

subject to $(5.1')$, $(5.2')$ and the employment constraint

$$n^S \leqslant n \tag{5.22}$$

Since the constraint is binding the solution determines the effective demands and supplies:

$$c^D = c^D (y^H, n^h, P, M, T) \tag{5.23a}$$

$$n^S = n \tag{5.23b}$$

$$\dot{m}^D = \dot{m}^D (y^H, n^h, P, M, T) \tag{5.23c}$$

The effect of the employment constraint is to introduce a new argument,

$$y^H = wn + \pi^H \tag{5.24}$$

into the consumption and money-demand functions. The new argument is the household's expectation of its constrained income. It is the income anticipated by the household when it perceives the employment constraint on wage income, n, and when its expectation of profit, π^H, allows for the fact that firms may be subjected to a sales constraint (see below). The wage rate does not appear separately in equations (5.23) because at the margin it is employment-rationing and not wage-rationing that governs income/leisure choice. The appearance of household income in equation (5.23a) makes it analogous to the consumption function of Keynesian theory.

When there is excess supply in the product market firms maximize (5.7′) subject to (5.8′) and the sales constraint

$$y^S \leqslant y \tag{5.25}$$

Since the constraint (5.25) is binding the firm's optimal strategy is to employ just sufficient labour to meet demand for the product. The effective labour demand and product supply functions are

$$\begin{aligned} n^D &= n^D (y) \\ y^S &= y \end{aligned} \tag{5.26}$$

and profit becomes

$$\pi^F = y - wn^D \tag{5.27}$$

The use of a capital superscript in (5.27) indicates that the profit is associated with a quantity-constrained production plan.

Constrained equilibrium (indicated by the superscript E) implies, amongst other things, that

$$y^D = y^S = y^H \tag{5.28}$$

All three variables are in turn identically equal to the equilibrium income y^E. Substituting the equation of aggregate demand (5.13′) and the consumption function (5.23a) into (5.28) yields

$$c^D (y^E, n^h, P, M, T) + g^d = y^E \tag{5.29}$$

Given P, M, T and G^d, this determines equilibrium income y^E. Equilibrium employment n^E and profit π^E may then be determined from equations (5.26) and (5.27).

A simple illustration of constrained equilibrium is given in Figure 5.2. Suppose that the economy is initially at full employment and that the money wage and money price level then increase in the same proportion. It may be imagined, for example, that a union-negotiated money wage increase is being passed on to consumers in higher administered product prices. Government expenditure and taxation are ignored, and the money supply remains constant.

Since the real wage remains unchanged, G and T are zero and M is constant, the only variables are P, which is exogenous, and the endogenously determined equilibrium output and employment, y^E, n^E. For small variations in P it is possible to examine the induced variations in y^E and n^E using the total differential of equation (5.29),

$$(\partial c^D/\partial y^E)\, dy^E + (\partial c^D/\partial P)\, dP = dy^E \tag{5.30}$$

Grouping terms in dy^E gives the multiplier formula:

$$dy^E = [1 - (\partial c^D/\partial y^E)]^{-1} (\partial c^D/\partial P)\, dP \tag{5.31}$$

This formula determines the quantity adjustment dy^E implied by an exogneous price change dP. The adjustment is equal to the change in consumption induced initially by the change in price, multiplied by the reciprocal of the household marginal propensity to save.

In Figure 5.2 price- and quantity-adjustments are separated into the left-hand and right-hand sides of the diagram. The schedule BB' in the top left-hand quadrant shows how consumption responds to price when employment is fixed at the full employment level n^e, while the schedule DD' in the top right-hand quadrant shows how consumption depends upon income when price is fixed at its full employment level P^e. An increase in the price from P^e to P_1 initially reduces consumption from c^e to c_1, as indicated by the movement along BB' from G to H. This is associated with an excess demand for real money balances of the same amount. This shifts down the schedule DD' in parallel fashion by $c^e - c_1$ to FF', creating an excess supply of output $y^e - y_1 = c^e - c_1$. The same effect would be produced in a Keynesian model by a fall in autonomous consumption. Firms are now sales-constrained and reduce output to y_1 to eliminate excess supply. They adjust along the production frontier OA, in the bottom right-hand quadrant, from N to Q reducing employment to n_1. The reduction in household income to y_1 now feeds back into the top left-hand quadrant, shifting the price-consumption locus

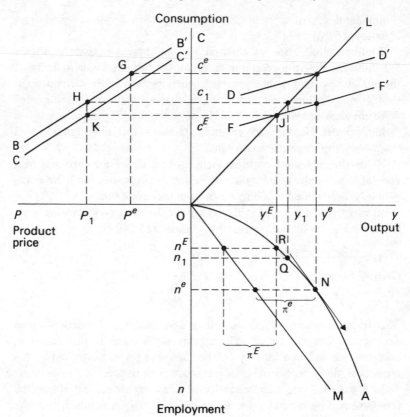

Figure 5.2. Demand-deficiency unemployment due to a too-high money
price level

Note: Strictly speaking the schedules BB′, CC′, DD′, FF′, apply only
over the range of price and output associated with notional excess supplies
in the labour and product market. Furthermore the schedules must be
regarded only as first-order linear approximations valid in the region of
the initial levels of price and output

BB′ downward and inducing a further fall in consumption. This in turn
feeds into the top right-hand quadrant, inducing a further contraction
of output. Equilibrium is achieved at J, the intersection of the consumption function FF′ and the 45° line OL. Given the new price P_1, income-
constrained consumption is just equal to the income which constrains
it: $c^E = y^E$. Associated with the new lower level of income is the new
price-consumption locus CC′, with households consuming at K.

There is one major difference between this and the conventional Keynesian unemployment equilibrium, and that is that the marginal product of labour is not equal to the real wage, but exceeds it. This is an immediate consequence of the binding sales constraint, which does not appear in Keynes' theory because he allowed price to be flexible (see section 6.4). In the bottom right-hand quadrant of the figure the angle MO*n* which the line OM subtends with the vertical axis measures the real wage. The slope of the production function OA, when referred to the vertical axis, measures the marginal product of labour. At the full employment equilibrium N the slope of the tangent to OA is equal to the slope of the line OM, indicating that the marginal product of labour and the real wage are equal. In constrained equilibrium firms produce at R, however, where the slope of the tangent to OA exceeds the slope of OM; this shows that in constrained equilibrium the marginal product of labour exceeds the real wage.

It can also be deduced from the diagram that if the real wage is fixed then as the sales-constraint tightens and employment is reduced, the level of profit diminishes but the share of profit in total income increases.

5.3 THE PERCEPTION OF QUANTITY CONSTRAINTS

There is one important aspect of the Barro and Grossman theory which has received surprisingly little emphasis: namely, the reason why households fail to respond to quantity constraints on the demand for money balances. Given the assumptions of the model, it is a consequence of generalized excess supply on the real side that there should be excess demand for money. If households perceived this they would modify their consumption and labour-supply strategy accordingly. Consumer demand would increase as money income originally intended to build up money balances was diverted into consumption, and labour supply would contract since one of the major uses of labour income would have been restricted. Thus household response would tend to diminish — and eventually eliminate — the excess supplies in product and labour markets. If this did occur then labour and product markets would adjust without any multiplier effect on income and employment.

The crucial point is that in the context of the money market households do not perceive that they are rationed. Although rationed in the aggregate, no household perceives this rationing itself. The reason is that the rationed asset, being a medium of exchange, is in continual circulation. Because of this continual circulation each household believes that it can, in principle, accumulate as large a money balance as it desires simply by maintaining money expenditure below money income for a sufficient period. What it fails to anticipate is that this strategy will reduce the money incomes of other households, who are indirectly the recipients of its own expenditure, and that they in turn, by reducing their own expenditures, will ultimately reduce its own income. Consequently in the aggregate the individual efforts of households to accumulate money balances are self-defeating. Thus underpinning the entire analysis is the fact that money balances circulate, and that for this reason households do not perceive that money balances are rationed.

5.4 REPRESSED INFLATION*

So far our analysis of the Mark II model has focused exclusively on the case of generalized excess supply. As Figure 5.1 indicates, however, there are three other regimes as well.

The top and bottom segments in the figure involve respectively an excess supply of labour associated with an excess demand for goods, and an excess demand for labour associated with an excess supply of goods. These cases are analogous to those examined in Chapter 3. In the first case unemployment results from a too-high real wage while in the second underemployment results from a too-low real wage. The existence of money balances introduces certain complications, however, which are considered in the following section.

The right-hand segment of the figure represents generalized excess demand — that is excess demand in both product and labour markets. This is a state of 'repressed inflation' where the rigidity of money wages and money prices prevents them rising to eliminate the excess demands.[3] As the figure shows, the repressed inflation is associated with an excess supply of money.

In repressed inflation firms experience an employment constraint, but have no difficulty selling their output since households are actively trying to run down their money balances through high levels of consumption. In fact because household labour supply is constraining firms' production, firms cannot produce sufficient to meet aggregate demand. It follows that if government is given priority over consumers when rationing output then households face a consumption constraint. Households are also constrained in their income, since the employment constraint reduces firms' profitability. To a certain extent this will reduce the significance of consumption rationing, since the income constraint will reduce effective consumer demand. Nevertheless it is assumed that some rationing will still remain.

The representative firm facing an employment constraint n has a constrained product supply

$$y^S = y(n) \tag{5.32}$$

and generates a constrained profit

$$\pi^F = y^S - wn \tag{5.33}$$

The representative household correctly perceives the firm's planned profit

$$\pi^H = \pi^F \tag{5.34}$$

and also perceives a consumption constraint

$$c = y - g \tag{5.35}$$

where y is the realized output. Its effective labour supply becomes a function of

$$\theta = \pi^H - t - c \tag{5.36}$$

which is the post-tax discrepancy between constrained profit income and constrained consumption. The variable θ represents the component of non-wage income which is available for building up money balances. The greater is the non-wage income available, the less is the wage income needed to achieve a given level of money balances, and so the lower will be effective labour supply. Thus effective labour supply is a decreasing function of θ.

Since there is excess demand in both product and labour markets

$$y^S = y \tag{5.37a}$$

$$n^S = n \tag{5.37b}$$

Substituting equations (5.32) to (5.35) and (5.37a) into (5.36) expresses θ as a decreasing function of n:

$$\theta = -wn - t + g \tag{5.38}$$

As employment increases, so both output and profits increase, but output increases faster than profits. Thus constrained consumption increases faster than profit income and so on balance θ diminishes as employment increases, as indicated by the negative coefficient on n.

Since effective labour supply n^S is a decreasing function of θ and θ is a decreasing function of employment n, n^S is an increasing function of n:

$$n^S = n^S (n, w, m, t, g) \qquad (5.39)$$

Substituting (5.37b) into the left-hand side of (5.39) gives an equation for n. The solution of this equation is illustrated graphically in Figure 5.3. The labour market equilibrium condition (5.37b) is represented by the 45° line OX while the effective labour supply function (5.39) is represented by the line AA'. It is assumed that AA' has a slope of less than 45° and intersects OX in the positive quadrant. The intersection G then determines equilibrium employment $n^E < n^e$.

This figure can be used to illustrate the 'supply multiplier', that is the impact on employment of an exogenous change in an economy where

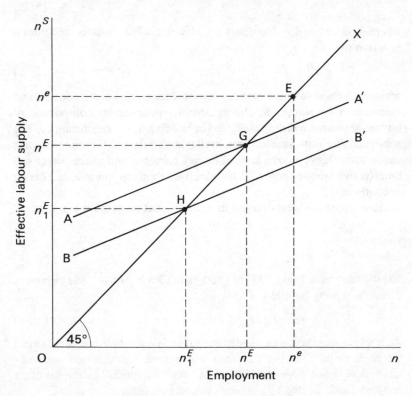

Figure 5.3. The supply multiplier

output is constrained by labour supply. It is readily established, for example, that an increase in government expenditure financed by an increase in the money supply will reduce employment, instead of increasing it as in the case where output is demand-constrained. An increase in government expenditure results in greater rationing of consumption, and so acts as a deterrent to labour supply. For there is no point in households earning additional wage income if they cannot use it for consumption, and if the value to them of any increase in money balances is less than the value of the leisure foregone. As individual households reduce labour supply, however, so they collectively reduce firms' output, and exacerbate consumption rationing, inducing a further contraction of labour supply. The secondary contraction of labour supply is not as great as the first, however, because the effect of increased rationing is offset to some extent by the reduction in profit income which follows from the reduced level of employment. In the figure the effect of the increase in government expenditure is to shift down the effective labour supply function from AA' to BB'. As a result of this the economy adjusts from G to H, which gives an equilibrium level of employment $n_1^E < n^E$.

The analysis of repressed inflation is relevant to situations where prices and incomes policies are used to stifle inflationary pressures built up by expansion of the money supply. It should be emphasized, however, that the case does not apply to stagflation induced by increases in negotiated money wages. Repressed inflation and cost-push stagflation differ in two important respects. In repressed inflation it is the upward rigidity of the money wage and money price level that causes problems, whereas in stagflation it is downward rigidity that is crucial. Also repressed inflation is associated with an excess demand for labour, while stagflation is normally associated with excess supply. In the constrained equilibrium generated by repressed inflation households are on their labour supply curve, so that underemployment rather than unemployment prevails. By contrast in stagflation households are off their labour supply curve and so unemployment prevails. Stagflation is analysed in some detail in Chapter 12.

5.5 THE DYNAMICS OF ADJUSTMENT*

The four regimes distinguished in Figure 5.1 are all based on a comparison of notional demands and supplies. At any point apart from the full employment equilibrium E, however, it is inevitable that either firms or households will experience a quantity constraint in one or other of the markets.

For reasons explained in section 3.7, the constrained transactor will transmit to each market a net demand which takes full account of the constraints binding in other markets, but ignores any constraints in the market to which the demand is transmitted. This means that an operational concept of equilibrium must be based on the Clower effective demands instead of the notional demands.

Consider for example the point F in Figure 5.4. The schedules AA', and BB' are the notional equilibrium loci for the product and labour markets, identical to those in Figure 5.1. The point F corresponds to a real wage above, and a value of money below, the full employment level. There is a notional excess demand for the product, and a notional excess

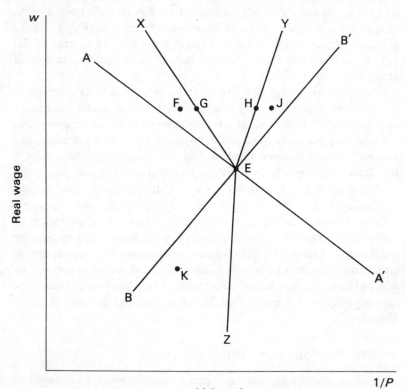

Figure 5.4. Taxonomy of equilibrium states

supply of labour. Households are constrained in both the labour and product markets, whereas firms are not constrained at all.

As shown, F corresponds to a very considerable notional excess supply of labour, and only a small excess demand for the product. This means that household effective demand for the product will be considerably less than the notional demand, with the probable result that the notional excess demand for the product will be replaced with an effective excess supply.

To restore equilibrium in the product market it would be necessary to either stimulate demand by increasing the value of money, or deter supply by raising the real wage. This would involve adjusting wages and prices to a point such as G lying to the right of, or above, the point F. In fact there is a whole set of such points, depending on the combination of wage and price adjustments used: the locus of these points is represented by the line XE in the figure.

Now consider the labour market. Since the household's notional demand for the product exceeds supply it faces consumption rationing, and this will reduce its supply of labour. Thus the effective labour supply is less than the notional labour supply. To bring the effective labour supply into line with the firms' notional demand for labour it would be necessary to stimulate effective labour supply either by increasing the real wage, or reducing the value of money. Thus equilibrium between the notional demand for labour and effective labour supply would be attained at a point such as H on the locus YE. As shown, H lies to the right of F, indicating that at the wage/price combination F, even when households express their effective labour supply rather than their notional labour supply there will still be an excess supply of labour.

Referring to Figure 5.4, it can be seen that the region in which households are effectively constrained in both labour and product markets, the interior of XEY, is much smaller than the region in which they are notionally constrained in both markets, the interior of AEB. At a point such as F in the interior of AEX the constraint on consumption becomes irrelevant once the impact of the employment constraint is felt. Similarly at a point such as J in the interior of YEB the employment constraint becomes irrelevant once the impact of the consumption constraint is felt. Here households would still like to consume more goods (because they would rather consume goods instead of accumulating money balances instead); conversely the rationing of consumption does not satiate their demand for employment (because they would rather accumulate money balances than enjoy leisure instead).

Now consider a point such as K, at which the real wage has been reduced to below its full employment level. There is a notional excess demand for labour and a notional excess supply of the product, indicating that firms are quantity-constrained in both labour and product markets. Households on the other hand are unconstrained. Since firms are employment-constrained they have an effective product supply below their notional product supply, and since they are also sales-constrained they have an effective labour demand below their notional labour demand. To maintain equality between effective product supply and notional product demand it is necessary to reduce product demand by reducing either the real wage or the value of money, while to maintain equality between effective labour demand and notional labour supply it is necessary to reduce labour supply either by cutting the real wage or increasing the value of money. The effect of this is to rotate the locus A'E clockwise, and the locus BE anticlockwise.

Now the firms do not have as many degrees of freedom as the households. Households are involved in three markets: for labour, goods and money balances, while firms are involved in only two: for labour and goods. A consequence of this is that a firm cannot be effectively constrained in both these markets at once. It follows that once effective demands come into force, the region of excess labour demand and excess product supply collapses into the line EZ. This locus describes the combinations of wages and prices at which the households will have notional demands and supplies compatible with the firms being able to produce on their production frontier.

It is apparent that when effective demands are introduced, the four regimes introduced in Figure 5.1 almost collapse into three. The regime of generalized excess supply expands from AEB to XEZ, the regime of repressed inflation expands from B'EA' to YEZ, while the regime of excess labour supply and excess product demand reduces from AEB' to XEY. A fourth regime still exists, but it is represented by a single line EZ.

In the literature the regime of generalized excess supply XEZ is usually referred to as a Keynesian unemployment regime. This identification is based on the view that generalized excess supply can be cured by Keynesian policies, such as stimulating government expenditure or increasing the money supply. Beyond this point, however, all similarity ends. Keynes' own theory does not regard prices as rigid but as flexible, so that the product market is always maintained in equilibrium. Moreover Keynes allowed that when there was unemployment the real wage would be above its equilibrium level. Consequently Keynesian unemployment should be identified with the locus XE rather than with the interior of XEZ. The precise position of the economy on the locus XE will be determined by the level of the money wage. An analysis of true Keynesian unemployment is presented in the following chapter.

CHAPTER 6

THE ROLE OF
INTEREST RATES

6.1 INTRODUCTION

An obvious criticism of the preceding model is that it is based on a one-period analysis of household and firm behaviour. As a consequence all questions of intertemporal allocation of resources are ignored. In particular, money balances are implicitly assumed to be of no value after the end of the current period. This means that the role of money as a store of value is not considered. It also means that the opportunity cost of nominal money balances in terms of current consumption is equal to the value of money, $1/P$. It is not until the possibility of borrowing and lending is introduced that the opportunity cost of money can be measured in terms of the rate of interest. These objections are met in full by the model developed below.

The model highlights an important distinction between the real rate of interest and the money rate of interest. Each of the two interest rates has a specific role in the macroeconomy, and it is important not to confuse them. The real rate of interest is an index of the opportunity cost of current consumption in terms of future consumption. The higher is the real rate of interest, the greater is the future consumption foregone as a result of a marginal increase in current consumption. The money rate of interest, on the other hand, measures the opportunity cost of holding money in terms of the money income foregone. This money income is the interest that would have been earned by holding a short-term bond (that is a bond that matures in one period — often called a bill). The real rate of interest governs the trade-off between present and future consumption, while the money rate of interest governs the trade-off between holding money and bonds. The real rate of interest determines how much wealth people wish to hold to provide for future consumption; the money rate of interest determines the form in which this wealth is held.

Although the two interest rates have quite distinctive roles, their values are related. This is a consequence of the way in which they are defined. Consider any commodity, and compare the spot price of that commodity with the price of a forward claim on it – specifically a claim to the same amount of that commodity one period hence. The own rate of interest on the commodity is defined as the percentage discount at which its forward price stands with respect to its spot price. Since the forward claim extends for only one period, this is a short-term rate of interest. The real rate of interest is, quite simply, the own rate of interest on goods, and the money rate of interest the own rate of interest on money.

There is however a difficulty in the measurement of the real rate of interest, namely that for reasons explained in Chapter 4, very few forward claims on goods are traded. Transactors wishing to establish a claim on future goods must proceed indirectly by purchasing a one-period bond and using the cash received on maturity to make a spot purchase of the product. In doing so they must allow for the fact that because of inflation, money may depreciate in value relative to goods.

Transactors cannot know what the rate of inflation will be but they may be able to form an expectation of it. They can therefore determine an implicit forward price for goods, based on the forward price of money adjusted for the expected rate of inflation. From this they can deduce an implicit real rate of interest which is equal to the money rate of interest less the expected rate of inflation.

In general, relations between interest rates are a reflection of price relativities. In the present instance for example it is the expectation of the future money price level relative to current money price level that relates the real to the money rate of interest. When money prices are flexible, the real and money interest rates can adjust independently. This is important, because in a competitive economy interest rate adjustments are instrumental in moving the economy toward a general equilibrium. Thus when money prices are flexible the real rate of interest can be set to achieve equilibrium in intertemporal consumption, while the money rate of interest can be set simultaneously to achieve a portfolio equilibrium, that is an equilibrium between holdings of money and bonds.

Suppose now that money prices are inflexible. For example, current prices may be fixed because they are administered prices which are not yet due for revision, while expectations of future prices may be inelastic.

With both current price and expected future price fixed, the expected rate of inflation is fixed as well. With fixed inflationary expectations the real rate of interest becomes entirely determined by the money rate: there are no longer two independent interest rates, but only one.

There is no guarantee that the real rate of interest determined in this way is compatible with intertemporal equilibrium. For example, if expected inflation is low then when the money rate of interest is high the opportunity cost of current consumption in terms of future consumption will be high and current consumer demand may well fall short of firms' planned output. This creates a deficiency of product demand which triggers off a downward employment multiplier.

Because of the bond market, the deflationary effects will be somewhat mitigated. The reduced transactions (or entrepreneurial) demand for money will encourage substitution into bonds, which will reduce the money rate of interest, and hence the real rate. This will encourage current consumption and so stimulate aggregate demand. Constrained equilibrium will finally be achieved with lower real and money interest rates than before.

This argument shows that fixed inflationary expectations are crucial in transmitting the effects of high money interest rates to aggregate demand. Although the argument has been couched in terms of consumer demand, a similar argument applies to investment demand. When allowance is made for inflation, it is apparent that an optimizing firm invests in response to the real rather than the money rate of interest (see Chapter 7). It is only when inflationary expectations are fixed that the firm will invest directly in response to the money rate of interest.

These points were well understood by 'classical' economists such as Fisher and Wicksell. It is unfortunate that their analysis was ignored by Keynes when developing his *General Theory*. Although in certain passages Keynes came close to recognizing the significance of the real rate of interest for the investment decision, his analysis of intertemporal consumption choice is deficient in this respect.

An important objective of this chapter is to synthesize classical and Keynesian insights into the significance of interest rates for macro-economic equilibrium. To simplify the analysis as much as possible investment continues to be ignored. It is often assumed that interest rate effects are channelled mainly through investment, but the empirical evidence for this is relatively weak. Interest rates affect consumption in much the same way as they affect investment, and so on both analytical and empirical grounds it is quite legitimate to focus on consumption instead. A full treatment of investment is given in the following chapter.

6.2 THE MARK III MODEL OF INTERTEMPORAL CHOICE

There are now four tradeable commodities – goods, labour, money and bonds – and three relative prices – the money wage W, the money price level P and the money price of bonds, U. A bond is a claim on money which matures one period hence; the money rate of interest is defined by

$$r = (1/U) - 1 \qquad (6.1)$$

All bonds are issued by the government. The nominal value of bonds outstanding at the beginning of period 0 is B; the nominal demand for bonds is B^d and the nominal supply is B^s. (To simplify the notation all time subscripts referring to period 0 are suppressed; only subscripts referring to period 1 are shown.)

There is also a nontradeable asset, equity, which constitutes a claim on the profits generated in the current period, Π, and in the next period, Π_1. Bonds and equities are perfect substitutes because both are assumed to be riskless assets. Consequently there is no loss of generality in assuming equities to be non-tradeable. Equilibrium between bonds and equities is guaranteed so long as equities are valued by the discounted sum of expected profits, where the discount rate is r, the money rate of interest.

Apart from the introduction of bonds and equity the structure of the economy is essentially unchanged from the previous chapter, and unless otherwise stated, the notation is also the same.

The representative household now plans over a two-period horizon. It pursues an integrated plan of consumption, saving, portfolio selection and labour supply. It maximises the well-behaved utility function

$$u = u(c^d, n^s, j, x^{hd}) \qquad (6.2)$$

where x^{hd} is the anticipated real value of wealth at the beginning of the next period. This wealth comprises money, bonds and equity, and is evaluated at the prices expected to prevail at the beginning of the next period.[1] It excludes anticipated future wage income.

Price expectations are assumed to be inelastic, that is the expected future money price level, P_1^h, is independent of the current price level,

P. Price expectations are held with complete conviction: no risk is perceived in converting money-denominated claims into claims on real output at a future date. The expected rate of inflation is expressed in proportional terms:

$$\dot{P}^h = (P_1^h / P_1) - 1 \tag{6.3}$$

The implicit real rate of interest is measured exactly by

$$\rho = (1 + r)/(1 + \dot{P}^h) - 1 \tag{6.4}$$

but when r and $\dot{P}^h$ are both small this may be approximated by the simpler formula

$$\rho = r - \dot{P}^h \tag{6.5}$$

that is the real rate of interest is equal to the money rate of interest less the expected rate of price inflation.

Expectations of future profit, Π_1^h, are fixed exogenously, an assumption which is justified in Chapter 10. On the other hand, expectations of current profit, Π^h, are equal to firms' current planned profit, Π^f. Given these assumptions, the household's expectation of its future real wealth is

$$x^{hd} = (M^d + B^d + \Pi_1^h)/P_1^h \tag{6.6}$$

The household maximizes utility subject to the real budget constraint for period 0:

$$c^d = wn^s + \pi^h - t - s^d \tag{6.7}$$

where s^d denotes real saving:

$$s^d = \dot{m}^d + \dot{b}^d/(1 + r) \tag{6.8}$$

and $\dot{b}^d$ is the demand for addition real bond holdings in period 0:

$$\dot{b}^d = (B^d - B)/P \tag{6.9}$$

Before deriving the first order conditions it is convenient to eliminate j from (6.2) using

$$j = m^d/c^d \tag{6.10}$$

The first order conditions then become

$$dc^d/dn^s = w \tag{6.11a}$$

$$-dc^d/dm^d = r/(1 + r) \tag{6.11b}$$

$$-\mathrm{d}c^d/\mathrm{d}x^{hd} = 1/(1+\rho) \tag{6.11c}$$

Condition (6.11a) describes equilibrium consumption/leisure choice: it equates the marginal rate of substitution between consumption and leisure to the real wage.

Condition (6.11b) describes equilibrium portfolio composition; it sets the marginal rate of substitution between consumption and the stock of real money balances equal to an increasing function of the money rate of interest. To confirm the formula, note that, working in real terms, a unit reduction in money balances must, to preserve future real wealth, be accompanied by the purchase of a unit bond. Since the money price of a bond is only U, this leaves $1 - U = r/(1+r)$ surplus real income, which can be used to finance additional real consumption. If the money rate of interest is low then, to a first approximation, the marginal rate of substitution is equal to the money rate of interest.

Condition (6.11c) describes equilibrium intertemporal allocation of consumption: it sets the marginal rate of substitution between consumption and future real wealth equal to an inverse function of the real rate of interest.

Equations (6.11), together with equation (6.4), determine the household demands and supplies c^d, n^s, $\dot{m}^d$, $\dot{b}^d$ as functions of the endogenous variables w, r, P, Π^h, and the exogenous variables P^h_1, Π^h_1, M, B, T.

As before, firms maximize profit

$$\pi^f = y^s - wn^d \tag{6.12}$$

subject to a technology constraint, and this determines the labour demand and product supply functions

$$n^d = n^d(w) \tag{6.13a}$$

$$y^s = y^s(w) \tag{6.13b}$$

The government budget constraint in real terms is

$$g^d = t + \dot{m}^s + \dot{b}^s/(1+r) \tag{6.14}$$

where

$$\dot{b}^s = (B^s - B)/P \tag{6.15}$$

There is still no investment, and so aggregate demand remains

$$y^d = c^d + g^d \tag{6.16}$$

Summing equations (6.7), (6.8), (6.12) and (6.14) gives GWL

for the economy:

$$z_y + wz_n + z_m + z_b/(1 + r) + (\pi^f - \pi^h) = 0 \qquad (6.17)$$

where

$$z_b = \dot{b}^d - \dot{b}^s \qquad (6.18)$$

For general equilibrium each of the four excess demands in (6.17) must be zero and household profit expectations must agree with firms' planned profits. The equilibrium conditions may be reduced to just three independent equations in the three endogenous variables w, r, P:

$$s^d (w, r, P) - g (P) + t (P) \;\; = 0 \qquad (6.19a)$$

$$\dot{m}^d (w, r, P) - \dot{m}^s (P) \;\;\;\;\; = 0 \qquad (6.19b)$$

$$n^d (w) - n^s (w, r, P) \;\;\;\;\;\;\; = 0 \qquad (6.19c)$$

The exogenous variables in (6.19) have been suppressed to simplify the presentation.

Equation (6.19a) is an aggregate saving condition. It is required for the compatibility of individual intertemporal consumption plans. It is a special case of the more general condition that the excess of saving over investment must equal the excess of government expenditure over taxation (that is, the budget deficit). Since by assumption aggregate investment is zero, in this case aggregate saving must equal the budget deficit. Equation (6.19b) describes an aspect of portfolio equilibrium: the equality of the demand and supply of additional money balances. Equation (6.19c) is the familiar condition for labour market equilibrium.

The solution of equations (6.19) determines w^e, r^e, P^e as functions of the exogenous variables P_1^h, Π_1^h, M, B, G^d, T, $\dot{M}^s$. The full employment levels of employment and output are derived by substituting w^e into equations (6.13).

To illustrate the role of interest rates and prices in macroeconomic equilibrium, Figure 6.1 demonstrates the effects of variations in r and P with w held constant at its full employment level. The locus AA' represents the combinations of r and P which are consistent with aggregate savings equilibrium. These variables influence aggregate savings through the intertemporal substitution effect.

To simplify the analysis it is assumed that the government balances its budget, so that, in equilibrium, aggregate saving is zero. Consider a hypothetical increase in the price level. Since price expectations are inelastic, an increase in P reduces expected inflation $\dot{P}^h$ and so increases

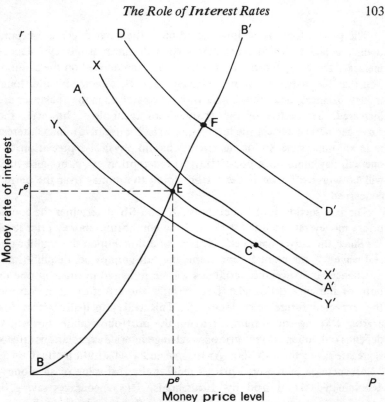

Figure 6.1. Money interest rate and money price level in full
employment equilibrium

the real rate of interest ρ. This stimulates saving and so increases household demand for bonds. To counteract this the money rate of interest
must fall to the point where the real rate of interest is restored to its
original level. Thus to maintain aggregate saving equilibrium the money
rate of interest must fall as the price level rises, that is the locus AA'
slopes downward from left to right.

The locus BB' representing portfolio equilibrium is derived as
follows. As the money price level P increases, the demand for nominal
money balances increases in the same proportion as individuals endeavour
to prevent transaction costs from rising. To maintain nominal demand
equal to the exogenous nominal money supply, the opportunity cost of
money balances must therefore increase, that is the money rate of
interest r must rise. This indicates that BB' must be upward-sloping
from left to right.

The precise form of the lower portion of the curve depends crucially upon the rate at which transaction costs diminish as money balances increase. The curve shown in the figure has been derived on the assumption that the marginal saving in transaction costs effected by additional money balances diminishes continuously to zero as money balances are increased. Irrespective of the transactions technology, however, the curve can never intersect the horizontal axis, for negative money interest rates are impossible, so long as money has no physical depreciation. No one will pay more for a bond than its redemption value, because they will be worse off than if they had stored the money over the period concerned.

The intersection E of the curves AA' and BB' determines the equilibrium money rate of interest r^e and the equilibrium money price level P^e. Since the curves have been drawn conditional upon the equilibrium real wage w^e, the point E represents the full employment equilibrium.

Changes in exogenous variables will be reflected in shifts in one or both of the curves. Consider for example the effect of an increase in the expected future price level P_1^h. This will principally affect the aggregate saving equilibrium, and not the portfolio equilibrium which depends only upon current prices. A change in price expectations affects aggregate saving through both an income and a substitution effect.

An increase in expected prices reduces the real value of all money-denominated claims held by households. This encourages saving in order to adjust future consumption toward its target level. In this way the income effect of the price change stimulates saving.

On the other hand an increase in expected prices raises inflationary expectations and thereby reduces the real rate of interest. This encourages the substitution of present consumption for future consumption, and so discourages saving.

If the income effect predominates then for any given level of current prices, a lower money rate of interest will be needed to discourage additional saving, and so the locus of aggregate saving equilibrium will shift down to YY'. If on the other hand the substitution effect predominates then a higher money rate of interest will be needed to encourage saving, and so the locus will shift up to XX'. If the two effects are equal, then a representative point of equilibrium, say C, will lie between XX' and YY', on the original locus AA'. As a result the macroeconomic equilibrium will be entirely independent of price expectations.

By contrast an exogenous increase in profit expectations will have a significant impact because it generates a pure income effect which discourages saving. To counteract this the money interest rate must increase substantially at a given level of money prices, thereby shifting the locus AA' up to DD', and moving the equilibrium to F. In this way higher profit expectations increase both the equilibrium money interest rate and the current money price level.

6.3 CONSTRAINED EQUILIBRIUM: AN IS/LM ANALYSIS

Suppose now that money wages and money prices are fixed at levels which create generalized excess supply on the real side of the economy. Households experience a binding employment constraint

$$n^S \leqslant n \tag{6.20}$$

while firms experience a binding sales constraint

$$y^S \leqslant y \tag{6.21}$$

To simplify the analysis it is assumed, once again, that household preferences are based on an exogenous estimate of employment n^h. Households maximize

$$u = u(c^D, n^h, j, x^{hD}) \tag{6.22}$$

subject to (6.7'), (6.8') and (6.20). The first-order conditions are similar to (6.11) except that (6.11a) is replaced by the equality of constrained labour supply and the binding level of employment. The portfolio equilibrium condition (6.11b') and the intertemporal equilibrium condition (6.11c') still apply. Solving these conditions determines the effective demands c^D, $\dot{m}^D$ and b^D as functions of the endogenous variables y^H, r and the exogenous variables, w, P, n^h, P_1^h, Π_1^h, M, B, T. The most important of these variables is y^H, the households' anticipated income allowing for the employment constraint (and for the impact of the sales constraint on firms' profitability).

The representative firm's profit-maximizing strategy is quite trivial: it employs just sufficient labour to meet product demand, y, so that

$$\begin{aligned} y^S &= y \\ n^D &= n^D(y) \end{aligned} \tag{6.23}$$

As a result its constrained profit is

$$\pi^F = y - wn^D \tag{6.24}$$

Government behaviour is unchanged, and so is the equation of aggregate demand.

Constrained equilibrium requires that all excess demands are eliminated and that household perceptions of profit agree with firms' planned profit. Taking equations (6.23) and (6.24) in conjunction with the equilibrium conditions for the labour market, product market and profits, allows the remaining equilibrium conditions to be reduced to

$$s^D(r, y) - g + t = 0 \tag{6.25a}$$

$$\dot{m}^D(r, y) - \dot{m}^S = 0 \tag{6.25b}$$

The first of these is the aggregate saving condition, which is shown graphically by the curve IS in Figure 6.2. The second is the portfolio condition, which is represented by the curve LM in the figure. The IS curve is downward sloping from left to right. When prices are rigid, a

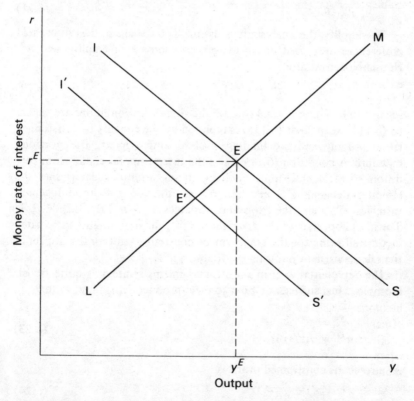

Figure 6.2. IS/LM analysis, showing the effect of a reduction in expected profit

high money rate of interest r corresponds to a high real rate of interest, which encourages saving. To maintain equilibrium, savings must therefore be discouraged by a low real income. Consequently the level of income is inversely related to the rate of interest, and so the curve is downward sloping.

The LM curve is upward sloping. With price fixed, the higher is real income the greater is the demand for money. To maintain the demand for money equal to its exogenous supply the opportunity cost of money must be increased, and so the money rate of interest must rise. Consequently the rate of interest varies directly with the level of income, and so the LM curve is upward sloping.

The intersection E of the IS and LM curves determines the equilibrium rate of interest r^E and the equilibrium output y^E. These equilibrium values are conditional on the exogenous values of w, P, n^h, P_1^h, Π_1^h, M, B, G^d, T.

The nature of the constrained equilibrium may be elucidated by considering the effect of a change in one of the exogenous variables. In view of later developments, it is instructive to consider the effect of a fall in expectations of future profit. A fall in profit expectations has two main effects on the household. It reduces expected real wealth, and so discourages consumption, both now and in the future. It also encourages saving to make good the loss of future income. This saving takes the form of an increased demand for bonds; if anything the demand for money is lower because of lower real wealth. The price of bonds is bid up and the money rate of interest falls until the excess demand for bonds has been eliminated. The interest rate is now so low, however, that, given the initial level of household income, there is an excess demand for money.

Consumer demand has fallen and so at the prevailing real wage there is now an excess supply of the product. Firms reduce employment to the level of consumer demand, and this in turn reduces household incomes. Equilibrium is achieved when the reduction in household income has eliminated the excess demand for money by its impoverishing effect.

Geometrically, the reduction in expected profits shifts down the IS curve to $I'S'$ and, with the LM curve unchanged, both the equilibrium money interest rate and the equilibrium output are lower than they were before. Unemployment is higher because employment has fallen while the notional labour supply has, if anything, increased.

It is evident that the constrained equilibrium of the intertemporal model provides a rigorous microeconomic foundation for the IS/LM analysis, which is the standard apparatus of Keynesian theory.[2] The omission of investment is of little consequence, for the behaviour of the model is determined by the excess demand for saving, and the arguments of the excess saving function are the same whether or not investment is introduced. It is of course to be expected that the introduction of investment will increase the interest-elasticity of the excess saving function, though as noted earlier the empirical evidence suggests that the change would only be marginal.

6.4 KEYNES AND IS/LM THEORY: A COMPARISON

Leijonhufvud's reinterpretation of Keynes emphasizes the distinction between Keynes' own macroeconomic model expounded in the General Theory and the fix-price IS/LM model described above.[3] The latter was developed by Hicks, Hansen, Klein and others from the summaries given by Keynes in Chapters 3, 15 and 18 of the General Theory. But in other chapters — notably 2 and 19 — it is quite clear that Keynes did not regard an assumption of fixed money prices as crucial to his theory. Once price is allowed to vary IS/LM analysis becomes much less powerful as a tool of analysis.

To obtain a model very similar to Keynes' own it is sufficient to relax the money price rigidity assumed in the previous section. The assumption of money wage rigidity is retained.[4] With W fixed, the equilibrium conditions for full employment (6.19) remain overdetermined, and so transactors will be quantity constrained. Attention is focused on the case of a notional excess supply of labour associated with a notional excess demand for money balances. In this case households are quantity-constrained but firms are not. It is assumed that price adjustments maintain equilibrium in the product market, and interest-rate adjustments maintain equilibrium in the bond market.

The constraint on employment is perceived by households but — as explained in section 5.3 — the constraint on the supply of money balances is not. The household decision problem is essentially the same as in the previous section, except that expectations of real income are now based on firms' unconstrained profits, π^h. To emphasize the difference a new variable is introduced

$$y^h = wn + \pi^h \tag{6.26}$$

to represent the household's perception of its constrained income. It is readily established that household effective demands c^D, $\dot{m}^D$, b^D are functions of the endogenous variables y^h, r, P and the exogenous variables W, n^h, P_1^h, Π_1^h, M, B, T. The only differences from before are the replacement of y^H by y^h, and the endogeneity of P.

The major difference concerns the firms, who are now unconstrained, and whose labour demands and product supplies are once again functions of the real wage (cf equations (6.13a and b)). However since the money wage is fixed the only endogenous variable on which they depend is the money price P:

$$n^d = n^d \ (P)$$

$$y^s = y^s \ (P) \tag{6.27}$$

Combining equations (6.26) and (6.27) with the usual conditions for a constrained equilibrium gives the three independent conditions

$$s^D \ (r, P, y) - g \ (P) + t \ (P) \ = \ 0 \tag{6.28a}$$

$$\dot{m}^D \ (r, P, y) - \dot{m}^s \ (P) \qquad = \ 0 \tag{6.28b}$$

$$y^s \ (P) - y \qquad = \ 0 \tag{6.28c}$$

Equations (6.28a and b) are the familiar conditions for saving and portfolio equilibrium, while equation (6.28c) is simply the condition that firms produce on their supply curve.[5] Equations (6.28a–c) constitute three equations in the three endogenous variables r, P, y. Their solution determines r^E, P^E and y^E as functions of the exogenous variables W, n^h, P_1^h, Π_1^h, M, B, G, T.

To analyse Keynesian equilibrium graphically it is best to substitute the aggregate supply condition (6.28c) into the saving and portfolio conditions (6.28ab), and so eliminate P. This reduces the equilibrium conditions to

$$s^{D*} \ (r, y) - g(y) + t(y) \ = \ 0 \tag{6.29a}$$

$$\dot{m}^{D*} \ (r, y) - m^s \ (y) \qquad = \ 0 \tag{6.29b}$$

The reduced form saving condition (6.29a) is represented in the top quadrant of Figure 6.3 by the line HT. Geometrically HT is obtained by rotating the IS curve of Figure 6.2 in a clockwise direction, giving it a steeper slope. The reason is that as output falls, the associated fall in price increases real balances and also raises inflationary expectations. The increase in real balances increases planned consumption both now and in the future; the increase in current consumption out of a given

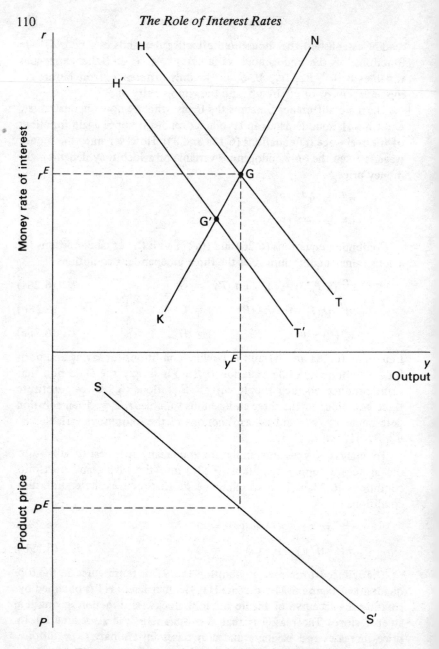

Figure 6.3. Reduced form of the Keynesian model

income leads to a fall in planned saving. This is reinforced by the effect of high inflationary expectations which encourages current consumption at the expense of saving. The price effects associated with a fall in output thus reduce the demand for saving, and so call for a substantial increase in the rate of interest to provide a compensating incentive to save. It is on this account that the HT curve is so steep.

The reduced-form portfolio condition (6.29b) is represented by the line KN, which corresponds to an anti-clockwise rotation of the LM curve. The rotation gives the line a steeper slope. The reason for the steeper slope is that, because the price level increases as output is raised, so the nominal demand for money increases more than proportionately to the increase in output. Since demand increases more rapidly, the interest rate must rise more rapidly in order to maintain equilibrium with the supply.

The intersection G of the HT and KN curves determines the Keynesian unemployment equilibrium r^E, y^E. The equilibrium price level P^E can be read off from the aggregate supply curve SS' shown in the lower quadrant.

Because the HT and KN curves are more interest-elastic than the IS and LM curves output will tend to show greater stability in response to exogenous change. This is intuitively reasonable, since the more markets that are free to adjust the greater should be the stability of the economy as a whole. For example when price is flexible an exogenous fall in profit expectations will shift equilibrium from G to G', which entails a much smaller contraction of output than before. The interest rate has adjusted more, but this is simply a reflection of the fact that price has adjusted too.

A key influence on the degree of stability is the price-elasticity of product supply. The lower the price elasticity, the greater is the burden of adjustment borne by price, and the less is the adjustment of output. For a profit-maximizing firm the price-elasticity of supply is a reflection of production technology, and in particular the speed with which diminishing marginal returns set in. In the Mark III model there is just a single variable factor − labour. Thus on Keynesian assumptions, the stability of output and employment depends quite significantly on the rate at which the marginal returns to labour diminish. The more steeply returns diminish, the greater the stability of output.

6.5 FULL EMPLOYMENT EQUILIBRIUM IN THE ADDI-LOG CASE*

Because of its complexity it is difficult to exhibit the 'inner workings' of the Mark III model in graphical terms. Graphical representation must be confined to reduced forms which often conceal more than they show. When the household has a logarithmically additive utility function, however, these difficulties are avoided because of the separability of different substitution decisions. Moreover when firms have a logarithimically additive production function it is possible to obtain simple algebraic expressions for demand and supply functions, and to solve explicitly for equilibrium values.

Although the addi-log case is highly restrictive, most of its restrictions contribute substantially to simplifying the model. Thus while the solution functions must be applied with caution in empirical work, the addi-log model remains very useful for expository purposes.

The representative household maximizes the utility function

$$u = A c^{d\alpha} (h - n^s)^\beta j^\gamma x^{hd\delta} \tag{6.30}$$

where h denotes the maximum number of hours that can be devoted to work. To ensure that the function is well-behaved it is assumed that the following restrictions apply to its parameters:

$$A, \alpha, \beta, \gamma, \delta > 0; \qquad \alpha > \gamma \tag{6.31}$$

Since utility is ordinal the function (6.30) is defined only up to a monotone transformation; without loss of generality it is therefore possible to set

$$A = \alpha + \beta + \delta = 1 \tag{6.32}$$

It is assumed throughout that government expenditure and taxation are zero. Maximizing (6.30) subject to the household budget constraint determines the notional demand and supply functions

$$c^d = (\alpha - \gamma) q \tag{6.33a}$$

$$n^s = h - (\beta q / w) \tag{6.33b}$$

$$m^d = \gamma (1 + r) q / r \tag{6.33c}$$

$$b^d = (\delta - \gamma/r) (1 + r) q - (\Pi_1^h / P) \tag{6.33d}$$

where q is a measure of real wealth which includes the imputed value of leisure:

$$q = wh + \pi^h + m + (b + \Pi_1^h/P)/(1 + r) \qquad (6.34)$$

The representative firm has a production function

$$y = n^\nu \qquad (6.35)$$

where $0 < \nu < 1$. Profit maximization determines the labour demand, product supply and profit functions

$$
\begin{aligned}
n^d &= (w/\nu)^{1/(\nu - 1)} \\
y^s &= n^{d\nu} \qquad\qquad (6.36) \\
\pi^f &= (1 - \nu) y^s
\end{aligned}
$$

Solving the general equilibrium conditions determines equilibrium employment and output

$$
\begin{aligned}
n^e &= h/(1 + \beta/(\alpha - \gamma)\nu) \\
y^e &= n^\nu
\end{aligned}
\qquad (6.37)
$$

The associated equilibrium 'price set' is

$$w^e = \nu n^{\nu - 1} \qquad (6.38a)$$

$$r^e = \gamma X^h/\delta M \qquad (6.38b)$$

$$P^e = r^e M/[(1 + r^e)\gamma y^e] \qquad (6.38c)$$

where M is the exogenous money supply and X^h is the exogenously determined nominal wealth,

$$X^h = M + B + \Pi_1^h \qquad (6.39)$$

The equilibrium solution has a number of important properties.

1. The equilibrium real wage — and hence employment and output too — depend only on 'real factors': the parameters of utility α, β, γ, the parameter of production technology ν and the maximum hours of work, h.

   Figure 6.4a exhibits the determination of the real wage. Consumption and output are measured vertically, work and leisure horizontally (from opposite ends of the axis). The representative household has a constant elasticity of substitution between consumption and leisure $(\alpha - \gamma)/\beta$ which is independent of portfolio decisions. Full employment is at the point of tangency E between the indifference curve BC

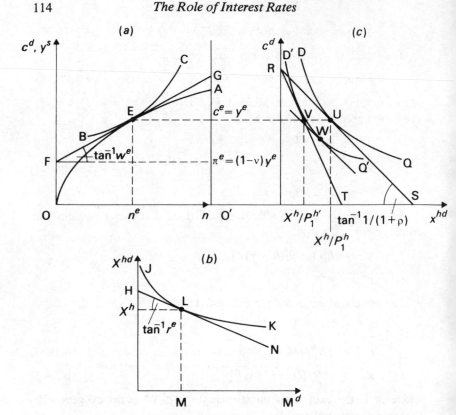

Figure 6.4. Full employment equilibrium in the addi-log case

and the representative firm's production function OA. The slope of the tangent FG determines the equilibrium real wage w^e. Its intercept with the left hand vertical axis determines the equilibrium real profit OF. Its intercept O'G with the right-hand vertical axis gives a measure of household real consumption gross of the imputed value of leisure.

2. The equilibrium money interest rate depends principally on 'monetary factors': the parameter of money utility, γ, and the ratio of the money supply M to the money value of wealth X^h; the only non-monetary factor is the parameter of future consumption utility, δ.

The determination of the money interest rate is illustrated in Figure 6.4b. The stock of nominal money balances is measured horizontally and the nominal value of wealth (inclusive of money balances) is measured vertically. The household has a constant elasticity of substitution γ/δ between real money balances and future real wealth. Since elasticities are defined in terms of percentage changes they are invariant to proportional change in the variables; hence the same elasticity applies between nominal money balances and the nominal value of wealth. The form of the trade-off is illustrated by the indifference curve JK.

Household equilibrium is achieved where the slope of the indifference map is equal to the opportunity cost of holding money balances, which is measured by the money rate of interest, r. For market equilibrium this condition must be satisfied at the point L representing the fixed endowments of money, M, and money wealth, X^h. The equilibrium rate of interest is therefore determined by the slope of the tangent HN to the indifference curve JK at L.

3. There are three important features of the equilibrium price.
   (a) Unlike the real wage and money rate of interest, the equilibrium price depends significantly upon both real and monetary factors. Its relation to each of these factors is one of either direct or inverse proportionality. It is directly proportional to the money supply M, inversely proportional to both the parameter of money utility, γ, and the equilibrium real output, y^e, and an increasing function of the money rate of interest r^e. When rearranged in the form

   $$[\gamma\,(1 + r^e)/r^e]\,P^e\,y^e = M \qquad (6.40)$$

   it resembles the modern quantity theory of money.
   (b) The general equilibrium relation (6.40) also resembles the partial equilibrium relation that is obtained, within the same model, by analysing the money market in isolation. The household demand for money in response to arbitrary parametric values of P and r is given by equation (6.33c). Using this demand for money function, the condition for partial equilibrium in the money market becomes

   $$[\gamma\,(1 + r)/r]\,P\,q = M \qquad (6.41)$$

   which resembles (6.40) if $P = P^e$, $r = r^e$ and $q = y^e$.

However, despite the formal similarity the behavioural interpretations of the equations are quite different. Equation (6.40) described how the three endogenous
variables P^e, r^e, y^e vary with respect to each other in a
cross-section of different equilibrium situations.
Equation (6.41) describes how a single endogenous
variable, r, adjusts when the economy is disturbed from
equilibrium by different sorts of exogenous variation in
P and q.

(c) A final property of the equilibrium price is that it is
completely independent of expectations of future prices.
This result applies only because of the addi-log utility
function. When expectations of future prices change
the income and substitution effects on planned current
consumption are equal and opposite. Thus current
consumer demand is independent of future price; and
since current output is also independent of future
price, expectations of the future price cannot influence
the current price.

This property is illustrated in Figure 6.4c. The vertical axis measures
current consumption and the horizontal axis the real value of inherited
wealth. The specimen intertemporal indifference curves DQ, D' Q' have a
constant elasticity of substitution $\delta/(\alpha - \gamma)$. Household equilibrium
requires that the marginal rate of intertemporal substitution is equal to
the opportunity cost of future consumption in terms of current consumption, $1/(1 + \rho)$. For market equilibrium the household must plan
intertemporal consumption at U, where it is compatible with the equilibrium output y^e in the goods market (cf Figure 6.4a) and with the
available stock of real wealth, X^h/P_1^h. Thus the slope of the tangent
RS at U determines $1/(1 + \rho^e)$. Given the equilibrium money rate of
interest r^e and the exogenous price expectations P_1^h, the current price
level P^e is determined by ρ^e.

Suppose now that price expectations double to $P_1^{h'}$, thereby halving
the real value of wealth. Market equilibrium now requires a household
consumption pattern represented by V. Given the constant elasticity of
substitution, the slope of the tangent RT to the indifference curve D' Q'
at V is exactly twice the slope of the tangent RS. This shows that a
doubling of expected future price results in a doubling of the equilibrium

relative price between future goods and current goods. It follows that the equilibrium current price is unchanged.

The argument can be expressed very simply in terms of income and substitution effects. When price expectations double, households experience an income effect which tends to reduce both present and future consumption, and a substitution effect which tends to increase current consumption at the expense of future consumption. In the figure the income effect shifts the household from U to W and the substitution effect from W to V. With addi-log utility the two effects are equal: they reinforce each other in halving future consumption, but cancel one another out where current consumption is concerned. Thus a doubling of price expectations has no effect on current consumption plans and so no effect on current equilibrium price.

6.6 UNEMPLOYMENT EQUILIBRIUM IN THE ADDI-LOG CASE*

Suppose now that the household faces a binding employment constraint which fixes effective labour supply at n. Suppose also that in determining its preferences between present and future consumption, and between consumption and money balances, the household assumes a fixed level of employment n^h independent of n. Thus the household maximizes

$$u = Ac^{d\alpha} n^{h\beta} j^{\gamma} x^{hd\delta} \tag{6.42}$$

subject to

$$y^h = c^d + \dot{m}^d + \dot{b}^d/(1+r) \tag{6.43}$$

where y^h is expected real income,

$$y^h = wn + \pi^h \tag{6.44}$$

The first order conditions determine the effective demand functions

$$c^D = (\alpha - \gamma) q'/\epsilon \tag{6.45a}$$

$$m^D = \gamma (1+r) q'/\epsilon \tag{6.45b}$$

$$b^D = (\delta - \gamma/r)(1+r) q'/\epsilon - \Pi_1^h/P \tag{6.45c}$$

where

$$q' = y^h + m + (b + \Pi_1^h/P)/(1+r)$$

$$\epsilon = \alpha + \delta \tag{6.46}$$

Suppose now that both the money wage and money price are rigid, and that there is generalized excess supply on the real side of the economy. In this case firms as well as households are quantity-constrained. Each firm faces a sales constraint and its profit-maximizing strategy is to supply exactly what is demanded, and to demand just sufficient labour to produce it with. If sales are constrained to y then

$$n^D = y^{1/\nu} \tag{6.47a}$$

$$\pi^F = y - wn^D \tag{6.47b}$$

The general equilibrium conditions imply

$$c^D = y^S = y = y^h \tag{6.48a}$$

$$n^D = n^S = n \tag{6.48b}$$

$$m^D = m^S = m \tag{6.48c}$$

In solving these conditions it is useful to make a change of variable from r to r', where

$$r' = r/(1 + r) \tag{6.49}$$

For small values of r the two variables are approximately equal, and so when interpreting the results we refer to r and r' indifferently as the money rate of interest. The advantage of the transformation is that some of the equilibrium conditions are non-linear in r but linear in r', and so are rendered more easily soluble.

Substituting (6.45a) into (6.48a) and solving for y gives the IS equation

$$y = \zeta \left[M + (B + \Pi_1^h)(1 - r') \right] / P \tag{6.50}$$

where

$$\zeta = (\alpha - \gamma)/(\gamma + \delta) \tag{6.51}$$

Substituting (6.45b) into (6.48c) and solving for y gives the LM equation

$$y = [-X^h + (\eta M + B + \Pi_1^h) r'] / P \tag{6.52}$$

where

$$\eta = \epsilon/\gamma \tag{6.53}$$

The IS and LM equations constitute a pair of simultaneous linear equations in the two unknown r' and y. Their solution is determined

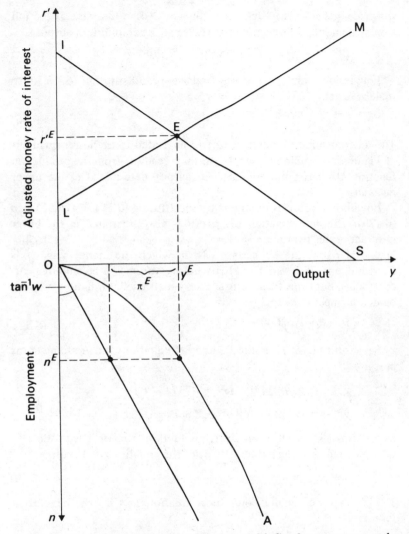

Figure 6.5. Unemployment equilibrium with fixed money wage and fixed money price in the addi-log case

graphically in Figure 6.5 by the intersection E. The equilibrium interest rate is

$$r'^E = [1 + (\gamma X^h / \delta M)]^{-1} \tag{6.54}$$

which on transforming back to r turns out to be the same as the full employment interest rate given by (6.38b). The equilibrium output is

$$y^E = \zeta \, [M + (B + \Pi_1^h)(1 - r'^E)] \, /P \tag{6.55}$$

Equilibrium employment is obtained by substituting (6.47a) into (6.48b) to get

$$n^E = y^{E \, 1/\nu} \tag{6.56}$$

The determination of employment is illustrated in the lower quadrant of Figure 6.5; equilibrium employment is read off from the production function OA using the equilibrium output determined in the upper quadrant.

Equilibrium profit is obtained by substituting (6.55) and (6.56) into (6.47b). The determination of profit is also illustrated in the lower quadrant of this figure.

Consider now the Keynesian case in which the money wage W is fixed but price P is variable. Households continue to be employment-constrained but firms are no longer sales-constrained. Firms now produce on their competitive supply curve

$$P = (W/\nu) \, y^{(1/\nu) - 1} \tag{6.57}$$

Substituting (6.57) into the IS and LM equations and grouping terms in y gives

$$\begin{aligned}
y^{1/\nu} &= (\zeta \nu/W) \, [M + (B + \Pi_1^h)(1 - r')] \\
y^{1/\nu} &= (\nu/W) \, [-X^h + (\epsilon M + B + \Pi_1^h) \, r']
\end{aligned} \tag{6.58}$$

Since firms also produce on their production frontier it is possible to substitute out y on the left-hand side of the equations (6.58) using

$$n = y^{1/\nu} \tag{6.59}$$

This gives a pair of simultaneous linear equations in n and r'. The solution for r' is

$$r'^K = [1 + (\gamma X^h/\delta M)]^{-1} \tag{6.60}$$

where the superscript K is used to indicate a Keynesian equilibrium. In this case however the equilibrium interest rate is the same as before: $r'^K = r'^E = r'^e$. The solution for n is

$$n^K = (\zeta \nu/W) \, [M + (B + \Pi_1^h)(1 - r'^K)] \tag{6.61}$$

Output is determined from the production function

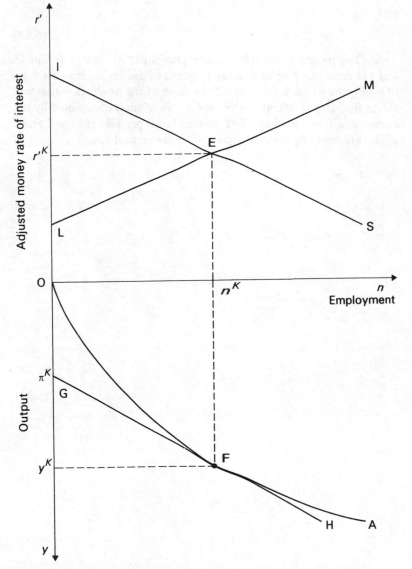

Figure 6.6. Keynesian unemployment equilibrium in the addi-log case

$$y^K = n^{Kv} \tag{6.62}$$

and since firms are producing on their supply curve it is readily established that

$$\pi^K = (1 - \nu) y^K \tag{6.63}$$

The Keynesian solution is illustrated graphically in Figure 6.6. The IS and LM curves are plotted against n instead of against y. Since the roles of n and y have been interchanged the graph of the production function OA in the lower quadrant is reversed. Equilibrium is determined by the intersection E of the IS and LM curves. Firms produce at F, and profit π^K is determined by the intercept OG on the vertical axis.

CHAPTER 7

INVESTMENT*

7.1 THE MARK IV MODEL

This chapter introduces investment into the Mark III model. It is important at the outset to distinguish between gross and net investment. Gross investment is the current output of goods which are to be added to the capital stock. Net investment is the period-on-period increase in the capital stock. The two concepts of investment coincide only in the absence of physical depreciation. When there is depreciation some of the gross investment must be used to replace depreciated stock before any net addition to the stock is made. Thus net investment is equal to gross investment less depreciation. Unless otherwise indicated, the term investment refers to gross rather than net investment.

As before there are just two periods: the present and the future. The restriction to two periods prohibits a fully comprehensive analysis of the investment decision. Nevertheless it is perfectly adequate for an analysis of its macroeconomic implications. Following the earlier convention, subscripts referring to the current period (period 0) are suppressed.

The introduction of investment, denoted i, means that there are now three components of aggregate demand:

$$y^d = c^d + i^d + g^d \tag{7.1}$$

The only other major difference is that firms as well as households now plan over a two-period horizon. The representative firm inherits a real capital stock from the past, k, and invests an amount i in the current period. Between the current period and the next an amount a of the capital stock physically depreciates, so that the capital stock at the beginning of the second period is

$$k_1 = k + i - a \tag{7.2}$$

123

The object of managers is to maximize the value of shareholders' equity. Given that bonds and equities are perfect substitutes, this is equivalent to maximizing the discounted sum of present and future dividend payments.[1]

In the present context the distinction between profits and dividends is important, because it is assumed that investment is financed by the retention of profit. The investing firm reduces the dividend paid out of current profit in order to acquire capital which is utilized to enhance future dividend payments. Thus the equity shareholders finance the investment, and it is management that decides the amount to be invested. Nowadays financing investment out of retained profit is quite usual, and so in this respect the model accords well with current practice.

The more traditional view is that investment is financed by the sale of bonds to households, and that households determine the scale of investment by their willingness to subscribe these bonds. Given the earlier assumption that households are indifferent between equity and bonds, however, it does not matter whether bond-holders or equity-holders finance the investment.[2] Furthermore because managers aim to maximize the value of equity, the amount of investment undertaken at a given money rate of interest will be independent of whether households or managers make the investment decision. For if in the aggregate managers decide to invest more than would the households, the households will compensate by reducing their demand for other assets, such as government bonds. This will reduce the price of bonds, raise the money interest rate, and reduce the equity valuation of the firms which are investing most. This creates a disincentive to investment which will persist until the total amount of investment has fallen into line with household savings plans.

The representative firm draws up an integrated plan of labour demand, product supply, investment and dividend distribution. In period 0 it demands n^d units of labour, generating an output y^s. It plans to invest i^d units of output, leaving $y^s - i^d$ units for sale to consumers and government. (If it plans to sell off inherited stock then investment may be negative.) As a result it generates a money dividend

$$D^f = P(y^s - i^d) - Wn^d \qquad (7.3)$$

Let P_1^f, W_1^f be respectively the money price level and the money wage rate anticipated by firms in period 1. For next period each firm plans to employ n_1^d units of labour, generating an output of y_1^s; and it plans to invest i_1^d, giving sales of $y_1^s - i_1^d$. As a result it generates an expected money dividend

$$D_1^f = P_1^f (y_1^s - i_1^d) - W_1^f n_1^d \tag{7.4}$$

The financing of investment by retained profit has implications for the household's budget constraint. The budget constraint for the current period becomes

$$Pc^d + \dot{M}^d + \dot{B}^d/(1+r) = Wn^s + D^h - T \tag{7.5}$$

where D^h is the dividend distribution anticipated by households. The anticipated real value of future inherited wealth becomes

$$X^{hd} = (M^d + B^d + D_1^h)/P_1^h \tag{7.6}$$

where D_1^h is the household's expectation of future dividends.

Summing the dividend function (7.3), the household budget constraint (7.5) and the government budget constraint

$$G^d = \dot{M}^s + \dot{B}^s/(1+r) + T \tag{7.7}$$

gives GWL for the economy. Normalizing with respect to current price, and indicating the normalized variables by small letters, this becomes

$$z_y + wz_n + z_m + z_b/(1+r) + (d^f - d^h) = 0 \tag{7.8}$$

where $d^f = D^f/P$, $d^h = D^h/P$ and, as before,

$$
\begin{aligned}
z_y &= y^d - y^s \\
z_n &= n^d - n^s \\
z_m &= \dot{m}^d - \dot{m}^s \\
z_b &= \dot{b}^d - \dot{b}^s
\end{aligned}
\tag{7.9}
$$

The only difference between (7.8) and (6.17) is that the excess demand for the product now includes a component of investment demand, and the error in household expectations relates to dividend distribution instead of profits.

7.2 THE MOTIVES FOR INVESTMENT

The capital stock adjustment principle asserts that the demand for investment is derived from the demand for capital stock. The objective of investment is to adjust the capital stock from its existing level to its target level.[3] This principle can be deduced from equation (7.2):

$$i^d = k_1^d - k - a \qquad\qquad (7.10)$$

It follows that the motives for investment are to be found in the motives for holding capital.

There are two main motives for holding capital: the user motive and the speculative motive. These two motives have been considered once already in the context of the demand for money. Money yields user services because it minimizes transaction costs, and it fulfills a speculative role because it is a store of value which is capable of appreciating in real terms. The theory of capital cannot be developed simply by generalizing the theory of money, however, for money has two characteristics which are not shared by all other assets. First, it is utilized efficiently only when circulated regularly between owners, whereas most assets are utilized efficiently only when there is continuity of ownership. Secondly it does not depreciate, which makes money of any age homogeneous in quality, and so very suitable for use as a medium of exchange; by contrast most other assets depreciate quite significantly over time.

The user motive and the speculative motive differ in importance according to the type of asset involved. Consider first an inventory — that is a stock of a good held in storage. The user motive for inventory may be illustrated by the way a stock of finished product facilitates an improved service to the customer.[4]

There are many instances in which customers cannot foresee their own requirements for the product, though once these requirements are known their demand must be satisfied immediately. If the demand is not met the customer's welfare is significantly reduced. So far as the firm is concerned, goodwill is lost by failing to supply the product immediately. On the other hand goodwill is also lost by making frequent price adjustments. Thus to maintain goodwill the firm must commit itself to supplying all that is demanded at a stable quoted price. It can do this either by adjusting output continually to meet demand, or by holding an inventory of the product. The first strategy destroys the continuity of production, and makes it necessary to hold labour in reserve to accommodate periods of peak demand. This problem is avoided by holding an inventory of the product instead.

Inventories also have an important speculative role.[5] If it is anticipated that future demand will be relatively high while future supply will be relatively low, then the price of the product can be expected to rise. This provides the inventory-holder with an opportunity to buy cheap today in order to sell dear tomorrow. It will be profitable to hold inventory up to the margin where the cost of storage is equal to the expected appreciation in value.

Consider now a producer durable, such as a machine which transforms raw material into a finished product. Producer durables are designed specifically with the user role in mind. They perform routine tasks more quickly and easily than manual labour, although the savings in manual labour are offset to some extent by increased demands on skilled labour for supervision and maintenance.

Producer durables may be held for speculative purposes if it is believed that they are likely to appreciate in value. If their current production cost is low in relation to their anticipated future production cost then firms may invest in new durables now even if they do not plan to utilize them till later, simply to achieve savings on the purchase price.

It is clear that both inventories and producer durables can perform either a user role or a speculative role, and possibly both at once. In each case the user role involves the substitution of capital for labour. This is obvious in the case of the producer durable, but more subtle where inventory is concerned. For analytical purposes therefore the distinction between the user motives and the speculative motive is probably more important than the distinction between inventories and producer durables.

The main difference between inventories and producer durables arises in connection with disinvestment. Disinvestment consists of running down the capital stock either by selling it off or otherwise consuming it; it reduces the capital stock by an amount over and above what is due to depreciation. Disinvestment may be regarded as negative gross investment. Since inventories are simply goods in store, and are readily liquidated, disinvestment of inventory poses no difficulties. But producer durables are usually highly specific and cannot be converted to alternative uses without enormous cost. In particular it is difficult to remodel producer durables into a form suitable for immediate consumption. Thus for practical purposes disinvestment in durables is zero.

7.3 INVESTMENT POLICY

This section develops a simple two-period model in which the representative firm invests to satisfy both the user motive and the speculative motive.

In the current period it has a fixed endowment of capital, k, and its production technology exhibits diminishing marginal returns to labour:

$$y^s = y(n^d, k) \tag{7.11}$$

where

$$\partial y^s/\partial n^d > 0, \partial^2 y^s/\partial n^{d2} < 0 \tag{7.12}$$

In the course of the period the capital stock can be either augmented through investment or reduced through disinvestment. In either case the consequences are not felt until the next period. This delayed reaction may seem a little implausible, particularly in respect of disinvestment. But in practice this assumption is unlikely to cause much difficulty because the stock of capital will normally be large in relation to the amount of investment or disinvestment concerned.

Between the current period and the next the capital stock depreciates. The proportional rate of depreciation is higher, the greater the size of the capital stock. This is due to the increasing marginal cost of storing stock and maintaining it in good condition. Depreciation is thus an increasing, and indeed accelerating function of the stock accumulated at the end of the current period:

$$a = a(k + i) \tag{7.13}$$

where

$$da/d(k + i) > 0, d^2 a/d(k + i)^2 > 0 \tag{7.14}$$

The future period offers the opportunity for capital-labour substitution. The firm has a well-behaved production technology, according to which both labour and capital have positive but diminishing marginal returns, isoquants are convex to the origin, and there are non-increasing returns to scale:[6]

$$y_1^s = y_1(n_1^d, k_1^d) \tag{7.15}$$

where

$$\partial y_1^s/\partial n_1^d, \partial y_1^s/\partial k_1^d > 0$$

$$\partial^2 y_1^s/\partial n_1^{d2}, \partial^2 y_1^s/\partial k_1^{d2} < 0$$

$$(\partial^2 y_1^s/\partial n_1^{d2})(\partial^2 y_1^s/\partial k_1^{d2}) - (\partial^2 y_1^s/\partial n_1^d \partial k_1^d)^2 > 0 \tag{7.16}$$

$$\lambda y_1^s < y_1(\lambda n_1^d, \lambda k_1^d) \text{ for } \lambda > 1$$

The capital good is produced using a similar technique to the consumption good, so that they are perfect substitutes in production. This means that the opportunity cost of the capital good in terms of the consumption good is equal to unity, whatever the combination in which the two goods are produced. Finally it is assumed that the capital good can be converted to consumption purposes without any difficulty, so that disinvestment is always possible. Since it is always efficient to disinvest as much as possible in the second period,

$$i^d = -k_1^d \tag{7.17}$$

Suppose that the firm operates in a competitive environment where wages, prices and interest rates are parametric. Management maximizes the equity valuation

$$V = D^f + D_1^f/(1+r) \tag{7.18}$$

subject to the investment equations (7.10) and (7.17), the production technologies (7.11) and (7.15), and the depreciation function (7.13). The first order conditions are

$$\partial y^s/\partial n^d \qquad\qquad = w \tag{7.19a}$$

$$\partial y_1^s/\partial n_1^d \qquad\qquad = w_1^f \tag{7.19b}$$

$$(1 - da/d\,(k + i^d))(1 + \partial y_1^s/\partial k_1^d) = 1 + \rho^f \tag{7.19c}$$

where

$$w_1^f = W_1^f/P_1^f$$
$$1 + \rho^f = (1+r)\,P/P_1^f \tag{7.20}$$

Conditions (7.19a) and (7.19b) equate the marginal product of labour to the real wage in each of the two periods. Condition (7.19c) equates the marginal product of capital, net of depreciation, to the implicit real rate of interest.[7] Solving these conditions determines the outputs y^s, y_1^s, labour demands n^d, n_1^d and investment i^d as functions of the current and anticipated real wages w, w_1^f, the implicit real rate of interest ρ^f and the initial capital stock, k.

The equilibrium of the firm is illustrated in Figure 7.1. Consider to begin with the case in which capital generates no user services, so that the marginal product of capital is zero. In this case investment is governed entirely by the speculative motive.

The top left-hand quadrant exhibits the determination of current output. The only variable factor is labour; as always, output and employment are set at B where the slope of the production function OA is equal to the real wage.

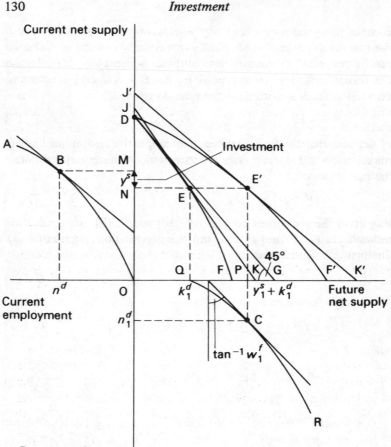

Figure 7.1. Intertemporal equilibrium of the firm

Because investment generates no user services, the future relation between output and employment is independent of investment policy: the future production function QR, shown in the bottom right-hand quadrant, depends on the same fixed factors, and hence has the same form, as the current production function OA. In the figure the production function QR has been translated from the origin O, for reasons which will become apparent later. Quite independently of this translation, future output and employment are set at C where the marginal product of labour, as measured by the slope of QR, is equal to the expected real wage.

Investment policy is determined by intertemporal equilibrium in the consumption of capital. This equilibrium is set at the margin where the costs of depreciation is just offset by the gains from anticipated real appreciation in the value of capital. In the top right-hand quadrant the vertical axis represents the net supply of goods to consumers and government in the current period, and the horizontal axis the net supply to them in the future period. If all current output and the entire endowment of capital from the past were liquidated and supplied to consumers in the current period, then the firm's investment policy would be represented by D. Net current supply would be $y^s + k$, there would be disinvestment of k, and the capital stock inherited by the future would be zero. By reducing net current supply the firm can increase the future capital stock, and thereby make a contribution to future net supply. The trade-off between current net supply and future capital stock is represented by the locus DF. In the absence of depreciation the locus would coincide with the 45°-line DG. But because of depreciation the locus DF lies within DG, and because depreciation accelerates as the capital stock is increased the locus DF is concave to the origin.

The straight line JK is a locus of the different combinations of net supply in the present and the future which provide the same valuation of equity. The slope of the 'iso-valuation' line JK is given by the implicit real discount factor $1/(1 + \rho^f)$. The point of tangency E between JK and DF determines the optimal investment policy. The firms sells ON units of current output to consumers and government, and invests the remaining MN units of output. When added to the initial capital stock MD this provides ND units of capital at the end of the current period. After depreciation the ND units produce OQ units of capital for the future. These units are disposed of, together with future output QP, to give a net supply of OP units in the future.

In this case of pure speculation the target capital stock k_1^d is determined solely by the implicit real rate of interest ρ^f. Investment is governed by the relation between the target stock and the initial endowment of capital k. Thus investment i^d depends solely on ρ^f and k, and is independent of the wage rates w, w_1^f. Investment is highest when both the real rate of interest and the initial capital stock are low; it is thus a decreasing function of both ρ^f and k:

$$i^d = i^d \; (\rho^f, \quad k) \tag{7.21}$$
$$(-) \quad (-)$$

It is important to note that speculative investment occurs only when the real rate of interest is negative, that is when the anticipated rate of inflation exceeds the money rate of interest. If the real rate of interest is zero or negative then, in the absence of user services, the cost of depreciation will deter any capital from being held over to the future period. This makes it apparent that purely speculative investment is a very special case which will not normally be observed except when price expectations are highly inflationary.

When the user motive is introduced investment will occur quite naturally when the real rate of interest is positive, although it remains true of course that the higher is the real rate the less will be the amount invested. The introduction of the user motive can be interpreted as an outward shift in the locus of intertemporal substitution from DF to DF'. At the same time the locus must now be reinterpreted as showing the trade-off, not between current net supply and future capital endowment, but between current net supply and future net supply. The difference arises because with the user motive present the future capital stock contributes directly to the production of additional future output. The magnitude of the horizontal displacement in DF is equal the volume of future output that can be produced with the inherited capital stock, assuming that it is combined with the optimal amount of labour. The optimal amount of labour, however, is conditional on the amount of capital available. The line DF has therefore been drawn on the assumption that the capital is combined with the amount of labour which is implied by the overall optimization of the firm's output and employment plans.

For reasons explained above, when analysing the user motive it is appropriate to assume a real rate of interest higher than that appropriate when analysing the purely speculative motive. This higher real rate of interest is reflected in the lower slope of the new iso-valuation line J'K'. The diagram has been simplified by choosing a real rate of interest which gives the same level of investment as before. Thus the point of tangency E' between the iso-valuation line J'K' and the locus of intertemporal transformation DF' has the same ordinate as E.

Current net supply is again OM and current investment MN. The capital stock inherited in the future is again OQ. The future employment—output relation, however, now depends on OQ. To further simplify the diagram it is assumed that the employment—output relation conditional upon OQ coincides with the production function assumed earlier, QR. In this case future employment is again set at C, where the marginal product of labour is equal to the real wage. Because of the assumptions on which the diagram is constructed, the resulting net future supply of the product OP is fully compatible with the firm's investment strategy represented by E'.

With the user motive present the target capital stock k_1^d now depends not only upon the implicit real rate of interest ρ^f but upon the expected real wage w_1^f. A high real wage has two effects. It reduces planned future output and so reduces the demand for both labour and capital; on the other hand it encourages the substitution of capital for labour, and so increases the demand for capital. The net effect on the demand for capital is indeterminate. Investment remains independent of the current real wage, and so the investment function is now of the form[5]

$$i^d = i^d \; (\rho^f, \quad w_1^f, \quad k \) \qquad (7.22)$$
$$\qquad\quad (-) \quad\;\; (?) \quad\; (-)$$

7.4 MACROECONOMIC IMPLICATIONS

The introduction of investment has two main effects so far as the macroeconomy is concerned. First it introduces a new component of aggregate demand. Secondly, the financing of investment through retained profit modifies household behaviour. The impact is chiefly on household aggregate saving plans, though portfolio composition and labour supply may be marginally affected as well.

The investment function (7.22) indicates that investment depends upon the implicit real rate of interest, the expected future real wage, and the initial capital stock. It has already been shown that household savings also depend upon the implicit real rate of interest. While savings depend on the implicit rate as perceived by households, however, investment depends on the implicit rate perceived by firms. The two implicit rates can differ if households and firms have different expectations of the future price level. Firms' expectation of the future price level may also influence their expectation of the future real wage, for expectations of the real wage are determined by expectations of price combined with expectations of the money wage. The effect of all this is that the introduction of investment adds three new exogenous arguments to the aggregate demand function: firms' expectations of the future price level, firms' expectations of the future wage rate, and the initial capital stock.

Profit retention has two effects on households. It alters their budget constraint because they receive only distributed profit, instead of all of the profit as before, and it alters the value of the wealth they expect to inherit at the beginning of the next period, because this wealth now includes the fruits of the investment financed with the retained profit. In general the greater is profit retention the lower is the saving that households plan to make on their own account. In other words, the greater is the saving that firms perform on their owners' behalf, the less is the saving that the owners will undertake for themselves. Formally, these effects are captured very simply, just by substituting expectations of dividends for expectations of profits in the household demand and supply functions.

There is a further change, which is of very little consequence, namely that firms' labour demand and product supply become functions of their initial capital endowment. This reflects the impact of the user services of capital on labour productivity. Since capital is just one of several fixed factors (for example, land), however, this is of no importance for macroeconomic behaviour.

The demand and supply functions in the markets for product, labour, money and bonds are as follows:

$$y^d = y^d \ (w, \ r, \ P, \ P_1^f, \ W_1^f, \ k, \ P_1^h, \ D_1^h, \ M, \ B, \ T, \ G)$$

$$y^s = y^s \ (w, \ k)$$

$$n^d = n^d \ (w, \ k)$$

$$n^s = n^s \ (w, \ r, \ P, \ P_1^h, \ D_1^h, \ M, \ B, \ T)$$

$$\dot{m}^d = \dot{m}^d \ (w, \ r, \ P, \ P_1^h, \ D_1^h, \ M, \ B, \ T) \qquad (7.23)$$

$$\dot{m}^s = \dot{m}^s \ (\dot{M}^s, \ P)$$

$$\dot{b}^d = \dot{b}^d \ (w, \ r, \ P, \ P_1^h, \ D_1^h, \ M, \ B, \ T)$$

$$\dot{b}^s = \dot{b}^s \ (G, \ T, \ \dot{M}^s, \ P)$$

Assuming that household dividend expectations are consistent with the dividends implied by firms' production and investment plans, application of GWL (equation (7.8)) reduces the four market-clearing conditions

$$z_y = z_n = z_m = z_b = 0 \qquad (7.24)$$

to three independent equations in three unknowns W, P and r:

$$s^d \ (w, \ r, \ P) - g^d \ (P) + t(P) = 0 \qquad (7.25a)$$

$$\dot{m}^d \ (w, \ r, \ P) - \dot{m}^s \ (P) \qquad \qquad = 0 \qquad (7.25b)$$

$$n^d(w) - n^s(w, r, P) = 0 \qquad (7.25c)$$

These equations are similar to those obtained before in the absence of investment. The only difference is that the saving must now be interpreted as saving by households exclusive of the saving made on their behalf by firms. If a new measure of saving, s'^d, is defined to include retained profit then equation (7.25a) may be rewritten

$$s'^d(w, r, P) - i^d(r, P) - g^d(P) + t(P) = 0 \qquad (7.26)$$

which is the more familiar form in which savings equilibrium is expressed.

Equations (7.25) can be solved as before to obtain the equilibrium real wage w^e, the money interest rate r^e and the price level P^e. Substituting the equilibrium values into equations (7.22) and (7.23) determines equilibrium employment n^e, output y^e and investment i^e as functions of the exogenous variables P_1^f, W_1^f, k, P_1^h, D_1^h, M, $\dot{M}^s$, B, T, G.

The main effect of investment on the full employment equilibrium is that firms' expectations of future wages and prices now influence the equilibrium. This is in contrast to the pure consumption model in which only household expectations are relevant.

The particular importance of firms' expectations is due to the fact that investment tends to be a very volatile component of aggregate demand. The most obvious reason for this is that investment demand is derived from stock adjustment. Any change in the target capital stock induces a change in investment of the same absolute amount. Over a short period of time the capital stock is almost invariably large in relation to output. A change in the target capital stock which is quite small in proportional terms may be quite large in relation to the demand for output. Consequently the change in planned investment due to a quite small proportional change in the capital stock may correspond to a very large change in aggregate demand for output. Thus because the capital stock is large in relation to output, a small change in firms' expectations can induce a major change in the level of aggregate demand.

Another reason for the volatility of investment may be that firms' expectations are revised more frequently than households', and exhibit a greater degree of unanimity. This may reflect the fact that managers are more alert to changes in the general economic environment than are other individuals. They monitor the news more carefully, and rely on basically similar sources of information. By contrast households do not monitor the news systematically, and rely for economic assessments mainly on their own experience. Household expectations are therefore more stable both because information is acquired less frequently, and because it is drawn from more diverse sources.

7.5 THE COMPATIBILITY OF EXPECTATIONS

It is interesting to inquire whether the existence of full employment equilibrium in the current period implies that the plans of firms and households will turn out to be consistent in the future period. In other words, does the existence of full employment equilibrium today imply that firms and households should have no need to revise their plans tomorrow? The answer to this is very definitely 'no'.

The answer is obtained most easily by seeking to extend GWL to the future period. Previously it has been assumed that households take no account of future wage income in planning their current demands and supplies. Suppose now that households draw up a comprehensive intertemporal programme which includes plans for future consumption, future money balances and future labour supply. This programme must satisfy not only the current budget constraint (7.5) but also the future budget constraint

$$P_1^h c_1^d + M_1^d = W_1^h n_1^s + D_1^h + M^d + B^d - T_1^h \tag{7.27}$$

where T_1^h is expected future taxation.

Assume for simplicity that no bonds are issued during the future period. Consequently the government's budget constraint is

$$G_1^d + B^s = T_1 + (M_1^s - M^s) \tag{7.28}$$

Equation (7.28) expresses the fact that government expenditure, together with the repayment of outstanding bonds, must be financed either through taxation or through an increase in the money supply.[8]

Summing the dividend equation (7.4), the household budget constraint (7.27) and the government budget constraint (7.28), and using the fact that the current money and bond markets are in equilibrium, gives

$$(P_1^h c_1^d + P_1^f i^d + G_1^d - P_1^f y_1^s) + (W_1^f n_1^d - W_1^h n_1^s)$$
$$+ (M_1^d - M_1^s) + (D_1^f - D_1^h) + (T_1^h - T_1) = 0 \tag{7.29}$$

An immediate consequence of equation (7.29) is that a meaningful equilibrium in the future goods and labour markets is impossible unless the wage and price expectations of households and firms agree. There is no reason why these expectations should agree for, as we have suggested earlier, the sort of information on which these expectations are based may well be different for firms and households. Only if households and firms were engaged in forward trading with each other would there be any tendency for expectations to converge on a common value. In this case each side would reveal their expectations to the other because of the different speculative positions they would take in response to different forward price quotations. As we have already seen, however, there are very high transaction costs in forward markets, and these constitute an effective deterrent to forward trading in goods and labour.

Suppose however that price expectations could be harmonized, so that

$$P_1^f = P_1^h = P_1 \text{ and } W_1^f = W_1^h = W_1 \tag{7.30}$$

Substituting (7.30) into (7.29), normalizing all nominal variables by P_1 and denoting the resulting real variables by small letters gives

$$(c_1^d + i_1^d + g_1^d - y_1^s) + w(n_1^d - n_1^s) + (m_1^d - m_1^s)$$
$$+ (d_1^f - d_1^h) + (t_1^h - t_1) = 0 \tag{7.31}$$

The sum of the first three terms in equation (7.31) is the total real value of excess demand in the future period, and for transactors' future plans to be in equilibrium it is necessary that this sum is zero. This implies that either households have correct expectations of both dividends and taxation, or that any overestimation of dividends is cancelled out by an equal overestimation of taxation. The probability that two errors will cancel each other out exactly is quite remote; if this possibility is rejected then it is necessary that households correctly estimate both dividends and taxation.

Predicting dividends is likely to prove extremely difficult. The problems encountered in formulating expectations of profit, discussed in Chapter 10, apply also to the formulation of dividend expectations. There is the added complication with dividends that it is necessary for households to make correct assumptions about the firms' profit retention policy.

There are stronger grounds for believing that households can predict future taxation. The nominal value of the bonds due for redemption in the future period is known, and it may be possible to infer the government's expenditure plans from its election commitments, or from statements made in the legislature. If in addition the government is committed to monetary targets then, using equation (7.28) it may be possible to deduce the tax implications of these plans. Alternatively the government may have a definite taxation policy, with monetary variables taking a residual role in balancing the government's account; in this case the future tax burden can be predicted directly from the taxation policy.

As noted above, however, the correct prediction of taxation is insufficient to guarantee future equilibrium. The difficulty of predicting dividends still remains. It is this, together with the problems of making wage and price expectations compatible, that makes the achievement of a future equilibrium practically impossible.

It follows that the full employment equilibrium derived in section 7.4 is essentially a temporary equilibrium. It harmonizes transactors' plans in the current period, but does not render compatible the judgements about the future which are implicit in these plans. These judgements can be rendered compatible only by a full and free flow of information between firms and households, involving forward contracts in both labour and product markets, and managerial announcements of the dividend implications of production and investment plans.

7.6 UNEMPLOYMENT DUE TO INVESTMENT DEFICIENCY

We turn now to the role of investment in an economy with rigid money wages (and possibly rigid money prices too). The formal analysis parallels exactly that of Chapter 6, and there is no need to rework that model simply with the inclusion of a new component of aggregate demand. It is sufficient to note that when the money wage is rigid and there is a notional excess supply of labour, the conditions for a constrained equilibrium are given by the IS and LM equations:

$$s'^d\,(r, P, y) - i^d\,(r, P) - g^d\,(P) + t(P) = 0 \qquad (7.32a)$$

$$\dot{m}^d\,(r, P, y) - \dot{m}^s\,(P) = 0 \qquad (7.32b)$$

Condition (7.32a) sets the excess of total saving (gross of profit retention) over investment equal to the government budget deficit. Condition (7.32b) equates the supply and demand for real money balances, and so determines equilibrium in household portfolio composition.

When the money price P is fixed, equations (7.32) can be solved for the equilibrium money rate of interest r^E and the equilibrium output y^E.

When money price is variable and firms produce on their supply curve

$$P = P(y) \qquad (7.33)$$

then P can be eliminated from (7.32) using (7.33). Equations (7.32) can then be solved for the Keynesian equilibrium values r^K, y^K; substituting y^K into (7.33) yields the Keynesian price level P^K.

In either case, substituting equilibrium output into the production function determines equilibrium employment, n^E and n^K respectively. Comparing this level of employment with the notional supply of labour at the prevailing real wage determines unemployment, as measured by the realized excess supply of labour.

Investment is important chiefly because it is a major potential source of disturbance to macroeconomic equilibrium. In the earlier discussions of unemployment exogenous disturbances have been assumed to originate with the household. For example it was shown that a downward revision of future profit expectations would lead to a reduction in current consumption, and a consequent deficiency of aggregate demand. It was also suggested that household anticipation of impending change may induce an increase the entrepreneurial — or precautionary — demand for money, which would also be at the expense of current consumption.

The effects of an exogenous change in investment may be analysed as follows. If managers become pessimistic about, say, future money prices, then they will tend to reduce investment. This will create an excess supply of goods. Suppose to begin with that money wages and money prices are flexible. Current prices will fall to eliminate the excess supply of the product, and to maintain equilibrium in the labour market the money wage must fall too. Stability will be achieved when the relation between the current price level and the expected future price level has been restored to what it was before. In this case the real rate of interest perceived by managers will return to its original level, investment will be restored to normal, and full employment will once again prevail.

If the money prices and money wages are fixed then this mechanism is inoperable. Unless business expectations can be changed, the only way of restoring full employment is for consumption or government expenditure to increase to make good the deficiency in aggregate demand. Households certainly have the income to finance additional consumption because, with investment reduced, profit retentions are lower and so dividends can be expected to increase. (If investments were financed by new bond issues then the money that would have been used to subscribe the new bonds becomes available for consumption instead.) But while households have the income to finance consumption they do not necessarily want to spend it in this way. For with investment reduced, and current dividends increased at the expense of future dividends, the value of equity-holders' claims on the future has been reduced, and it is therefore natural that they should want to make good this reduction by increasing their holding of government bonds. But the supply of government bonds is, by assumption, fixed, so that the only effect of increased demand is to increase the price of bonds and reduce the money rate of interest. This reduction in the money rate of interest may help to stimulate investment demand, but there is no guarantee that it will be sufficient to restore investment to its previous level. Thus while profit retentions may increase marginally, households are still left with some surplus income to invest. Because the money rate of interest has fallen it is now attractive to invest in additional money balances. Only when sufficient income has been directed to meet the increased demand for money balances will the rest of the income be diverted to alternative uses, that is to increased consumption.

It follows that the induced increase in consumption is much less than the initial decrease in investment. The net effect is that aggregate product demand diminishes while an excess demand for money balances is created. The deficiency of aggregate demand imposes a sales constraint on firms, who reduce employment as a consequence. This reduces labour incomes and so feeds back on consumption. Output and employment fall through a multiplier process until constrained equilibrium is achieved in the product market and, at the same time, the excess demand for money balances is eliminated.

A similar argument applies if the money price is flexible but the money wage is rigid, for although a reduction in the money price assists the equilibrating process, it cannot prevent unemployment occurring altogether. Each reduction in money price induces a contraction of output by firms. Given a fixed money wage, this leads to an excess supply of labour.

CHAPTER 8

QUANTITY ADJUSTMENT VERSUS PRICE ADJUSTMENT

8.1 LIMITATIONS OF THE NON-RECONTRACTING APPROACH

There is no doubt that the rejection of recontracting has been a powerful liberating influence on macroeconomics. By weakening the assumptions of competitive theory it has made economic analysis much more flexible. Its emphasis on the informational aspects of market trading makes possible a more realistic account of transactors' behaviour.

The rejection of recontracting, however is by itself inadequate as a basis for a new macroeconomics. This inadequacy stems from the very generality of the theory: the fact that in principle it applies to nearly all markets. In the real world there are very few markets where transactors respond to notional rather than to realized excess demands. Thus in the absence of recontracting almost all markets are susceptible to disequilibrium. The evidence suggests, however, that some markets are much more prone to disequilibrium than others. For example, the labour market appears to suffer more from disequilibrium than does the typical product market, while most financial markets seem to be maintained close to equilibrium. One reason may be that the frequency of exogenous change is much greater in some markets than in others, but this does not account fully for observed differences in market behaviour. The main reason seems to be that prices adjust at different speeds in different markets. To explain this it is necessary to complement the non-recontracting approach with some sort of analysis of price adjustment.

In the preceding chapters some very extreme assumptions have been made about price adjustments. It has often been assumed that transactors do not adjust price at all in response to realized excess demands. Thus money wages and money prices remain fixed throughout the time in which successive contractions of output and employment occur — that is throughout the entire multiplier process.

One way of rationalizing this is to regard the multiplier process as a purely imaginary one, in the sense that the economy adjusts to equilibrium within a single period. For the multiplier process to work in this way, however, transactors must be involved in a kind of recontracting in order to revise their quantity plans, so that these quantity plans are mutually compatible when they are put into effect. All that the theory has done is to replace recontracting in terms of prices with recontracting in terms of quantities. Since recontracting has already been rejected for price adjustments it is most unsatisfactory to revive it for quantity adjustments. It is difficult to see how recontracting can be impossible with prices but perfectly easy for quantities.

It should be emphasized that while the choice of quantity adjustment rather than price adjustment implies a stable market price, price stability may be due to many other things beside quantity adjustment. For example the price in a perfectly competitive market will be stable in response to horizontal shifts in demand and supply if either the demand or supply schedule is very elastic. Many writers have sought support for fix-price macroeconomic models on these very grounds. Such explanations rely explicitly on an equilibrium framework, however; they do not question the use of price adjustment, but merely argue that the price adjustment required is very small.

To justify the disequilibrium approach it is necessary to explain why transactors respond to realized excess demands by adjusting quantity instead of price. This chapter investigates the conditions under which such behaviour will occur.

8.2 QUANTITY ADJUSTMENT AS AN OPTIMIZING POLICY

It is usually assumed that in the absence of constraints a rational transactor will always choose price adjustment rather than quantity adjustment. Failure to adjust price is attributed to exogenous limitations on the transactor's freedom of action. Thus most applications of the fix-price theory have assumed that price rigidity is a consequence of government price controls: the analysis has been used to examine the effects of prices and incomes policies, and also the fixing of consumer goods prices in Soviet-type economies.[1] If these were the only ways of explaining price rigidity the fix-price theory would have a very limited range of applications.

An alternative approach is to explain price rigidity in terms of oligopolistic behaviour. It is argued that the managers of oligopolistic firms perceive a kinked demand curve for output because they expect rival firms to respond strategically to any price changes they initiate. An oligopolist will be reluctant to increase price following an increase in industry demand because he believes that his rivals intend to keep their prices stable in order to increase their market share at his expense. This approach is evaluated in section 8.3. The main difficulty is that, under the assumptions of the theory, on the few occasions when price changes are actually initiated the anticipated response will not materialize, so that if managers learn by experience they will modify their expectations. If their expectations were correct they would not perceive any kink in the demand curve, and prices would not be rigid.

It is argued below that quantity adjustment may not be due either to regulatory constraints or to the subjective constraints inherent in oligopolistic rivalry. Instead quantity adjustment may be a well-informed transactor's response to other transactors' information costs. A transactor may well evaluate price and quantity adjustment and decide, quite correctly, that it is in his long-term interests to adjust quantity rather than price.

The well-informed transactors are firms, and the not-so-well informed transactors are households. Prices are administered by firms and they maintain prices stable in order to secure 'goodwill' from the households. Three variants of this 'goodwill theory' are presented in sections 8.4–8.6.

The first is concerned with price stability as an informationally efficient substitute for futures markets and insurance markets. Ideally a household would like to be able to plan an intertemporal programme of consumption and work, with built-in insurance against various contingencies. The household would enter into contracts for its labour services to be supplied, and its consumer goods delivered, in specific amounts at particular dates according to conditions which prevail on or before these dates. But the information required to undertake such planning is far too much for a household with limited search time and limited mental capabilities. One way round the difficulty is for firms (or other intermediaries) to offer the household regular work and regular consumption supplies at relatively stable spot prices. This provides the household with the insurance it requires but without the information-processing costs. The household will prefer to trade with a firm offering such services, even though the cost of the service is ultimately included in the price. Consequently price stability becomes just one feature of the quality of service offered by the representative firm.

The second model is concerned with price stability as a policy for reducing a firm's turnover costs. It is much cheaper for a firm to supply established customers than it is to take on new ones; and it is much more profitable to employ established workers, who have acquired firm-specific skills, than it is to take on new workers who have to be trained. In general the firm cannot recover the losses it sustains when customers or workers quit: they are 'external costs' borne by the firm and originating from customers' and workers' decisions.

It is argued that customers and workers are most likely to quit when there is an adverse movement in the price or wage quoted to them. Thus the firm minimizes its turnover costs by avoiding such adverse movements. It does not increase its prices or reduce its wages when competitive circumstances are favourable to it; and it recovers its losses by not reducing prices or increasing wages when competitive circumstances are unfavourable to it.

The third model emphasizes the importance of advertising in economizing on household's search costs. It is argued that advertising is most effective when the firm guarantees a high degree of short-term price stability.

Different reasons for quantity-adjustment have different behavioural implications. It is sometimes suggested that there is a unified theory of quantity-adjustment for all fixed-price models, but this is far from the truth. In particular we shall show that the 'goodwill' theory of price stability may be inconsistent with the principle that quantities are set at the short end of the market. It is only the non-recontracting approach which is always in accord with this principle.

8.3 OLIGOPOLY

A possible rationalization of quantity-adjustment is to be found in the theory of oligopoly. It is discussed at this stage for the sake of completeness, but it will not play any further role in our analysis. Oligopoly is undoubtedly a common form of market structure, and the kind of behaviour described below may well be typical of oligopolistic industries. The approach to quantity-adjustment through oligopoly cannot readily be integrated into the theme of this book, however, and since the subject has been treated fully elsewhere, we shall not pursue it in any detail.[2]

An oligopolistic industry consists of a small number of price-setting firms. The firms produce a basically homogeneous product, so that customers will substitute between firms in response to very small price differentials.[3] Consequently each firm's pricing decision depends crucially on other firms' pricing decisions, which in turn depend upon its own. The manager of each firm believes that if he raises his price then other firms will not follow suit; consequently almost all his customers will be lost to other firms. On the other hand, he believes that if he reduces his price then other firms will follow suit so that his share of the market will remain unchanged; thus the firm has the same customers as before, though each of them buys a little more because the price is lower. As a result the manager perceives the firm's demand curve to be highly elastic above the prevailing price, and much less elastic below it, that is there is a kink in the demand curve at the prevailing price.

Suppose that the manager is a profit-maximizer, producing where marginal revenue is equal to marginal cost. Assuming he charges a uniform price, the existence of a kink in the demand curve implies a discontinuity in the marginal revenue schedule (see Figure 8.1). It follows that over a wide range of variable costs the optimal strategy is to charge the prevailing price and to produce the amount demanded at that price.

Under certain conditions this analysis can be used to explain the

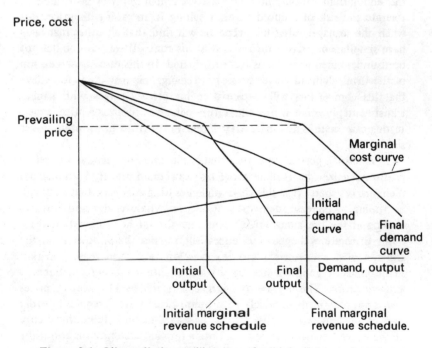

Figure 8.1. Oligopolistic equilibrium: the 'kinked' demand curve

invariance of price not only with respect to cost changes but with respect to demand changes too. Suppose that the manager anticipates that if industry demand increases then other managers will still be prepared to maintain their prices constant, hoping thereby to gain market share at his expense when he raises his own price. In this case, as the industry demand curve shifts to the right the price at which the kink occurs remains unchanged. The manager's optimal response is to leave price unchanged and increase output to meet the increased demand. The only qualification is that the marginal cost at the new output should not exceed the prevailing price; if it does then price as well as quantity should be adjusted. If all managers act the same then the price remains unchanged and each manager's expectations of the others' behaviour is fulfilled. In this sense the behavioural responses actually reinforce belief in the assumptions on which they are based.

It must, however, be recognized that the analysis would seem to have rather limited application in inflationary conditions. Suppose that money wage inflation causes marginal cost to exceed the marginal revenue at the equilibrium output. In this case each manager will be willing to tolerate the risk of reduced sales resulting from raising his price. But when the manager raises his price he will find that all other managers have simultaneous raised theirs, and so his competitive position has not been undermined as much as he anticipated. In this case his perception of the firm's demand curve is likely to change. He may come to believe that his competitors will respond to his price changes with similar adjustments; in other words each firm perceives itself as a price leader. In this case there is no longer any incentive for firms to maintain prices stable.

It is also important to note that while each manager is himself a profit-maximizer, he assumes that his rivals' main priority is to increase their market share. It is this that underlies his assessment that they will be willing to increase their output to meet whatever demand is forthcoming at the prevailing price. But why should he believe that these other firms are willing to increase their market share, possibly at the expense of their profits? One explanation is that increasing market share builds up goodwill among a larger clientele and so contributes to *long-run* profits. The increase in market share achieved by keeping prices low is an investment in which short-term profits are foregone in order to increase long-term profits. This suggests that underlying the theory of the kinked demand curve are certain implicit assumptions about the 'goodwill' motive. It is to the analysis of this motive that we now turn.

8.4 GOODWILL THEORY I: PRICE STABILITY AS INSURANCE

This theory is concerned with the role of firms in simplifying household decision problems, and insuring them against risk.

In conventional microeconomics the firm is concerned chiefly with the management of production. Because of complementarities between factor inputs, and economies of scale, production activities centre on the firm rather than the household. This is the rationale for the firm in a static and perfectly certain world. But in an uncertain and changing world firms have another role. This originates from an obligation firms accept to provide income stability for factor owners, and short-term price stability for consumers. This service encourages consumers and factor owners to channel their transactions through firms, even where the physical transformation effected by the firm is relatively trivial. One way in which this commitment manifests itself is in the 'price quotation' role of the firm. Typically firms quote prices to households in product markets and quote wages to workers in the labour market. It is most unusual for customers to quote prices to firms; similarly firms advertising vacancies quote wage rates, while workers seeking jobs normally do not. The obligation to trade at the quoted prices means that the owners of firms become specialized bearers of market risk. Thus there is a tendency for the least risk-averse individuals to become shareholders in firms, while the more risk-averse remain simply as customers and employees. The risk-bearing services of shareholders are rewarded by a risk premium included in the long-run normal rate of profit.[4]

To understand why firms have assumed this role it is necessary to explain why short-term price and wage stability is the most appropriate way of simplifying household decision problems and insuring them against certain categories of risk. From a theoretical standpoint price and wage stability is certainly not the ideal method. In order to achieve maximum welfare a household should in theory plan its lifetime consumption and work programme in advance, down to the finest detail. It would enter not just into spot contracts but also into forward contracts. A typical forward contract would specify the supply of a given amount of labour at a particular date, or the delivery of a given amount of a particular good at a particular date. Conversely the typical firm would be committed to supply specific amounts of output at specific dates; the output would be produced using labour and other factors which the households have committed themselves to supplying at these dates.

There would be a market for each type of spot or forward claim, in which the price of the claim was determined.

Of course, both households and firms would like some flexibility built into the contracts so that they can adapt to unpredictable changes of circumstance. One way of accommodating uncertainty about the future is to make each contract contingent on the circumstances which prevail up to the time it is completed. The typical contingent forward contract is to supply a given amount of a good or service at a given date if a given set of circumstances prevail. If these contracts cover all conceivable contingencies then once all the forward contracts have been set up the production and distribution of goods under all conceivable circumstances is completely determined.[5]

An idealized economy of this kind has two very important properties. The first is that each household can insure itself against any adverse contingency, provided this contingency can be specified precisely enough. This is a highly desirable feature of the economy. The second is that once the futures contracts have been set up there is no reason for subsequent spot contracts to be made: all future transactions are triggered off automatically by the maturing of forward claims at various dates. Thus future transactions in their entirety are 'telescoped' into a single period. But in this single period an enormous range of claims have to be traded; the number of different spot claims, though very large, is negligible compared to the number of different types of contingent forward claim. In practice households do not have the time, or mental capability, to process the enormous amount of information that would be required to set up a comprehensive intertemporal programme of consumption and work. There are also other practical difficulties in trading forward claims, which were considered in Chapter 4.

The question arises as to how the benefits of insurance can be secured without the informational complexities created by a complete set of contingent futures markets. One way of organizing partial insurance with economy of information is to replace contingent forward contracts in a commodity with a guarantee of stability in future spot prices of the commodity. Given the choice between buying forward claims on a consumer good, or purchasing from a producer that guarantees a reasonable degree of spot price stability, the typical household may well prefer to undertake a sequence of spot transactions. In this case trading in forward markets will be very thin, and given the fixed costs of market organization, many forward markets will cease to exist altogether. Similarly given the choice of entering into forward commitments for labour supply, or working for an employer offering a reasonable degree of spot wage stability, the representative household may prefer the spot wage stability. Analysis of this case is complicated, however, by the fact that there are specific legal problems in enforcing forward contracts in labour. Nevertheless the general point remains that stability of spot prices and wages may be an important feature of the services which a firm offers to its customers and its employees.

8.5 GOODWILL THEORY II: PRICE-STABILITY AS A QUIT-DETERRENT

Suppose that transactors on one side of a market have very limited information about transactors on the other side. It is costly for them to discover the price at which they can transact with different traders, and to discover the non-price attributes of the commodities that the different traders demand or supply.[6] In such cases a rational policy is to find a trader with whom satisfactory terms can be negotiated, and then to continue trading with him. Development of a regular purchasing routine also helps the consumer in planning his daily programme of consumption and work. It also enables both purchaser and supplier to learn of each other's specific requirements, and so improve the quality of service and the profitability of supply, to their mutual benefit.

With all traders following this policy the market will become segmented, with pairs of traders repeatedly transacting with each other, and with no-one else. These repeat transactions may be governed by nothing more than habit, or they may involve a formal contract which specifies the terms on which repeated transactions take place.[7]

The consumer will continue with his routine until he has reason to believe that his regular supplier is no longer as competitive as he was. Since the consumer is not actively scanning the competition, he is likely to initiate a search for alternative supplies only if his existing supplier's service deteriorates, either by an increase in price, or a failure to meet demand. Thus the supplier will retain regular customers to the extent that he can maintain price stability, and adjust production to meet whatever quantity is demanded at this price.

From the supplier's point of view it is much cheaper to service established customers than it is to service new ones. Suppose that consumer demand increases, and competitive forces indicate that price should rise in the short run. Firms may recognize that if they raise their prices then there is a risk of breaking regular customer's habits. Customers may experiment with other suppliers and, although they may in fact get no better service than before, they may decide to stay with the new supplier simply to avoid the cost of switching back to the original one. The original supplier will of course have no difficulty in replacing his established customer with a new one — probably someone who has quit trading with a competing firm which has also raised its price. The effect on each supplier is that his stock of customers 'turns over' — a proportion of his regular customers quit, and these customers are replaced by a similar number of new ones. But customer turnover imposes costs on the firm: it is necessary to screen new customers for credit-worthiness, learn their habits, adapt to their particular requirements and so on. The long-run profit-maximizing strategy for the firm may therefore be to forego short-run price adjustments, and maintain prices stable in order to retain its existing clientele.

A similar argument applies if demand contracts. If the contraction is expected to be temporary then the firm which cuts its price immediately can anticipate having to raise it again later if it is to earn normal profits in the long run. When the price increases later on clients may still initiate a search of competitors, since they may think it is possible that other firms that cut their prices have not raised them again. Thus a firm which cuts its prices when demand contracts runs the risk of losing its regular customers should it wish to increase its price again once demand recovers.

The idea that firms will attempt to restrain search by maintaining price stability is also applicable to the labour market. The long-term relationship between the firm and its established customer has its analogue in the relationship between the firm and its employee.[8] The long-term nature of the relationship is more obvious because it is not an informal one based on habit, but a formal one in which a contract for recurrent supply of services is made. The contract is normally terminable on notice from either side. The more formal nature of the contracts in the labour market probably reflects the very high cost of labour turnover, relative to the cost of customer turnover.

The 'set up' costs of taking on a new employee comprise chiefly advertising costs, screening costs and training costs. Advertising costs tend to be greater the more specialized is the job, since the advertisement must distinguish carefully the type of applicant required, and must be circulated widely enough to reach the small number of job seekers likely to be eligible. Screening costs are exemplified by the costs of interviews, taking up references, etc. and are related to the responsibility of the job. The training costs borne by the firm tend to be related to the amount of firm-specific skill required. None of these costs is recoverable if the worker quits.

When the worker is not actively monitoring the labour market he will continue with his regular employer so long as he believes that he is receiving a competitive wage. By analogy with the regular customer, the employee is likely to initiate job search in response to a reduction in the money wage. If he requires time off work for interviews, and needs to quote his employer as a referee, then he may feel, once job search has begun, that his prospects in his existing employment are diminished. It will be taken as a sign of economic weakness by his employer if he cannot get a job elsewhere, and so he becomes committed to taking a new job even if it is no better than his old one. Thus to minimize turnover the employer must deter the initiation of search, and the best way of doing this is to provide wage stability.

The theory of quit-deterrence suggests that wage stability will be extended on preferential terms to workers in skilled, specialized and responsible jobs, for it is in these jobs that the costs of recruiting and training a replacement for the worker are greatest. On the one hand, by offering wage stability the firm is reducing its flexibility to respond to adverse changes in its competitive position, and so is increasing its risks; but on the other hand by reducing the turnover of skilled labour it is reducing its costs and enhancing its ability to cope with competition from other employers. Overall, the net cost of wage stability to the firm is very low; the benefits of wage stability can therefore be passed on to the skilled employees in return for only a small sacrifice in their average wage.

Skilled employees have a strong incentive to accept wage stability when it is offered by employers both because it is cheap and because there are few alternative ways of insuring their income. Unskilled workers on the other hand have much less incentive to do so. The benefits to the firm of reducing the turnover of unskilled workers are much lower, and so the cost of wage stability which has to be borne by the worker is that much greater. The unskilled worker may also attach much less value to insurance because his consumption habits lead him to take on fewer financial commitments. Moreover because his wages are lower than those of the skilled worker he may feel that state benefits (both in money and in kind) provide adequate insurance, so that it is unnecessary to seek insurance from his employer. The theory therefore predicts that the unskilled worker will not negotiate wage stability to the same extent as does the skilled worker.

The implications of this view, and the qualifications to which it is subject, are considered in detail in Chapter 9.

8.6 GOODWILL THEORY III: PRICE-STABILITY AS AN ADJUNCT TO ADVERTISING

The previous section was concerned with price stability in the context of repeat-trading, that is where two parties transact time and again with each other. This model is appropriate for commodities which are purchased regularly by the representative household. But there are many commodities which are only purchased occasionally, in particular specialized durable goods.

When commodities are purchased regularly, consumers' price information is easily maintained up to date. The price of the last purchase is a guide to the price of the next one; in other words, a by-product of each transaction is a prediction of the future price. This does not apply to occasional purchases, for which price information must be obtained by other means.

In a developed economy an occasional purchase may involve a choice between a wide range of differentiated products. To evaluate each product calls for an investment in search. Because the purchase is only 'one-off' it is important for the household to economize on search costs. One way of doing this is to evaluate only products for which reliable price information is readily available. Unless information networks between households are exceptionally good, the information must be obtained through advertising.

The representative producer recognizes that he cannot secure a sale without first encouraging evaluation, and that to encourage evaluation he must advertise. As an advertiser he recognizes that consumers will compare the prices quoted at the point of sale with their recollection of the advertised price. Given the time involved in search, this price may have been advertised some time ago. Nevertheless if there is a substantial discrepancy between them then the customer will react unfavourably. The customer will feel that the producer has defaulted on his original offer to trade at the advertised price, and the sale will be lost. In such cases price stability is an integral part of the firms' marketing strategy. The optimal period over which stability is sustained will depend, upon other things, on the consumer's price-consciousness and his retentiveness of price information.

8.7 QUANTITY DETERMINATION IN THE GOODWILL MODEL

The goodwill theory suggests certain qualifications to the maxim that quantity is set at the short end of the market. It can be shown that firms which maintain prices fixed to generate goodwill may in certain cases set quantity at the long end of the market.

Consider first the product market. When price stability is administered by firms in order to promote goodwill, each firm will normally be committed to supply all the product demanded at the quoted price. This applies to each variant of the goodwill model described above.

To begin with, an essential complement to price stability is an assurance of continuity of supply at that price. It is pointless for a firm to insure its customers against price movements unless supplies are actually forthcoming at the regular price. Unless the supply is guaranteed the typical customer is likely to find that just when the regular price is most favourable relative to the short-run equilibrium price, the increased demands of other customers result in quantity rationing. Secondly, it is impossible to retain established customers by avoiding price increases if they have to find alternative supplies because some of their demand cannot be met. Finally there is no point in building up goodwill by advertising the product price if the product is out of stock when customers decide to purchase. Thus a commitment to price stability is inseparable from a commitment to supply all that is demanded at the quoted price.

A partial analysis of goodwill in the product market is illustrated in Figure 8.2. If price exceeds the equilibrium level (at say $P_1 > P^e$) then quantity is set at the short end of the market, as before: $y_1 = y_1^d$. But if price is too low (at say $P_2 < P^e$) then firms still supply what is demanded, even though this exceeds the competitive supply, and output is set at $y_2 = y_2^d$. This is because firms are maximizing long-run profit rather than short-run profit. Instead of producing an output which equates marginal production cost to price (that is producing on the supply curve) they invest in goodwill by foregoing some of their short-run profits. The profits foregone by producing at the long end rather than the short end are measured by the shaded area in the figure. Thus the firms themselves bear the entire cost of their supply commitment. It follows that the locus of price-quantity combinations actually observed in the product market is given by the demand curve (the solid line in the figure); the supply curve exerts no influence on the outcome unless, or until, price adjustment is initiated.

A similar argument linking price stability to quantity commitment

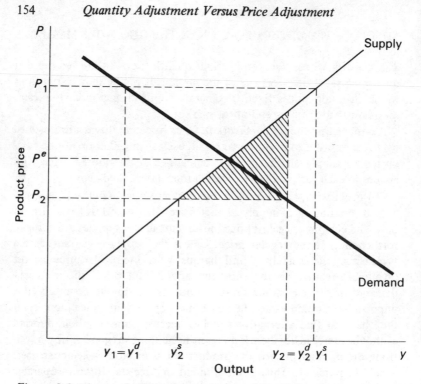

Figure 8.2. The goodwill model: partial analysis of the product market

can be applied to the labour market. The stability of the wage is apparent in agreements, both individual and collective, to renegotiate wages only after stated intervals of time, usually one year. Our argument suggests that wage stability motivated by goodwill will normally be accompanied by employment guarantees. If it were not, the goodwill built up through wage stability would be lost as a result of instability in employment. There is the additional consideration that workers kept fully employed have less time to search for jobs. While workers in employment can scan wage quotations which appear for advertised vacancies, they cannot assess the non-income attributes of jobs without investigating them personally, and this is much more difficult to do when the worker is fully employed. Consequently a worker with guaranteed employment has less alternative to shop around for vacancies, and so the probability that he will quit is reduced.

A partial analysis of employment guarantees is illustrated in Figure 8.3. The demand and supply curves are drawn conditional upon a given money price level. At the money wage W_1 above the equilibrium level

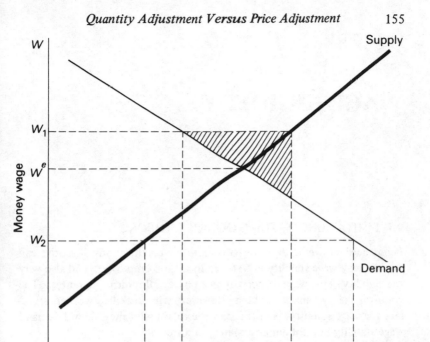

Figure 8.3. The goodwill model: partial analysis of the labour market

W^e, firms offer all the employment workers demand, and so actual employment is $n_1 = n_1^s$. Employment exceeds firms' competitive demand for labour n_1^d because the firms are following long-run profit maximization rather than short-run profit maximization, and so the marginal conditions underlying the short-run competitive demand curve do not apply to them. The short-term profit foregone by employing at the long end rather than the short end is measured by the shaded area in the figure. At the money wage W_2, below the equilibrium wage, firms are actually constrained by labour supply. Since households have no reciprocal commitment to supply all the labour firms require, employment is now set at the short end of the market: $n_2 = n_2^s$. It follows that the locus of wage-employment combinations actually observed is given by the supply curve (the solid line in the figure). The demand curve is relevant only in determining the direction in which competitive pressure will tend to adjust the wage over time.

CHAPTER 9

WAGE RIGIDITY

9.1 LIMITATIONS OF THE GOODWILL THEORY

It has been shown in the previous section that the goodwill motive can explain why wage stability is offered to skilled employees, and also why the stability of the wage is accompanied by employment guarantees. The goodwill theory cannot explain, however, why unskilled workers stipulate for wage stability. Neither can it explain why they should demand wage stability but not employment guarantees.

It seems that there is more to wage stability than the goodwill motive alone indicates. There must be another factor which explains why wage stability is also found in unskilled occupations. This is not to say that the factor must be exclusive to the unskilled: it may be a subsidiary factor reinforcing wage stability among the skilled as well. But it must differ from the goodwill theory is one salient feature: that wage stability alone is regarded as being adequate, without employment guarantees.

It must be admitted at the outset that this kind of wage stability is difficult to rationalize. Given the usual assumptions about individual preferences which are made in neoclassical economics, it is difficult to see how stipulating for wage stability can be an efficient policy for the unskilled worker.

Take for example the conventional view that workers prefer both a high expected real income and a low variation of income. Wage income depends upon both the wage rate and the amount of employment offered at that rate. A worker who stipulates for a fixed real wage is vulnerable to competition from other workers who are willing to work for less (for example those in lower paid jobs, or the unemployed). Even if there is no direct competition in the labour market, the worker may be threatened by adverse developments in the product market, for example a decline in demand due to a switch in tastes to another product. Workers who refuse to accept wage cuts reduce their employers' ability to respond by cutting costs, and so imperil employment in their own industry. Although the expansion of another industry may create vacancies for unskilled workers, there is no guarantee that, given a fixed wage, the number of vacancies will be sufficient to absorb all the redundant workers.

In general therefore the greater is wage stability the greater is the tendency toward employment instability. There is no doubt that wage stability reduces employers' short-run profitability, since it constrains them to adjust quantities when they would prefer to adjust prices instead. In the long run these costs of wage stability are passed on to the employees in terms of lower wage rates. Wage stability — though bought at a price — does not necessarily benefit the worker, however, because the instability of employment is increased. The net effect on the stability of wage income will depend on the wage elasticity of labour demand. If the elasticity is high then employment instability will be increased significantly by wage stability and income stability will therefore be reduced. Only if competitive forces are so muted that the elasticity of demand for the individual worker is less than unity will the stability of wage income be increased. Thus unless the elasticity of demand for labour is low, wage stability reduces both the average wage and the stability of wage income. In this case, stipulating for wage stability without employment guarantees is a demonstrably inefficient strategy for the worker.

9.2 THE ROLE OF TRADE UNIONS

In practice trade unions have an important role in the negotiation of wages. The conventional economic view of the trade union is that it is a combination of employees who negotiate collectively in order to exploit their monopoly power.[1] Those who ascribe unemployment to a too-high real wage often cite trade-union power as the reason for the maintenance of an excessive real wage.

When analysing union bargaining it is important to distinguish between national negotiations over basic rates and local negotiations over bonuses, etc. The function of national bargaining appears to be to establish a minimum wage throughout the industry, leaving individual groups to bargain at the plant level to secure further concessions from the employer.

At the national level unions tend to negotiate for wages which apply to all workers rather than just to union members. The rationale for this is presumably that it eliminates wage competition from non-union labour in the same industry. It has the disadvantage, however, that it reduces the incentive to join the union because it allows non-union members a 'free ride' on the union. From the point of view of the union members themselves it would be preferable to bargain directly for employment guarantees. Since the guarantees would be confined to union members, the employer's ability to adjust employment would be only slightly impaired. It would mean simply that he would discriminate against non-union labour when recruiting or laying-off workers. This arrangement would also benefit union officials since it would increase the incentive to join the union, and so increase membership and give the union greater control of the labour force.

An alternative strategy is for the union to bargain for a closed shop. While this is nowadays quite common in Britain, it is much more characteristic of plant bargaining than national bargaining. Furthermore in most cases the closed shop merely represents the consolidation of a situation in which a high degree of unionization has already been achieved. Cases in which discrimination against non-union members has been used conspicuously to increase recruitment have so far been relatively few.

This suggests that union objectives are somewhat wider than the short-run advancement of members' economic interests. Most unions are willing to tolerate the spill-over of benefits to non-union labour. Such behaviour raises the possibility of a degree of altruism is union motives — a possibility which is quite alien to the spirit of neoclassical economics. A strictly neoclassical view of the union would see its attraction for the worker as similar to the attraction of a cartel to producers. It would suggest that in setting wages the union follows similar principles to those of a cartel which fixes prices. This may be true of certain aspects of plant bargaining, but it cannot fully explain union behaviour at the national level.

The beneficial spill-over effects of union activities may explain the extensive political support that unions have received. At a time when producers' cartels have been outlawed, unions have received positive encouragement in many ways, notably in legal immunities. Where unionization has been weak governments have often established statutory bodies to regulate conditions of employment. Of all union activities it appears that the one with most widespread support is the setting of a national minimum wage in each industry. In many countries, governments have intervened to establish wages boards in non-unionized industries, with the specific objective of setting a national basic wage in the industry.[2]

9.3 THE LIVING WAGE

Public support for the minimum wage can be explained on two grounds. First, in unskilled occupations where unionization is weak the minimum wage often represents a 'living wage'. It permits the worker to achieve a standard of living which society deems acceptable. This standard is a reflection of the prevailing culture. In some cases it may be literally a subsistence wage. In other cases it may permit the worker not only to subsist but also to live with his family in reasonable accommodation, commute to work, benefit from health insurance and so on.

The living wage may be established out of altruism, and also to control the externalities of extreme poverty, such as vagrancy and disease. More generally still, it could be regarded as a means of defending the existing economic order. The contract of employment is in a sense a microcosm of the social contract by which the worker opts in to society. His chief contribution to society is the work he performs for his employer and his reward is the satisfaction generated by the job and the income that he receives for it. If a worker cannot obtain a living wage by selling his labour then he may repudiate the social contract, and seek his rewards by going outside the law and the constitution, for examply by resort to crime or violent revolution. Those who benefit most from the market system have a strong incentive to ensure that those who benefit least receive at least sufficient to make the system acceptable to them. Since the low paid benefit least from the market system, the employers and highly-paid employees, who benefit most, may encourage the low-paid to substitute away from crime and violence by guaranteeing a living wage.

The main weakness of the living wage as an instrument of social policy is that it carries with it no guarantee of employment. It is for this reason that the post-war welfare state has extended similar benefits to the unemployed, and to those unable to participate in work at all. Nevertheless it can be argued that in the long run society will endeavour to maintain a differential between benefits to non-workers and the 'living wage' offered to the lowest paid employees. First there is a natural desire to control the disincentive to work created by these benefits.[3] Secondly there is the 'work ethic' which suggests that those who work ought justly to receive more than those who do not. Finally there is the fact that dissatisfaction among low-paid workers is more of a threat to society than is dissatisfaction among the unemployed. The workplace is a natural centre around which to organize labour for political purposes;

it is much more difficult to organize the unemployed since they are widely scattered and have no social tendency to agglomerate. In any case the low-paid workers are in a stronger position to disrupt the economy than are the unemployed, who have no strike-threat power. On both counts, society has much more to fear from the political mobilization of the low-paid than it does from the mobilization of the 'army of the unemployed'. It may be concluded that while social security and unemployment benefit are the most comprehensive forms of income maintenance available, they are not regarded as an adequate substitute for the living wage. Furthermore they are unlikely to be regarded as such in the foreseeable future.

9.4 WAGE DIFFERENTIALS AND THE OCCUPATIONAL HIERARCHY

The second ground for public support for the minimum wage is that it lends stability to the occupational hierarchy. An important expression of a culture is the status that is accorded to various occupations.[4] There may be widespread agreement in society that status should be reflected in the wage or salary level of the occupation. The wage rate becomes an index of the social valuation of the services provided by that occupation. The valuation may simply be based on how well each individual thinks he could do other people's jobs, given the usual standards achieved and the conditions under which the work has to be performed.[5] The fact that the criteria used in making this valuation may be loose and ill-defined does not matter. Indeed the very looseness of the concept may help in achieving a consensus on occupational status.

Cultural factors alone, however, are not normally sufficient to determine the status of all occupations. Some occupations may be difficult to compare with others on grounds of skill, responsibility, and so on. But for those who work in these occupations it may be essential to know their status, since the status of their occupation may be an important influence on their welfare. If status is supposed to be reflected in wage rates then it is natural, in the absence of other criteria, to use the wage rate as a measure of status. In this way the wage differential between two occupations may come to be taken as defining their relative status.

By negotiating a national minimum wage in each industry, unions may be performing an important social function. The national minimum wage provides an index by which the worker can assess the status of his occupation. His wage, relative to that of other occupations, is taken to reflect society's opinion of the importance of the work he does. It is quite possible that in fact there is no unanimous opinion of this kind; but what matters is only that the worker perceives his relation to society in these terms. Because of the role of wage relativities as social and cultural indicators, it may be unacceptable to adjust them in response to short-run changes in the competitive position of individual industries. Differentials can change only in the long run, as new occupations appear, and existing occupations either prosper or go into decline.

Suppose that each union perceives its primary role as furthering the long-term interests of a particular occupation rather than the short-term interests of those who happen to be in this occupation at the time. Since the status of the occupation is believed to be reflected in its basic wage the maintenance of status demands at very least the preservation of existing differentials. While the union may be unable to influence long-term trends in the fortunes of the occupation, it can certainly avoid employers taking advantage of a short-run excess supply of labour to secure a cut in the basic wage. So far as union officials are concerned, the fact that some workers are prevented from entering the industry, and that others are forced out into lower status occupations, may be a price they are willing to pay to avoid any long-term damage to the status of the occupation.

The maintenance of fixed relativities between basic wage rates does not eliminate short-run competition in the labour market – it merely changes its form. Wage competition is replaced by competition for places in high-wage industries. Firms offering high-wage employment siphon-off the more highly qualified and able workers, forcing the remaining workers into lower-wage (and lower-status) employment. An occupation which suffers a short-run decline in demand relative to other occupations will maintain its wage differentials but will offer fewer job opportunities. Employers will make redundant the less able workers, and recruit only the very able. The redundant workers, and the workers who would normally have expected to enter the industry, will go into other occupations where demand has increased. Thus the effect of a contraction of demand in a given occupation is to increase the average quality of the workforce employed at the given wage, while the effect of a corresponding expansion of demand in the other occupations is to reduce the quality of the workforce at the prevailing wage. So far as the employers are concerned, a contraction of demand reduces average labour costs by increasing the productivity of labour rather than by reducing the wage rate, while an increase in demand increases average labour costs by reducing the productivity of labour instead of by increasing the wage rate.

Suppose now that there is a general contraction in demand, associated with excess supply in both labour and product markets. Demand for labour contracts in the high-status occupations, preventing many highly qualified entrants to the labour force from getting jobs there, and making other workers redundant. Only the very best workers are recruited to, or retained in, these occupations. The others move down the occupational hierarchy to compete for lower-status jobs. Employers prefer the more highly qualified workers to those they usually recruit, and so the less-well qualified workers either fail to get recruited as they usually do, or if they have already been recruited they are liable to be made redundant. As everyone moves one step down the occupational hierarchy it is the unskilled that are forced out at the bottom. They cannot bid down the wage, for firms cannot offer jobs at below the living wage, and so they become unemployed.

The main conclusion is that in many respects trade-union objectives are a reflection of underlying social attitudes towards the occupational hierarchy. This hierarchy is reflected in the relativities between the basic wage rates in different occupations. Such importance is attached to this hierarchy that no group is willing to accept a short-run deterioration in its relative wage merely to maintain employment prospects and to avert redundancy. While the costs of unemployment are high, the costs of instability in the occupational hierarchy are perceived to be even greater.

If trade-union behaviour merely reflects social attitudes then it is possible that the restriction of trade-union power would not lead to any significant change in behaviour. Workers who felt that they had suffered a decline in status might spontaneously reduce the effort they put into work. The cost to the employer of monitoring effort is so high that it may be cheaper to maintain relativities and reduce the workforce, rather than reduce wages, and endure a lower level of productivity. Thus even where trade-union power is slight employers may prefer to maintain relativities in order to benefit from high morale in the workforce.

9.5 DOWNWARD MONEY WAGE RIGIDITY

In the preceding sections it has been implicitly assumed that wages are fixed in real terms, whereas in fact wages are almost invariably denominated in money terms. This is done to reduce transaction costs. Considerable savings are achieved by using the medium of exchange as unit of denomination (see Chapter 4). If instead wages were denominated in a cost of living index then employers would have the administrative costs of converting the index into monetary equivalents each time wage payments were made. They would also be exposed to greater risks because one of their prime costs would be indexed to the cost of living while their output prices would presumably continue to be denominated in money terms. In the long run the additional cost of administration and risk-bearing would be passed on to workers, because employers would only accept indexation if it were accompanied by a compensating reduction in the real wage.

Because wages are denominated in money terms, labour is likely to become overvalued at a time when money prices fall. Variations in the real wage due to changes in prices can only be avoided by increasing the frequency with which wages are negotiated. This in turn increases negotiation costs, however, thus it is normally only in situations of extreme inflation or deflation that employers or trade unions press for renegotiation of the wage more than once a year.

Because basic rates are minimum rates on top of which groups or individuals can negotiate bonuses, there is no constraint on employers increasing the money wage at times of labour shortage. As noted earlier, most unions do not seek to supplant individual bargaining altogether, merely to constrain workers from bidding down the wage below a certain level. Thus while the frequency of negotiation constrains the downward adjustment of the money wage, it does not constrain upward adjustment to anything like the same extent.

The reluctance of unions to negotiate a cut in the money wage cannot be explained by their attitudes toward the frequency of negotiation. Nor is it immediately obvious why the maintenance of relativities prevents them agreeing to a cut in the money wage. For if all money wages are cut in the same proportion then relativities are unaltered. It has been suggested, however, that because wage bargains in different industries are sequential, no union can ever be sure that if it negotiates a money wage cut then other unions will follow its lead. Indeed the very reverse tends to be the case, with each union citing the highest rather than the lowest of previous wage settlements in their negotiations with employers. Thus any union that negotiates an absolute cut in the money wage is likely to experience a relative reduction in the real wage. In order to achieve a money wage cut across the board it would be necessary for all wages to be negotiated simultaneously.

Another reason why money wage cuts may be resisted is that they would redistribute income away from the recipients of contractual income (that is employees) to the recipients of residual income (that is the owners of firms). It must be recognized, however, that if pressure for money wage cuts arises from lower money prices then it is likely that residual income-earners have already suffered relative to contractual income-earners. Thus the redistribution may only serve to restore the status quo. Workers though are unlikely to perceive the situation in this light.

One reason is connected with political attitudes towards profit-income. To many people profit is a surplus appropriated by the creators of the capitalist system — the entrepreneurs. A recession which reduces profits is merely a manifestation of a flaw in the system. Responsibility for this lies ultimately with the entrepreneurs themselves. It is unacceptable on ideological grounds to attribute the recession to an excessively high real wage. It only needs one group of workers to adopt this line — perhaps under the influence of a militant trade-union leadership — and to resist a cut in money wages. For other workers who wish to maintain their differentials with this group must then follow suit, in resisting cuts in their own industry. Thus a political ideology which is strong among just one group of workers can — when coupled with social pressures on differentials — lead to a hardening of attitudes toward wage cuts throughout the entire economy.

It is also possible that a fall in money prices is not correctly perceived by the workers. It may be that they do not perceive changes in the general price level at all, though this seems unlikely. It is more probable that they register price increases more than they do price decreases, so that there is a tendency to underestimate deflation and overestimate inflation. Money illusion of this kind will cause wage cuts to be resisted at all times, particularly among the unskilled who will see it as a threat to the living wage. If the basic wage of the unskilled worker cannot be cut then the other wages tied to it through differentials cannot be cut either.

9.6 THE MARK V MODEL OF A DICHOTOMIZED LABOUR MARKET*

The Mark V model is a modification of the Mark IV model designed to take account of the theory of quantity adjustment developed in this chapter. The main modifications are to the structure of the labour market, as specified below.

1. The representative household has endowments of both qualified labour, n_q, and unqualified labour, n_{uq}. Qualified labour can perform both skilled and unskilled work, while unqualified labour can perform only unskilled work. The household is indifferent between the non-income attributes of skilled and unskilled work. The supply of qualified labour is fixed at $\bar{n}_q$, but the supply of unqualified labour n_{uq}^s is variable.

2. There is a well-behaved production technology relating output y to employment in skilled work, n_s, and employment in unskilled work n_{us}. Qualified labour is more productive in unskilled work than is unqualified labour, but only marginally so. There are positive but diminishing marginal returns to both skilled and unskilled employment, and the marginal rate of substitution between skilled and unskilled work diminishes continuously as the proportion of skilled to unskilled work increases. Finally, when both kinds of employment are increased in the same proportion there are decreasing returns to scale:

$$y^s = y\,(n_s^d, n_{us}^d) \tag{9.1a}$$

$$\partial y^s/\partial n_s^d,\ \partial y^s/\partial n_{us}^d > 0 \tag{9.1b}$$

$$\partial^2 y^s/\partial n_s^{d2},\ \partial^2 y^s/\partial n_{us}^{d\,2} < 0 \tag{9.1c}$$

$$(\partial^2 y^s/\partial n_s^{d2})\,(\partial^2 y^s/\partial n_{us}^{d\,2}) - (\partial^2 y^s/\partial n_s^d\,\partial n_{us}^d)^2 > 0 \tag{9.1d}$$

$$\lambda y^s < y\,(\lambda n_s^d,\ \lambda n_{us}^d)\ \text{for}\ \lambda > 1 \tag{9.1e}$$

Suppose to begin with that the skilled workers are offered wage stability and employment guarantees while unskilled workers are offered neither. Suppose furthermore that the amount of skilled employment guaranteed, n_s^g, represents an equilibrium in the sense that it is just sufficient to keep all qualified labour fully employed, that is

$$n_s^g = \bar{n}_q \tag{9.2}$$

It follows that so far as firms are concerned, qualified labour is simply a fixed factor which is employed exclusively on skilled work.[6] Unqualified labour is the only variable factor and it is employed exclusively on unskilled work. Thus the production function (9.1a) may be rewritten to express output simply as a function of a single variable input, unqualified labour,:

$$y^s = y(n_{uq}) \qquad (9.3)$$

It follows from equations (9.1b)–(9.1e) that the production function (9.3) has the same properties as those assumed of the production functions in earlier chapters; the only difference is that it relates output to unqualified labour instead of to labour input as a whole.

As before there are two main kinds of household income: a variable income and a fixed income, the latter comprising the quasi-rents distributed to households as the owners of fixed factors. The variable income consists of the wage income of unqualified labour, while the fixed income comprises the wage income of qualified labour and residual income, that is distributed profit. Comparing this to the Mark IV model shows that unqualified wage income, as the variable income, is analogous to the labour income of the Mark IV model, while total quasi-rent, as fixed income, is analogous to the dividend income of the Mark IV model.

The existence of two different kinds of work — skilled and unskilled — does not materially affect household preferences, since by assumption they are indifferent between the non-income attributes of the two kinds of work. The only difference is that in measuring leisure it is necessary to subtract from the maximum possible hours of work both the supply of labour to skilled work and the supply of labour to unskilled work. Since by assumption the supply of skilled work is equal to the household's fixed endowment of qualified labour, this is equivalent to reducing the maximum number of hours that are available for unskilled work by an amount equal to the household's endowment of qualified labour.

Taken together these remarks show that when qualified labour behaves as a fixed factor, the dichotomized labour market can be modelled simply by reinterpreting the variables in the Mark IV model. Unqualified labour replaces total labour as the single variable factor of production and total quasi-rent replaces dividends as the household's fixed income. The supply of unqualified labour replaces total labour supply in household preferences. The actual level at which the skilled wage is fixed is of no consequence at all; changes in the skilled wage merely redistribute income between the owners of different kinds of fixed factors which, under the assumptions of the model, have no effect on firm or household behaviour.

9.7 UNEMPLOYMENT AND ITS INCIDENCE IN THE MARK V MODEL

This section, examines the equilibrium of the Mark V economy under varying degrees of money wage and money price flexibility.

Let there be a nationally negotiated basic money wage for unskilled work $\bar{W}_{us}$ and also a basic wage for skilled work

$$\bar{W}_s = (1 + \chi) \, \bar{W}_{us} \tag{9.4}$$

where $\chi > 0$ is the basic wage differential. In each case the basic wage sets a lower bound on the wage actually paid. To simplify matters it is assumed that the wage actually paid to unskilled workers is always less than the skilled workers' basic wage:

$$\bar{W}_{us} \leqslant W_{us} < \bar{W}_s \tag{9.5a}$$

$$W_s \geqslant \bar{W}_s \tag{9.5b}$$

Suppose to begin with that the unskilled money wage is fully flexible within the limits set out in (9.5a), and that money price is flexible too. By analogy with the Mark IV model, there is an equilibrium money wage W_{us}^e and an equilibrium money price level P^e and money interest rate r^e which will provide full employment for the unqualified labour force. If W_{us}^e lies within the limits (9.5a) then this full employment equilibrium will be attained. It should be emphasized, however, that this equilibrium is conditional upon qualified labour behaving as a fixed factor. There is no guarantee that, from a long-run point of view, either firms or households will perceive the existing levels of employment and remuneration of skilled labour as being in equilibrium. Subject to this qualification the mechanism by which unqualified employment is determined is exactly the same as the mechanism which determines the full employment equilibrium in Chapter 7.

Given equilibrium unqualified employment n_{uq}^e and the equilibrium price level P^e it is possible to determine from the production function (9.1a) the marginal value product of qualified labour. The equilibrium money wage for skilled work, W_s^e, can then be determined as the greater of the basic wage $\bar{W}_s$ and the marginal value product of qualified labour.

Consider now the case in which the full employment wage W_{us}^e lies below the basic wage $\bar{W}_{us}$. As a result, downward money wage rigidity is encountered once the wage has fallen to $\bar{W}_{us}$. By analogy with Chapter 7, unqualified labour experiences Keynesian unemployment. The only difference from the Mark IV model is that the present model predicts an unequal incidence of unemployment. Because qualified labour is covered by employment guarantees, the burden of unemployment falls exclusively on the unqualified.

Suppose now that downward rigidity of the money wage is coupled with a fixed money price level. Prices are inflexible because they are administered by firms to secure goodwill. Unlike the Mark IV model, firms are committed to supplying all that is demanded at the quoted price. In the case we are interested in, however, where generalized excess supply prevails, this modification is of no consequence because consumers demand less than firms would wish to supply anyway. Thus once again the results follow by analogy with Chapter 7. *De facto* the money wage is fixed equal to the basic wage for unskilled work, and the money price is fixed at the level administered by firms, a level which creates a notional excess supply in the product market. Firms are demand constrained, households are supply constrained, and the fix-price multiplier determines equilibrium employment and output at levels below those of the flexible-price Keynesian model.

Finally, consider the case in which the guarantee of skilled employment falls short of the stock of qualified labour. Suppose also that the employment guarantee is actively constraining firms, in the sense that their profit-maximizing demand for skilled employment is less than the guaranteed level of skilled employment. At the same time there is an excess supply of unskilled employment as well. Although these assumptions are very restrictive, they are appropriate to the sort of recessionary situations in which unemployment is likely to occur. The analysis can be extended without difficulty to examine the many other sorts of situation that could occur.

Because there is an excess supply of qualified labour the skilled wage will be bid down to the basic rate. Because workers are indifferent between the non-income attributes of skilled and unskilled work, qualified labour which cannot find skilled employment will seek unskilled employment instead. And because qualified workers are marginally more productive than unqualified workers in unskilled work, they will gain priority in hiring by employers. As a result, some of the unqualified who could previously have obtained unskilled work are displaced by qualified workers.[7] These workers bid down the unskilled money wage until the basic wage is reached, whereupon wage competition ceases. If the equilibrium unskilled wage lies below the basic wage then some of the unqualified workers will be unemployed.

The unemployment equilibrium as a whole exhibits the following characteristics:

> 1. there is overemployment in skilled work, equal to the discrepancy between the profit-maximizing demand for skilled labour and the level of guaranteed skilled employment;

2. there is disguised unemployment, in the sense that qualified labour performs unskilled work rather than the skilled work it has been trained for;

3. there is unemployment among unqualified labour.

As in the previous case, the incidence of unemployment is entirely on the unqualified. Because employment guarantees are now more limited, however, qualified labour is also adversely affected because some of it has to be diverted to unskilled work.

These results provide an interesting example of the way in which the theory of quantity adjustment can provide predictions not only about the aggregate volume of unemployment, but about the incidence of unemployment on different groups of workers. It is argued in Chapter 12 that these disaggregated predictions are a good deal more accurate than the corresponding predictions derived from alternative theories of unemployment – notably from the neoclassical theory of unemployment.

CHAPTER 10

PROFIT EXPECTATIONS

10.1 INTRODUCTION

This chapter is concerned with the way in which household profit expectations influence employment. The explicit consideration of profit expectations marks a departure from the mainstream literature on disequilibrium economics.

The significance of household profit expectations is that they influence the household's perception of its budget constraint, and thereby affect its product demand and labour supply.

It is argued below that household profit expectations may not always be consistent with firms' production plans. In the short run they may be at least partly exogenous. Changes in profit expectations can be a major source of disturbance to the economy, in just the same way as changes in tastes and technology.

The exogeneity of profit expectations effects a significant change in the structure of macro-theory. Simple Walras' Law – that the total value of net excess demands is zero – no longer applies. This makes it possible even in a non-monetary economy, for unemployment to be associated with excess supplies of both labour and the product. It can be shown that when profit expectations are pessimistic unemployment can occur with the real wage at, or even below, its full employment level. Unemployment occurs in this case because pessimistic profit expectations lead to a deficiency of product demand. Previous writers have suggested that demand-deficiency unemployment can only occur in a monetary economy. Our analysis shows that this is not so; it can occur in a non-monetary production economy provided household profit expectations are sufficiently pessimistic. The problem in this case is not the existence of money, but the delegation of production decisions to firms, and the restricted flow of information from firms back to the households. Thus it is not only money, but the prevailing form of capitalist organization, which is capable of generating demand-deficiency unemployment.

10.2 THE UNPREDICTABILITY OF PLANNED PROFIT

In general equilibrium theory it is assumed that household profit expectations always adjust to firms' planned profits. Each time the Walrasian auctioneer announces a trial price the household calculates the profit that will be generated by firms' planned response to these prices, and uses this profit figure in determining its budget constraint.

The disequilibrium literature has to date simply extended this assumption to the profits generated by firms' sales-constrained production plans. At any given level of prices the household calculates the firms' response to the quantity constraints that they face, and uses the implied level of profit to determine its budget constraint. To make this point clear we have throughout the book distinguished carefully between the profits generated by constrained and unconstrained production plans.

In each case, as markets adjust to equilibrium, household expectations of profit adjust in line with the modifications to firms' production plans, so that when equilibrium is achieved, and firms' planned profits are realized, households' anticipation of profit is correct. Equilibrium — with or without quantity constraints — is achieved only because household profit expectations are revised continually as part of the adjustment process.

It is, however, quite remarkable that the mechanism by which households learn of firms' planned profits, and by which this information is updated, has not been analysed in any detail. Various possible mechanisms are considered below and it is shown that all of them are unsatisfactory in one way or another.

1. Households could predict current profit from past realized profit. In a stationary economy such predictions would be correct. Given that the economy was already in equilibrium they would allow the equilibrium to be perpetuated. But as we have already seen, one of the crucial features of the macroeconomy is that it is continually subject to change, and there is no completely reliable way of predicting the magnitude and direction of change. Consequently there is no way in which predictions based on past realized values can guarantee complete accuracy.

2. Households could infer profits from the prevailing prices of the firms' inputs and outputs. This inference, however, requires a knowledge of the production function. Knowledge of the production function is usually derived from a knowledge of technology, which is specialized with firms and is indeed often protected as a trade secret. Furthermore, when firms face quantity constraints it would be necessary to know what the constraints are and how they are likely to modify the firms' production plans.

3. Managers could publish forecasts of profit for shareholders' benefit. In order to fulfill their primary role of maximizing profit, however, managers need to know only the differences in profit associated with alternative production strategies, and not the absolute level of profit generated by the optimal strategy. Thus the preparation of profit forecasts is an additional managerial function, involving resource costs which will ultimately be borne by the shareholders. Shareholders will wish to trade-off the increasing cost to management of preparing profit forecasts in greater detail against the diminishing returns to greater accuracy. Thus even if profit forecasts are prepared it is unlikely that they will be a completely accurate reflection of the profits implied by firms' production plans.

4. It could be argued that the existence of a stock market, in which rights to profit (equities) are traded, would enable firms' expectations to be communicated to households. The price of equity would reflect firms' planned profits, and even if a household did not actively trade in the market, it could learn equity prices easily through the financial news media.

It is households, however as the owners of firms, and not the managers, who set the price of equity. Thus the valuation of equity will reflect households' expectations, not those of managers. Only if the managers of firms are involved in insider trading will there be a tendency for the valuation of firms to be brought into line with their managers' own expectations. The rewards to insider trading are undoubtedly great, and schemes for employee-ownership may well encourage it. But the obstacles to insider trading are in many cases even greater — one obstacle is its illegality in most countries.[1] When the deterrents to inside trading are effective, equity prices simply reflect household expectations: households can learn nothing from them about managerial expectations.

5. Another possibility is to invoke the Walrasian auctioneer. If the auctioneer were to quote not only a trial wage but an associated trial profit figure too then both firms and households would necessarily have the same perception of profit.

But modifying the role of the auctioneer in this way implies a change in the behaviour of firms. They would now be motivated to set labour demand and product supply, not to maximize profit, but merely to realize the target profit figure. The outcome would be the same only if the auctioneer calculated the target figure so that it was always consistent with firms' maximizing efforts. This involves a significant extension of the role of the auctioneer. Not only does he adjust trial prices according to notional excess demands, he also calculates the profit implied by these prices and communicates it to households. But since his primary role in initiating price adjustments has already been rejected, it is only consistent to reject this secondary role too.

6. Finally it is necessary to dispose of a fallacious argument based on a confusion of *ex ante* and *ex post* variables. It is undoubtedly true that what firms generate as profit is equal to what households receive as profit income. In the context of national income accounting this is an identity (provided that retained profits and capital gains are treated consistently). However, what households receive as profit after a given set of transactions has been completed is not the same as what households anticipate profit to be when deciding how much to transact at prevailing prices.

Of the arguments considered above, it is the third and fourth which have the greatest plausibility. The publication of profit forecasts, and 'insider trading' on the equity market, will both help to keep households in touch with the profit implications of firms' production plans. In practice, however, information costs and legal obstacles to insider trading will prevent household profit expectations from achieving the degree of accuracy assumed by the theory. If the disequilibrium approach, with its emphasis on information costs — is to be applied consistently then it is important to recognize not only that prices do not adjust instantaneously, but that profit expectations do not adjust instantaneously either.

10.3 PROFIT EXPECTATIONS IN A NON-MONETARY ECONOMY

It is instructive to examine the role of profit expectations in the Mark I model of a non-monetary economy. The simplicity of the model serves to highlight the significance of profit expectations for macroeconomic equilibrium. Throughout the discussion it will be assumed that the real wage is rigid and that both consumption and leisure are normal goods, so that an increase in profit income will increase the demand for both. In the light of the discussion in Chapter 8 it will be assumed that firms are willing to enter into quantity commitments to consumers. They do not offer employment guarantees to labour, however. Alternatively it may be assumed that skilled labour is covered by employment guarantees but is regarded by both firms and households as a fixed factor. The variable factor is unskilled labour, which is not covered by employment guarantees. On the latter interpretation it is necessary to read 'unskilled labour' for 'labour' throughout the following.

In Figure 10.1 the full employment equilibrium is at E where the indifference curve DD′ is tangent to the production function OA. Employment is n^e and output y^e. The equilibrium real wage w^e is given by the slope of the tangent BC and equilibrium profit π^e by the intercept OB.

Suppose now that household profit expectations become pessimistic. For example households may anticipate that depletion of resources will result in lower output and lower profits this period. Their expectations of profit are revised down from OB to OG, and the budget constraint they perceive shifts down from BC to GH. Household consumption plans are set at the point of tangency J between GH and the indifference curve FF′. Households plan to supply n_1^s units of labour and consume y_1^d units of product. However since the real wage is unchanged firms still plan to produce at E. Consequently there is an excess supply of labour $n_1^s - n^e$ and an excess supply of goods $y_1^d - y^e$. In other words, the fall in profit expectations to below the full employment level has created generalized excess supply on the real side of the economy.

Employment is set at the short end of the labour market and so remains at n^e. Household demand is less than product supply, so that while output is y^e sales are only y_1^d. Thus firms effectively produce at K, which lies within the production frontier.

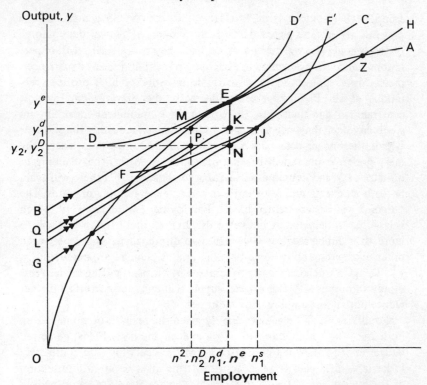

Figure 10.1. Unemployment due to pessimistic profit expectations

If the product is durable then the unsold output can be added to inventory. If it is perishable then it goes to waste. In the first case the profits distributed by the firm fall to OL, with BL being retained to finance the inventory. In the second case total profits fall to OL and nothing is retained. Thus so far as the households are concerned, their expectation that profits will fall is at least partially self-fulfilling. It must be recognized, however, that profits do not fall by as much as was anticipated, and subsequent household behaviour will depend upon how expectations are revised in the light of this.

The representative firm is not in equilibrium at K. Next period it will react to the sales constraint, and if its expectations of sales are stationary it will produce no more than has just been sold (if unsold output has just been added to inventory it may decide to produce even less). For example, it may decide to produce at M, the point on the production frontier where output is just sufficient to satisfy the demand of the previous period. This gives a demand for labour, n_2^D, lower than before.

Household plans will depend upon how they revise their profit expectations and how they respond to the employment constraint experienced previously. Suppose the households do not modify their profit expectations at all. If they perceive correctly the previous employment constraint n^e and their expectations of the employment constraint are stationary, then they will plan to consume somewhere along the segment GN of the budget constraint GH. Given the assumed preferences, the most preferred point will be the end point N. With firms planning to produce at M and households planning to consume at N there will again be both an excess supply of labour and an excess supply of goods. The outcome will be represented by P. Employment will be $n_2 < n^e$ which is less than anticipated by households. On the other hand, profit will be more than anticipated, at OQ. The two discrepancies will cancel each other out, leaving households to consume as planned an amount $y_2 = y_2^D$. Demand will be less than anticipated by firms, resulting in an excess supply of output MP. This excess supply will encourage firms to further reduce output and employment next period.

Equilibrium will be achieved only when the realized outcome lies on both the firms' production function and on the households' perceived budget constraint. When household profit expectations are completely inelastic with respect to realized profit this must be at an intersection of the budget line GH with the production function OA. As shown in Figure 10.1, there are two such intersections, at Y and Z. However because households cannot be forced to supply more labour than they wish, or to consume more output than they wish, households can be in equilibrium only on the segment GJ of the budget constraint. In this case the intersection Y represents the unique constrained equilibrium.

It is not always the case that the equilibrium is unique. For example if the point of tangency J lay on the other side of the intersection Z, then Z would be an equilibrium too. The only guarantee of uniqueness is if firms are unwilling to give either supply commitments to consumers or employment guarantees to workers. In this case firms will be unwilling to produce anywhere on OA above the point E. Since the slope of the segment OE is everywhere either greater than or equal to the slope of the budget line GH, there can only be one point of contact between the segments OE and GJ.

In the case where profit expectations are overoptimistic there may be no equilibrium at all. For example if profit expectations were revised upward from OB, while the real wage remained unchanged, then there would be no point of contact at all between the budget constraint perceived by the household and the production function OA. The situation would be unlikely to persist for long, however, because realized profits would be much lower than anticipated, and would fall at an ever-increasing rate. Thus sooner or later profit expectations would be revised downward. An equilibrium state would once again exist, even though the economy might take some time to adjust to it.

All of the constrained equilibria described above are characterized by the equality of expected profit and realized profit. In conventional analysis this equality is achieved by assuming that households correctly perceive firms' planned profits, so that when all markets are in equilibrium and firms' planned profits are realized, household profit expectations turn out to be correct. In other words, expectations are correct because they adjust automatically to realized values. In the present analysis this direction of causation has been reversed: instead of expectations adjusting to realized profit, realized profit adjusts to make expectations self-fulfilling. The adjustment of realized profit is effected by changes in the levels of employment and output; these adjustments continue until household profit expectations have been validated.

10.4 EVALUATION OF THE PROFIT EXPECTATIONS MODEL

There is an interesting parallel between the preceding model and the simple model of a fixed-price monetary economy presented in Chapter 5. An exogenous fall in expected profit has the same effect as an exogenous increase in money prices, namely it reduces aggregate demand and leads to an excess supply in both goods and labour markets. The similarity is apparent from GWL (equation (5.14)). The Mark II model sets $\pi^h = \pi^f$ but sets $z_m > 0$, while the profit expectations approach sets $z_m = 0$ and sets $\pi^h < \pi^f$; these are just alternative ways of accommodating generalized excess supply (z_y, $z_n < 0$) on the real side of the economy. In either case a constrained equilibrium is attained through a reduction in real income, whose impoverishing effect either eliminates the excess demand for money balances, or brings realized profit into line with expectations.

Despite the formal similarity the models have radically different implications for both theory and policy.

In the Mark II model the existence of money is crucial to the entire analysis, while the profit expectations model applies to a non-monetary economy as well as to a monetary one. The exogeneity of profit expectations is a consequence of the delegation of production decisions by the owners (the households) to the managers, and the restricted flow of information back from the management to the owners. Thus demand-deficiency due to inappropriate profit expectations can be attributed to the specialization of the ownership and management functions. It is not money, but the prevailing form of capitalist organization, which makes possible demand-deficiency unemployment in this model.

In the Mark II model the existence of unemployment depends crucially on money wage and money price rigidities. If both money wages and money prices are flexible the economy will adjust to full employment. In the profit expectations model unemployment does not depend upon wage or price rigidity. When profit expectations are exogenous equilibrium can be achieved only when profits have fallen to the level anticipated by households. If household expectations are incompatible with the full employment level of profit then there is no way in which the economy can adjust to full employment, even though wages and prices are flexible.

This result has important implications for wages policy. Indeed it is possible to strengthen the result still further, and show that in certain circumstances wage adjustments may be counterproductive. Under certain conditions unemployment will be exacerbated by a reduction in the real wage, and may be reduced (though not eliminated) by an increase in the real wage.

Suppose to begin with that changes in the real wage have no effect on household profit expectations. Figure 10.2 illustrates an initial state of unemployment D. In Chapter 3 (Figure 3.2) this was said to represent unemployment due to a too-high real wage. Implicit in this view is that household profit expectations are always consistent with firms' planned profits. In other words it is assumed that if the real wage is reduced firms' profits will increase and the economy will adjust to full employment at E.

But if household profit expectations remain unchanged when the real wage is reduced then the perceived household budget line, instead of becoming tangent to the production frontier OA at a point such as E to the right of D, will rotate about the intercept H. The new budget line will be HK instead of HJ, and household equilibrium will move down to L. L cannot be a general equilibrium, however, because firms are producing within the production frontier. Employment will therefore con-

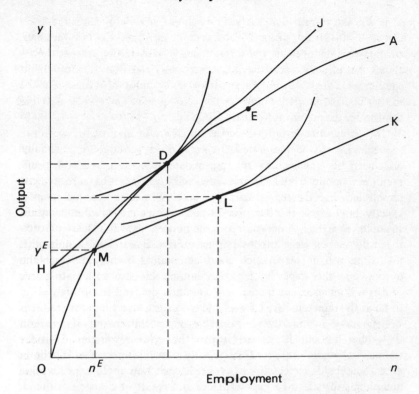

Figure 10.2. Effect of a real wage cut on unemployment

tract and a downward multiplier process will bring the economy to equilibrium at M, the point of intersection between the budget line HJ and the production frontier OA. Unemployment at M is higher than at D even though the real wage is lower.

A further application of wage cuts would reduce employment even more. Only an increase in the real wage back to its original level will restore employment. Thus at the unemployment equilibrium L a reduction in the real wage will further reduce employment, while only an increase in the real wage will increase it.

This proposition is reminiscent of underconsumptionist arguments.[2] Typical of these arguments is that profit income is not fully converted into aggregate demand, that is profit income constitutes a leakage from the circular flow of income. While these theories correctly view the role of profit as central, their analysis is almost invariably impaired by a failure to distinguish properly between *ex ante* and *ex post* variables, and between endogenous and exogenous variables. The present theory argues that profit expectations are exogenous and that unemployment equilibrium is achieved only when output and employment have adjusted so that realized profit is equal to expected profit. Only when stated in this form is the argument logically sound.

The assumption that profit expectations are invariant with respect to the real wage may be questioned, however. If every reduction in the real wage were accompanied by an appropriate increase in expected profit then the economy would adjust to full employment. It has already been established that the representative household will be unable to infer exactly the change in profit implied by any given change in the real wage. It could be argued, however, that the household will at least perceive that a lower real wage implies higher profits. But this in turn assumes that firms will not experience sales constraints if they increase their output, and this depends on *other* households also anticipating that profits will increase, and increasing consumer demand accordingly. Thus so far as the representative household is concerned, a cut in the real wage will encourage an upward revision of profit expectations only if it believes that other households also anticipate that profits will rise. Thus the rational household's expectation of profit depends upon what it believes other households expectations to be. If each household expects other households to raise their expectations as a result of a wage cut then it will raise its own expectations too. But if it believes that other households' perception of the macroeconomy is too simplistic, or that they — like itself — are cautious in revising profit expectations upward, then its own expectations may remain unchanged; they may even be revised downward. Thus the prima facie case for supposing that real wage cuts will enhance profit expectations is very weak.

10.5 PROFIT EXPECTATIONS IN A MONETARY ECONOMY

It is often suggested that money is somehow a source of instability in the economy. The analysis in Chapters 5 and 6 indicates that this is so only in so far as money wages and money prices are inflexible. When wages and prices are flexible money is effectively neutral as regards economic stability.

This result is strengthened quite remarkably when profit expectations are exogenous. In this case money may actually be a stabilizing influence on the economy. Unemployment which would occur in the absence of a monetary asset may be mitigated or eliminated altogether when a monetary asset exists. This result depends upon both money wages and money prices being flexible. If they are inflexible then money simply acts as a transmission mechanism by which profit expectations create unemployment; it does not itself exacerbate their impact.

Consider first a flexible-wage and flexible-price economy. A reduction in household profit expectations will lead to a reduction in planned consumption, and also to a reduction in the demand for money balances and an increase in labour supply. At the initial wages and prices this creates notional excess supplies of product, labour and money balances. Since money is a circulating medium, however, the excess supply of money balances will not be perceived. The reaction in the labour and product markets will, therefore, be to bid down the money wage and the money price in order to restore equilibrium. This increases the real value of money balances and so encourages households to run them down further by increasing their consumption relative to labour supply. Equilibrium will eventually be achieved when the excess supply of money balances is equal to households' underestimation of firms' planned profits. At this point the reduction in consumption due to lower anticipated income is exactly compensated by the increase in consumption generated by the planned running down of money balances. Each household finds that its unanticipated profit income exactly makes good the planned reduction in money balances induced by the lower price level. The equilibrium real wage is virtually the same as it was to begin with, and output and employment are maintained close to their initial levels too.

The actual magnitude of the money wage and money price reductions will depend upon whether household profit expectations are fixed in real or monetary terms. The denomination of expectations in money terms implies a degree of money illusion by households. In the present context money illusion will have a stabilizing effect on price, for as price falls so anticipated real profit rises, and real consumption increases along with it. As the underestimation of real profit is reduced so the magnitude of the compensating excess supply of money balances required for equilibrium is reduced too, and the reduction in the equilibrium price is much less than it would otherwise be.

The argument may be expressed formally by modifying the Mark II model of Chapter 5. The household notional demand and supply functions are still given by equations (5.6)

$$c^d = c^d (w, \pi^h, m, t) \tag{10.1a}$$

$$n^s = n^s (w, \pi^h, m, t) \tag{10.1b}$$

$$\dot{m}^d = \dot{m}^d (w, \pi^h, m, t) \tag{10.1c}$$

where either expected real profit π^h or expected money profit Π^h is now exogenous.

As before, the notional demand and supply functions of the firm are

$$\begin{aligned} y^s &= y^s (w) \\ n^d &= n^d (w) \end{aligned} \tag{10.2}$$

and the equation of aggregate demand is

$$y^d = c^d + g^d \tag{10.3}$$

GWL (equation 5.14) is still

$$z_y + wz_n + z_m + (\pi^f - \pi^h) = 0 \tag{10.4}$$

but the equilibrium conditions (5.18) are reduced to

$$z_y = z_n = 0 \tag{10.5}$$

Substituting (10.5) into (10.4) gives the relation between unanticipated profit and the excess supply of money:

$$z_m + (\pi^f - \pi^h) = 0 \tag{10.6}$$

This is a weaker form of the equilibrium conditions used in Chapter 5 because it allows the money market to be in disequilibrium when household expectations are incorrect. Unless this weaker concept of general equilibrium is used, however, there is no possibility of equilibrium at all. For as noted in Chapter 2, when household profit expectations are incorrect it is impossible for all markets simultaneously to be in equilibrium.

Substituting equations (10.1a), (10.1b), (10.2) and (10.3) into the equilibrium conditions (10.5) gives

$$\begin{aligned} z_y \, (W, P; \Pi^h, M, T, G^d) &= 0 \\ z_n \, (W, P; \Pi^h, M, T) &= 0 \end{aligned} \tag{10.7}$$

where, as before, a semi-colon separates the endogenous and exogenous variables. Alternatively one of the conditions (10.5) may be replaced by the condition (10.6). In either case there are two simultaneous equations in the two endogenous variables W and P. These can normally be solved to express the equilibrium money wage W^e and the equilibrium money price P^e as functions of, amongst other things, household expectations of money profit Π^h (or in the absence of money illusion, π^h).

The introduction of a bond market into the model does not affect the argument, provided that the bond market is always maintained in equilibrium by adjustments of the money rate of interest, r. In this case the equations (10.7) are replaced by three simultaneous equations in the three unknowns W, P and r. Equilibrium is achieved with the goods, labour and bond markets in equilibrium, and the notional excess supply of money equal to the household's underestimation of profit income.

When the money wage is fixed, and price is flexible, price adjustments will induce a contraction of the supply of output, and consequent employment rationing for households. In this case employment in a monetary economy is only slightly more stable than it is in a non-monetary economy.

Finally, when both money wages and money prices are fixed then the existence of a monetary asset contributes nothing to employment stability. Just as in the non-monetary economy, profit expectations are a source of exogenous disturbance which has a direct effect on employment and output, unmitigated by adjustments elsewhere in the system.

10.6 RELEVANCE OF PROFIT EXPECTATIONS

It is possible to question the relevance of the preceding theory on a number of grounds.

It may seem counterintuitive that profit expectations can exert such an important influence on the macroeconomy when in practice the typical household derives very little income directly from profits. In this context a typical household consists of a prime-age working head of household and his or her dependents. Such households normally have few accumulated savings, and those they do have are usually invested in financial intermediaries such as banks and pension funds. The bulk of profit income accrues to a minority of atypical households, containing very wealthy people, or those approaching retirement age. For these households, however, profit income is a far more important determinant of consumption than is wage income. As a result, simply grossing up the effects of profits on the typical household will severely understate the significance of profits for aggregate household consumption.

The relevance of profits for household behaviour is not impaired by the fact that profits are channelled to households through intermediaries such as pension funds. All that intermediation means is that households form expectations of profit at one remove. For example, their immediate expectations may relate to their pension income, but their expectations of future pension income will in turn be based on their expectations of profit.

A much more serious objection arises from the fact that in the simple model developed above investment has been ignored. An increase in household profit expectations will increase their valuation of the existing stock of productive assets, and this will be reflected in higher values of corporate equity. Managers of firms will perceive that shareholders' valuation of existing assets has risen relative to the supply price of newly produced assets and so, acting in their shareholders' interests, they will increase investment demand, until the cost of production of the marginal asset has become equal to the value of an existing asset.

Ultimately this additional investment must be financed by the households. If firms make use of retained profit then households must finance a postponement of their dividend income; if firms do not retain profit then households must subscribe to new issues of corporate debt. In either case, household saving must increase, and this must be at the expense of current consumption. Thus once investment is allowed for, higher profit expectations may actually reduce, rather than increase, household consumption.

Because household profit expectations have increased, however, their reduction in consumption is likely to be less than their increase in saving, and so aggregate private sector expenditure (consumption plus investment) will increase. Thus aggregate private expenditure will vary directly with household profit expectations.

In principle the relevance of household profit expectations can be tested using data on equity prices. As noted earlier, equity prices reflect households' expectations of profit, not those of the management. If equity investors perceive no risks then in an efficient market the price of equity will equal the discounted sum of expected nominal profits. This discounted sum depends upon (a) the discount factor, which is determined by the price of bonds, (b) the expected rate of money price inflation, and (c) the expected stream of real profit income.

In order to isolate the impact of real profit expectations on the equity price it is necessary to eliminate the effects of changes in the discount factor and in the expected rate of inflation. The effect of changes in the discount factor can be eliminated by normalizing the equity price with respect to the price of a bond, that is by focusing upon the equity price relative to the bond price. To eliminate the effect of inflationary expectations it is necessary to have price information on an asset yielding a fixed income denominated in real terms, for example an indexed bond. The price of the indexed bond relative to the price of an ordinary bond reflects inflationary expectations, whilst the price of the equity relative to the price of the indexed bond reflects the state of profit expectations. Thus the impact of profit expectations on private expenditure is essentially an empirical question – namely the extent to which equity prices, normalized by indexed bond prices, are leading indicators of private expenditure.

Unfortunately there are few economies for which indexed bond prices are available, though at least one economy – Israel – has reliable data. Surrogate measures of expected inflation are widely available, however, for example inflation forecasts, the rate of money supply growth, and so on.

There is evidence that, in the absence of normalization, equity prices function well as leading indicators of private expenditure. It is also established that movements in equity prices are only weakly correlated with movements in inflation indicators. This lends indirect support to the view that profit expectations are an important influence on private expenditure.

Fluctuations in equity prices are known to have a fairly large amplitude over a wide range of frequencies (which suggests that they follow a random walk in which the average step is large). It is not unreasonable to ascribe some of these fluctuations to exogenous changes in the state of profit expectations. On this assumption, exogenous changes in profit expectations are both frequent and large, and thus could be an important destabilizing influence on private expenditure, and hence on employment and output.

10.7 SUMMARY

The theory of profit expectations illustrates an important case in which unemployment may be truly involuntary, in the sense discussed in section 1.6. If household profit expectations are exogenous then attempts by individual workers to bid down wages in response to an excess supply of labour may exacerbate demand-deficiency by reducing aggregate wage income. In this case the efforts of individual workers to secure employment through wage-competition are collectively self-defeating. Since wage-competition is their chief method of securing employment, their unemployment is truly involuntary.

This proposition was demonstrated for a non-monetary economy in section 10.3. The result must be qualified to some extent for a monetary economy, for the existence of a monetary asset tends to stabilize employment. In a monetary economy workers will bid down money wages rather than real wages, and this can stimulate real consumer demand in two ways. First, if profit expectations are fixed in money terms household expectations of real profit will be increased as money prices fall. Secondly the real value of money balances will increase and this will stimulate households to run down money balances by increasing real consumption relative to their anticipated real income.

If both these effects are large then money-wage and money-price adjustments may succeed in maintaining the economy at full employment. Thus exogenous changes in household profit expectations will alter the money wage and the money price level, but leave the real wage, and hence output and employment, unchanged. Under these circumstances variations in household profit expectations form the basis for a theory, not of unemployment, but of wage and price fluctuation in a full employment economy.

In practice, however, both effects are likely to be quite small. This will certainly be the case if household profit expectations are denominated in real rather than money terms, and if households are far from satiating their demand for real money balances. In this situation it is likely that money wages and money prices will have to fall very substantially in order to maintain a full-employment equilibrium.

In principle it is quite possible that money wages and money prices could fall to zero and still no equilibrium would be achieved. This case would be unlikely to occur except under very extreme conditions, such as if real profit expectations actually fell as money wages were reduced. It does illustrate, however, a hypothetical state of true involuntary unemployment in a monetary economy.

In practice, long before money wages had fallen to zero institutional constraints would come into operation. The first of these is trade union opposition to cuts in basic money wages, and similar opposition by wages boards in non-unionized industries. If this first line of opposition were removed then the second line would be the unwillingness of workers (and possibly employers too) to denominate labour contracts in a currency whose real value was so volatile. The search for an alternative unit of denomination would tend to increase the risks associated with the currency as a store of value, and perhaps lead to its eventual replacement by another currency instead. In practice, therefore, the extent of money wage and money price adjustment will be constrained by institutional factors. This has suggested to some observers that these institutional constraints are the primary cause of unemployment. The analysis of profit expectations suggests, however, that in many respects these constraints merely mitigate some of the adverse effects of the underlying cause, which is pessimistic expectations, and the inability of the economic system to correct them quickly enough.

CHAPTER 11

DYNAMICS OF EMPLOYMENT AND OUTPUT*

11.1 INTRODUCTION

The preceding analysis has stressed the importance of expectations in determining employment and output. For example Chapter 7 showed how firms' expectations of prices influence the level of investment demand, and Chapter 10 explained how household expectations of profit influence consumer demand. In both these chapters expectations were assumed to be exogenous – more precisely, they were assumed to be inelastic with respect to changes in current levels of prices and profits. This assumption was necessary in order to exhibit the role of expectations in a comparative static framework. By assuming that expectations are inelastic it is possible to show how a change in the state of expectation can shift the economy from one equilibrium to another.

The assumption of inelastic expectations is very strong, however – particularly in the long run, when individual transactors have plenty of time to learn from experience. It is more plausible to assume an adaptive expectations mechanism, in which expectations are modified each period by some proportion of the previous period's 'forecast error' – in other words expectations are changed by some proportion of the discrepancy between the value expected for the current period and the value actually realized. The adaptive mechanism contains inelastic expectations as a limiting case – the case in which the proportion of forecast error used in revising expectations is zero. The other limiting case is that of stationary expectations in which the proportion of the forecast error used is unity. In this case expectations are revised fully in the light of the realized value; the expectation for next period is equal to the value realized in the current period.

Analytically the advantage of the adaptive mechanism is that it contains both endogenous and exogenous elements. It can therefore explain how following an exogenous change in the state of expectation, expectations are revised over time in the light of experience. In a closed economic system this 'experience' itself reflects the impact on the economy of the initial change in expectations.

Expectations influence economic behaviour in a variety of ways. The impact of price expectations on investment behaviour and the impact of profit expectations on household behaviour are only two particular examples of this, albeit important ones. The analysis of Chapters 5 and 6 directs attention to another kind of expectation which is perhaps even more important than the other two — namely expectations of quantity constraints. These expectations did not appear explicitly before, because in the comparative static analysis quantity constraints were regarded as completely endogenous variables which are perceived with complete accuracy by firms and households alike. In dynamic analysis, however, it must be recognized that transactors must often plan without a knowledge of the quantity constraints to which they will be subject. It is only after the event that plans can be revised in the light of the quantity constraints that have been experienced.

11.2 HOUSEHOLD EXPECTATIONS OF INCOME

Consider to begin with the dynamics of household behaviour under conditions of generalized excess supply. Each period the household draws up a consumption and saving plan not knowing the employment constraint it will face in the labour market. It knows the maximum amount of labour it would be willing to supply at the prevailing wage, but not how much of its labour firms will actually demand. This must be estimated on the basis of past experience of employment, together with any other information that the household believes relevant. The level of employment anticipated last period represents the household's interpretation of all employment experience and other information that was available prior to the last period. Expectations for the current period will be based on this, together with any new information available since then. This new information comprises last period's employment experience, together with any news about employers' intentions received during the same period. Response to last period's employment experience will be adaptive, as indicated above. On the other hand important news may induce an exogenous change in expectations over and above the adaptive change. Thus the household's estimate of current wage income depends partly on a lagged endogenous variable — the previous period's employment — and partly on a current exogenous variable, representing the impact on expectations of news received during the previous period.

In order to plan consumption and saving the household needs to predict not only its wage income but also its non-wage income, that is profits. A similar kind of reasoning applies to the formulation of profit expectations. The previous period's expectations reflect the accumulated experience and knowledge of the earlier periods. Thus current profit expectations will be based on the previous period's expectations, modified in the light of the previous period's realized profit, and of any news of profit prospects received during that period.

By combining its expectations of wage and non-wage income the household can determine expected total income, and thereby draw up its consumption and saving plans. In fact when the proportion of forecast error used to modify expectations is the same for both wage and non-wage income a further simplification can be achieved. In this case wage and profit expectations are determined by the respective mechanisms

$$
\begin{aligned}
wn_t^H &= wn_{t-1}^H + \lambda \, (wn_{t-1} - wn_{t-1}^H) + e_t \\
\pi_t^H &= \pi_{t-1}^H + \lambda \, (\pi_{t-1} - \pi_{t-1}^H) + f_t
\end{aligned}
\tag{11.1}
$$

and so it follows by addition that

$$
y_t^H = y_{t-1}^H + \lambda \, (y_{t-1} - y_{t-1}^H) + e_t + f_t
\tag{11.2}
$$

where the superscript H denotes, as before, the household's expectation of a constrained variable, the subscript t refers to the time period, $0 \leqslant \lambda \leqslant 1$ is a parameter of the adjustment process, and e_t, f_t are exogenous changes in expectation induced by news or opinion regarding employment and profits respectively. Equation (11.2) asserts that expected household income is determined adaptively from previous expectations and previous income, as well as by reaction to extraneous news.

11.3 FIRMS' OUTPUT AND INVESTMENT POLICIES

The significance of firms' expectations depends upon several technological parameters, notably the lags involved in changing the rate of output, and in commissioning and installing new capital equipment. The role of expectations also depends upon whether the firm's capital requirements are met from its own output, or by purchases from other firms.

A variety of different assumptions can be made about firm behaviour.

This section presents the conventional view of firms' output and investment policies, which is associated with the 'accelerator' theory of investment. The next section presents an alternative theory which emphasizes production lags and the role of inventories. The implications of the two theories are compared in later sections of the chapter.

In conventional macroeconomic literature it is usual to ignore production lags and to assume that firms can respond instantaneously to fluctuations in demand by hiring additional labour and increasing the utilization of existing fixed factors. Consequently while the firm is demand constrained, it has no need to forecast demand in order to plan production.[1]

The only need for predicting demand is in connection with the firm's investment policy. While production lags may be ignored, it is recognized that there is a gestation lag for newly installed capital equipment. As a result of this the target capital stock for the beginning of period $t + 1$ must be decided at the beginning of period t, in time for investment to be undertaken during period t.

The target capital stock is determined by the firm's anticipated output requirements. The firm is committed to supplying all that is demanded at a given price, because of the goodwill motive. This demand cannot be met by running down inventories (for example because the product is perishable). It must therefore be met out of current supply, the cost of which is minimized by maintaining the capital stock in a fixed proportion to the level of output. Since supply is always adjusted to demand, this means that the target capital stock depends upon anticipated aggregate demand.

At the time the investment decision is made, at the beginning of period t, the opening value of the capital stock, k_t, is known, but the most recent realized value of demand that is known is that of the previous period, y_{t-1}^D. Ignoring depreciation of the capital stock, investment demand will be set to make good the discrepancy between the target capital stock k_{t+1}^d and the initial capital stock k_t:

$$i_t^d = k_{t+1}^d - k_t \tag{11.3}$$

where k_{t+1}^d is proportional to anticipated aggregate demand,

$$k_{t+1}^d = v_t y_{t+1}^F \tag{11.4}$$

where $v_t > 0$ is the cost-minimizing capital-output ratio. The expectation y_{t+1}^F is formed by adapting the expectation held in period $t-1$ in the light of realized demand:

$$y_{t+1}^F = y_t^F + \mu (y_{t-1} - y_{t-1}^F) \qquad (11.5)$$

where $0 \leqslant \mu \leqslant 1$ is a parameter of the expectation adjustment process.

The consequences of this pattern of firm behaviour are examined in section 11.5. It is shown that in the limiting case where both firms' and households' expectations are stationary, their interaction is described by the familiar 'multiplier—accelerator' model.

It must be recognized, however, that the model presented above is subject to a number of qualifications. The most important of these concern the nature of the capital stock. To begin with, although the capital goods produced are clearly durable, the capital good producers do not hold inventories of their output. If they did, other firms' investment demands could be met from stock, and it would no longer be necessary for the output of capital goods to adjust fully each period to current demand. Even though instantaneous adjustment of output is possible it may well be costly, so that adjustment of inventory is preferable. The argument usually advanced for not holding inventories is that many capital goods are designed specifically to individual customers' requirements, which are difficult to foresee, and so the capital goods must be built to order.

This argument does not apply to consumer goods, however; here the lack of inventories is usually explained in terms of the perishability of the goods. This line of argument leads to the conclusion that the products of the economy are extremely heterogeneous. Consumer goods and producer goods differ in their degree of perishability, while producer goods take many different forms depending on individual customers' requirements. It becomes extremely difficult to see how this conclusion can be squared with the assumption that all units of output are perfect substitutes and are therefore sold at a uniform price.

The heterogeneity of capital also makes it difficult to see how disinvestment can occur. Depreciation may result in net disinvestment, but gross disinvestment can really only occur by the conversion of capital back into consumption. When producer goods are highly specific it is usually prohibitively expensive to convert them to a form in which they can be consumed. Once the theory is modified to take account of the impracticability of gross disinvestment, the analytics of the multiplier—accelerator interaction become much more complex.

11.4 INVENTORY INVESTMENT

It is desirable to formulate an alternative model which affords an internally consistent treatment of capital, and gives a central role to inventory adjustment. The simplest model interprets capital as an inventory of finished product. By focusing on the finished product, rather than raw materials or work in progress, the analysis of disinvestment is simplified because the finished product is by definition immediately transformable into a consumer good.

The user motive for holding inventory is to accommodate unpredictable changes in demand while avoiding the costs of short-run adjustments of the rate of output. It is assumed for simplicity that wages and prices are fixed, so that the speculative motive for holding inventory is not applicable.

In contrast to the previous model, it is assumed that there is a one-period lag in the adjustment of output, arising from the firm's desire to exploit economies of continuity in production. In planning output for the next period the firm has to anticipate two distinct components of demand. The first component is final demand originating from consumers and government; the second is investment demand arising from the desire to adjust inventory to its target level. It is assumed that each firm meets its investment demand from its own output: no inventories are traded between firms.

Firms are committed to meeting all final demand if they possibly can. If there is excess demand for output then inventories are run down, while if there is excess supply then the unsold output is added to stock. Assuming that the inventory is never totally depleted, consumer demand and government will always be satisfied:

$$c_t^D = c_t, \qquad g_t^d = g_t \qquad (11.6)$$

In predicting final demand for the next period the firm has only current demands, and its earlier expectations of them, to go on. It is assumed that expectations are normally adaptive, though they may be subject to exogenous change from time to time:

$$c_t^F + g_t^F = c_{t-1}^F + g_{t-1}^F$$
$$+ \xi \left[c_{t-1} + g_{t-1} - (c_{t-1}^F + g_{t-1}^F) \right] + \phi_t \qquad (11.7)$$

where $0 \leqslant \xi \leqslant 1$ is a fixed parameter of the adjustment process and ϕ_t is a disturbance factor which is normally zero.

The firm's target capital stock depends upon the variability of demand, as estimated from past data. It is set at the margin where the additional cost of holding inventory is equal to the expected additional value of goodwill generated by serving customers from stock. The figure for the target capital stock is not revised continuously, but only occasionally when the statistical evidence indicates a significant change in the long-run pattern of demand. Thus

$$k_{t+1}^d = k_t^d + \psi_t \tag{11.8}$$

where ψ_t is a disturbance factor representing the impact of statistical reassessment, and is normally zero.

Assuming generalized excess supply, firms are not constrained by the supply of labour. Consequently they can always achieve their planned supply of output. Thus total output, and hence total household income, is

$$y_t = c_t^F + g_t^F + i_t^d \tag{11.9}$$

It is quite possible that firms' expectations of final demand will turn out to be incorrect. The accounting identity describing sources and uses of output is

$$y_t = c_t + i_t + g_t \tag{11.10}$$

where i_t is realized investment:

$$i_t = k_{t+1} - k_t \tag{11.11}$$

Comparing equation (11.11) with the equation of planned investment

$$i_t^d = k_{t+1}^d - k_t \tag{11.12}$$

and using (11.8) gives

$$i_t^d = i_{t-1}^d - i_{t-1} + \psi_t \tag{11.13}$$

This is the fundamental equation governing the dynamics of the firm's investment behaviour. It asserts, quite simply, that each period planned investment is designed both to make good the unplanned disinvestment of the previous period, and to respond to any change in the target capital stock arising from a reassessment of the long-run variability of demand. This investment policy, coupled with adaptive expectations of final demand, determines how the firm's output varies over time. Output represents a lagged response to both endogenous and exogenous changes; the endogenous change is in household final demand, while the exogenous changes are in government demand, the target capital stock, and the firm's own expectations of final demand.

Section 11.6 explains how the firm's investment and output behaviour interacts with household consumption behaviour to generate cycles in income. The theory is extended further in section 11.7 to allow for price changes administered by firms. It is shown that if firms integrate their policies for investment behaviour and price adjustment then the stability of the economy will be significantly increased. It is argued that the resulting theory offers a plausible account of the influence of pricing, output and inventory policies on the level of employment.

11.5 THE MULTIPLIER–ACCELERATOR MODEL

The multiplier–accelerator model synthesizes the theory of household behaviour developed in section 11.2 with the theory of output and investment behaviour developed in section 11.3.[2] It is assumed throughout that money wages and money prices are fixed, and that generalized excess supply prevails on the real side of the economy. The effects of changes in government expenditure and taxation on the real side of the economy are assumed to be transmitted only through the product market; no repercussions on the real side of the economy result from induced changes in the money rate of interest.

It is assumed that consumer demand is a linear function of expected income

$$c_t^D = a + cy_t^H \tag{11.14}$$

where $a \geq 0$, $0 \leq c < 1$ are fixed parameters. It is also assumed that expectations are stationary (that is $\lambda = 1$ in equation (11.2)):

$$y_t^H = y_{t-1} + \iota_t \tag{11.15}$$

where ι_t is an exogenous disturbance reflecting changes of opinion about employment and profits. Substituting (11.15) into (11.14) gives the consumption function

$$c_t^D = a + cy_{t-1} + \omega_t \tag{11.16}$$

where $\omega_t = c\iota_t$. Equation (11.16) expresses consumer demand as a lagged function of income. It has an autonomous component a and is subject to a disturbance ω_t which is normally zero.

Government expenditure is normally constant, though it may be subject to exogenous disturbance from time to time:

$$g_t^d = g + \sigma_t \tag{11.17}$$

where σ_t is a disturbance factor which is normally zero. Taxation is fixed on a lump sum basis at a level which normally ensures a balanced budget. The impact of taxation on consumer expenditure has already been allowed for in fixing the value of autonomous consumption in equation (11.14).

Firms always adjust supply to meet aggregate demand, so that realized income is

$$y_t = c_t^D + i_t^d + g_t^d \tag{11.18}$$

This implies, amongst other things, that since investment is not supply constrained, the target capital stock is always realized:

$$k_t = k_t^d \tag{11.19}$$

Combining equation (11.19) with equations (11.3) and (11.4) shows that when the capital-output ratio v is constant, investment demand is equal to the change in expected aggregate demand $y_{t+1}^F - y_t^F$, scaled up by v:

$$i_t^d = v\,(y_{t+1}^F - y_t^F) \tag{11.20}$$

Finally it is assumed that firms' expectations of aggregate demand are stationary (that is $\mu = 1$ in equation (11.5)):

$$y_{t+1}^F = y_{t-1} \tag{11.21}$$

Substituting equation (11.21) into (11.20) gives the accelerator theory of investment

$$i_t^d = v\,(y_{t-1} - y_{t-2}) \tag{11.22}$$

Equation (11.22) asserts that investment demand is proportional to the lagged change in output.

Substituting the consumption function (11.16) and the accelerator equation (11.22) into the product market equation (11.18), and setting

$$\omega_t = \sigma_t = 0 \tag{11.23}$$

gives

$$y_t - (c + v)\,y_{t-1} + v y_{t-2} - (a + g) = 0 \tag{11.24}$$

This is a second order linear difference equation whose solution is

$$y_t = A_0 + A_1\,\theta_1^t + A_2\,\theta_2^t \tag{11.25}$$

where

$$\theta_1 = \tfrac{1}{2}\,(c + v + \tau), \qquad \theta_2 = \tfrac{1}{2}\,(c + v - \tau) \tag{11.26}$$

with

$$\tau = \sqrt{((c + v)^2 - 4v)} \tag{11.27}$$

In the special case where $\tau = 0$ we have $\theta_1 = \theta_2$ and the solution becomes instead

$$y_t = A_0 + A_1 \, \theta_1^t + A_2 t \theta_1^t \tag{11.28}$$

In each case the constants A_0, A_1, A_2 are determined by the initial conditions y_0, y_1, y_2.

If $\tau > 0$ then income either grows or decays geometrically, while if $\tau < 0$ it oscillates at a constant frequency. The economy is stable only if $\nu < 1$. The equilibrium to which it converges may be found by substituting $y_t = y_{t-1} = y_{t-2}$ into equation (11.24). The equilibrium income is

$$y^E = (a + g)/(1 - c) \tag{11.29}$$

This is the familiar multiplier formula expressing equilibrium income as the product of exogenous demand and the reciprocal of the marginal propensity to save.

In this model the fluctuation of income is governed principally by the efforts of entrepreneurs to maintain their capital stock in fixed proportion to the expected level of output. The dynamics of income are usually analysed by assuming an exogenous increase in government expenditure, but it is more in line with the theme of this book to consider instead an exogenous reduction in household income expectations, due for example to greater pessimism about profits. Suppose therefore that there is a temporary reduction in household profits expectations: $\omega_0 < 0$. Consumer demand is reduced, and so is firms' output. Expectations of future output are revised downward, the target capital stock is reduced and firms plan to disinvest. At the same time the lower level of output has reduced household income, though by not so much as was anticipated. Household income expectations are adjusted to the realized level, generating a consumer demand which is slightly greater than before, but still lower than its original level. As a result aggregate demand is likely to fall still further, generating a lower level of output, and consequently a lower target capital stock and lower household income. This secondary reduction in the target capital stock may not be so great as the first, however, and so planned disinvestment may be less than before. The reduction in disinvestment may be sufficient to offset any further fall in consumption, and so next period aggregate demand may actually increase. In this case income will move over time along a cyclical path, with an amplitude which either increases or diminishes, depending on the relation between the marginal propensity to consume and the capital-output ratio.

Most estimates of the capital-output ratio suggest a figure of at least three or four, which implies that the economy should be highly unstable.[3] But the evidence suggests the contrary: most exogenous changes generate cycles which are damped, and sooner or later the economy converges to equilibrium. The theory can be modified to take account of this by postulating that investment is planned to only partially adjust the capital stock toward its target figure.

Although modifications such as these enhance the predictive power of the theory, they do so only at considerable cost in terms of complexity. In particular restrictions on disinvestment in producer goods, discussed in section 11.3, are incompatible with a simple analytic solution of the model, such as that exhibited in equation (11.25). Thus although the multiplier–accelerator theory affords valuable insights into economic dynamics, it is difficult to make further progress by extending and modifying the theory. What is needed instead is another equally simple theory which complements the multipler–accelerator theory on those points where it is weakest.

11.6 A THEORY OF INVENTORY FLUCTUATION

Suppose now that the capital stock consists of a homogeneous inventory of finished product, held for the motives described in section 11.4. The main change is that firms' expectations of final demand are now assumed to be stationary. Substituting $\xi = 1$ into equation (11.7) and combining with (11.9) gives the output equation

$$y_t = c_{t-1} + g_{t-1} + i_t^d + \phi_t \tag{11.30}$$

Household behaviour is assumed to be the same as in the multiplier–accelerator model.

Substituting equations (11.6), (11.10), (11.16), and (11.17) into the fundamental equation (11.13) and setting

$$\phi_j = \psi_j = \omega_j = \sigma_j = 0 \qquad (j = t-3, \dots, t) \tag{11.31}$$

gives a third-order linear difference equation

$$y_t - 2cy_{t-2} + cy_{t-3} - (a + g) = 0 \tag{11.32}$$

The solution of equation (11.32) determines the time path of output:

$$y_t = A_0 + A_1 \, \epsilon_1^t + A_2 \, \epsilon_2^t + A_3 \, \epsilon_3^t \qquad (11.33)$$

The A_i ($i = 0, 1, 2, 3$) are constants determined by the initial conditions y_i ($i = 0, 1, 2, 3$) and the ϵ_m ($m = 1, 2, 3$) are the roots of the cubic equation

$$\epsilon^3 - 2c\epsilon + c = 0 \qquad (11.34)$$

In the case where the roots of (11.34) are not distinct, some modification of (11.33) is required, along the lines of equation (11.28).

Assuming $c > 0$ there is one and only one negative real root, say ϵ_1, so that the second component on the right hand side of (11.33) continually oscillates in sign. The other roots are either real and positive, or complex, depending upon whether $c \lessgtr 27/32$. If the roots are real and positive the third and fourth terms in (11.33) will exhibit steady geometric growth or decay, while if they are complex then the sum of these two terms will oscillate with a frequency greater than two periods.

The system tends to be unstable; the necessary and sufficient condition for stability[4] is $c < \frac{1}{3}$. If this condition is satisfied then all the oscillations are damped, with the lower frequency oscillations being damped more heavily than the two-period oscillations. Thus the system converges to equilibrium, alternating from above to below the equilibrium level for large values of t. Substituting $y_t = y_{t-2} = y_{t-3}$ into equation (11.32) shows that the equilibrium income is

$$y^E = (a + g)/(1 - c) \qquad (11.35)$$

just as in the multiplier–accelerator model.

To illustrate the fluctuation of income, consider the effect of an exogenous fall in households' expectation of profit. Consumer demand is lower than anticipated by firms and unplanned inventory investment occurs. Since output is unchanged, however, household income is unchanged (though the distribution of profit will be reduced to finance the inventory investment). Because household income expectations are stationary, next period consumer demand returns to its previous level, but since the capital stock exceeds its target, firms plan to disinvest. Since firms' expectations of final demand are stationary, output is lower than before, and since they underestimate final demand unplanned inventory disinvestment occurs. Next period firms seek to correct this by increasing investment. Because household incomes have fallen, firms overestimate final demand, and so realized investment is actually greater than planned. As noted above, if the marginal propensity to consume is very small then the process converges eventually to an equilibrium, with the alternation between unplanned investment and unplanned disinvestment dominating the asymptotic behaviour. In other cases the amplitude of the fluctuations will increase geometrically over time.

The instability of the model is a serious drawback to its application, just as it was with the multiplier—accelerator model. The instability problem can be solved, however, by allowing firms to adjust price as well as output when responding to changes in demand.

11.7 DYNAMICS OF ADMINISTERED PRICES

Suppose now that whilst money wages are fixed, money prices are flexible. The representative firm administers the product price P_t which it revises every period. The price for each period is set at the end of the preceding period, and once it has been set it cannot be revised in the light of subsequent information.[5] To simplify the analysis it is now assumed that government expenditure and taxation are fixed exogenously in real and not money terms.

Competitive forces oblige the firm to set a price which it believes will be in line with the prices administered by other firms next period. It believes that its competitors will set a price which will equate supply to expected demand next period. It also believes that other firms have the same perception of the market situation as itself.

The firm's supply curve is specified conditional on the money wage, and is assumed to be linear:

$$P_t = \alpha + \beta y_t^s \tag{11.36}$$

where y_t^s is product supply and $\alpha, \beta \geqslant 0$ are fixed parameters.

The firm recognizes that final demand will be influenced by prices. Apart from price changes, it expects that final demand will normally be the same as before. Thus expectations of final demand are given by

$$c_t^F + g_t^F = c_{t-1} + g_{t-1} - \delta (P_t - P_{t-1}) + \phi_t \tag{11.37}$$

where $\delta > 0$ is the estimated price-sensitivity of final demand.

The firm plans to produce on its supply curve, any imbalance between supply and demand being accommodated by unplanned inventory investment; thus

$$y_t^s = y_t \tag{11.38}$$

It is assumed that the firm's capital stock is adjusted only in the light of long-run changes in the price level; it does not respond to period-to-period changes in administered prices. Long-run price expectations are stationary, and so the target capital stock is fixed in the manner described by equation (11.8) above.

Equating the aggregate demand anticipated by the firm to its aggregate supply determines the administered price P_t as a function of the previous period's final demand $c_{t-1} + g_{t-1}$, the anticipated exogenous change in final demand, ϕ_t, planned investment, i_t^d, and the previous period's price level, P_{t-1}.

Assuming the true price-sensitivity of final demand is given by the parameter d in the consumption function

$$c_t = a + cy_{t-1} - dP_t + \omega_t \tag{11.39}$$

the dynamics of the system may once again be derived from equation (11.13). As before, income satisfies a third order linear difference equation, namely

$$(1 + \beta\delta)y_t + 2\beta(d - \delta)y_{t-1} - (2c + \beta(d - \delta))y_{t-2} + cy_{t-3} - (a - d\alpha + g) = 0 \tag{11.40}$$

In the special case where firms' perceptions of price elasticity are correct, $\delta = d$, this simplifies to

$$(1 + \beta d)y_t - 2cy_{t-1} + cy_{t-3} - (a - d\alpha + g) = 0 \tag{11.41}$$

It can be seen that apart from the factor βd in the first bracket and the term $d\alpha$ in the final bracket this equation is identical with (11.32). The additional factor βd is the product of the price-sensitivity of final demand, d, and the reciprocal of the price-sensitivity of aggregate supply, $1/\beta$. This factor is greater the greater is the price-sensitivity of final demand and the smaller is the price-sensitivity of supply (that is the steeper the product supply curve). Conversely, the factor βd approaches zero as either final demand becomes insensitive to price (d tends to zero) or supply becomes infinitely price-elastic (β tends to zero).

The solution of equation (11.41) has the same form as equation (11.32), although the values of the roots ϵ_1, ϵ_2, ϵ_3 will normally differ. The properties of these roots may be established simply by substituting $c/(1 + \beta d)$ for c in all the propositions advanced in section 11.6. The most important feature is that the stability of the system is markedly increased. For example if $\beta d \geq 2$ then the system is stable for all positive values of c less than unity. When the system is stable it converges over time to the equilibrium income

$$y^E = (a - d\alpha + g)/(1 - c/(1 + \beta d)) \tag{11.42}$$

This is the multiplier formula (11.35), adjusted to take account of the price sensitivity of aggregate demand and supply.

The time-variation of price, as well as its equilibrium value can be obtained simply by substituting the income equations into the equation of the supply curve (11.36).

The dynamics of income are basically the same as before, though with price fluctuations enhancing the degree of stability. Because of its upward-sloping supply curve the firm tends to substitute price- for quantity-adjustment. When demand is expected to increase it raises its price, and thereby deters demand. The increase in demand is not so great as it would otherwise be, and so the increase in output is smaller. Though the firm's expectations may be wrong, they will be wrong by a smaller margin, and so the amount of unplanned investment (or disinvestment) will be less. The repercussions of an expected change in demand will be damped down over time, and eventually the system will return to equilibrium.

11.8 EXPECTATIONS AND INFORMATION NETWORKS

The preceding analysis has emphasized four main types of exogenous disturbance:

1. a change in household expectations of income, due either to a change in profit expectations, or to a change in expectations regarding the severity of the employment constraint;
2. a change in firms' target capital stock due for example to a reassessment of the variability of demand;
3. a change in firms' expectations of final demand, due for example to a change of opinion about household savings behaviour;
4. a change in government expenditure, due for example to a change of government, or to the efforts of government to maintain or enhance its popularity.

In all cases except the last the disturbances consist of changes in the state of expectation of firms or individuals. The exogenous disturbance represents a discretionary element in the revision of expectations which is superimposed on a routine process, such as the adaptive mechanism described above. The element of discretion is necessary because no rule of expectation formation could take account of all relevant contingencies that might arise.

It may, however, be questioned whether these discretionary revisions are truly exogenous. For ultimately any revision of expectations must be based on upon the interpretation of information about current or past events. The only exception is where individuals rely on prophecy or mysticism.

There are two main reasons for regarding an economic variable as exogenous. The first is that the determinants of the variable are entirely non-economic, in the sense that there is no feedback at all from the economy to the variable concerned. This is unlikely to apply to the expectations referred to above, which are often strongly influenced by news of current economic events. The second is that the feedback mechanism is so complex that it is impossible for the modeller, or any other economic agent, to comprehend it fully. In this case exogeneity must be assumed because the modeller has reached the limits of his theoretical competence.

The second case almost certainly applies to expectations, because of the enormous amount of information that is of potential relevance to expectations, and the difficulty of predicting what kind of information will be of greatest relevance at any particular time. Individuals cannot actively monitor all potentially useful sources of information, but neither can they afford to ignore altogether any source that might prove important. They may therefore choose to operate with a threshold of awareness that information must surmount in order to be noticed and acted upon. Their field of observation is large, but only significant changes catch their attention. One day it may be a large increase in the price of oil, the next an unexpected fall in bank reserves, and so on.

The threshold of awareness may be partly psychological, but mainly it is effected by intermediating institutions which filter information before it is passed on to individuals. Most individuals do not collect primary data, but rely on secondary and tertiary sources. Secondary sources collect, summarize and interpret primary data, and publish their conclusions for a selective audience. Tertiary sources scan the output of secondary sources, select the most remarkable items and publish these in a form suitable for a mass audience. By subscribing to just one tertiary source the individual may be able to obtain a digest of information on major economic changes covering an extremely wide field.

It is almost impossible for a theorist to predict the news of economic relevance disseminated by a tertiary source. Even if the criteria used in the selection of information were known, it would still be necessary to generate detailed predictions of primary news to which these criteria could be applied. It is simply not economic to model the economy to the degree of accuracy that would be required. Indeed if it *were* possible, the theorist would have a strong incentive to 'endogenize' his activity in pursuit of private profit. By doing so he would alter the dynamics of the economy, and so invalidate the use of his model by any other theorist.

Tertiary sources tend to reduce economic stability by creating uniformity in the state of expectation. If individuals had to rely on primary data alone, different individuals would normally take different samples of data, each of them fairly small. Sample variation would create a divergence of opinion, and also reduce each individual's confidence in his own views. Consequently the magnitude of exogenous changes induced by the revision of expectations would be considerably reduced.

It should not be inferred from this that the existence of tertiary sources is undesirable, however, for may well help to improve the functioning of markets at the microeconomic level, and hence reduce some of the other sources of economic instability.

CHAPTER 12

SUMMARY AND
POLICY IMPLICATIONS

12.1 SUMMARY

In Chapter 1 a number of issues were raised concerning the nature of
unemployment and the appropriate policies to deal with it. It is the
object of this chapter to apply the analysis of Chapters 2–11 in order
to answer these questions. We begin by summarizing the main results of
the analysis.

1. Unemployment may be defined as a realized excess
   supply of labour, that is an excess of notional labour
   supply over actual employment. Households are off their
   supply curve because they are subject to a quantity
   constraint in the labour market. An unemployment
   equilibrium is a constrained equilibrium in which effective
   labour demand is equal to effective labour supply, but
   effective supply is less than notional labour supply.[1]

2. In a non-monetary economy two main kinds of unemployment are possible: classical unemployment due to a too-high
   real wage, and unemployment due to pessimistic profit
   expectations. With classical unemployment, only households experience quantity constraints: firms can hire as
   much labour as they require and sell as much output as
   they like. A necessary and sufficient condition for curing
   classical unemployment is a reduction in the real wage. On
   the other hand, with unemployment due to profit-
   pessimism both households and firms experience quantity
   constraints. Households cannot supply as much labour as
   they would like in order to make good their anticipated
   loss of profit income, and firms cannot supply as much

205

output as they would like because households reduce consumption in anticipation of lower income. Unemployment cannot be cured by adjustment of the real wage: it is necessary that profit expectations be revised upward to their full employment level.

3. Classical unemployment applies also to a monetary economy, but the results for profit-pessimism differ according to whether money wages and money prices are flexible are not. If they are flexible then demand deficiency can often be cured by money wage and money price adjustments. A fall in money prices causes households to dis-save, and this offsets the deflationary effect of profit pessimism; a corresponding fall in money wages ensures that the real wage remains unchanged, so that the demand for labour does not contract as a result of lower money prices. Thus when wages and prices are flexible profit pessimism induces a fall in prices which may well be sufficient to restore full employment.

4. In a monetary economy price adjustments stabilize the economy through both the money market and the bond market. A fall in money prices reduces the transactions demand for money and so encourages households to run down nominal money balances. The effect on the bond market depends on the way that product price expectations are formed. If price expectations are stationary then a fall in price increases household real wealth and so stimulates current consumption through an 'income' effect. If price expectations are inelastic then a fall in prices reduces the implicit real rate of interest and so stimulates current consumption through an intertemporal substitution effect. Thus repercussions in both the money market and the bond market serve to stimulate current consumption, though the mechanism involved depends on the nature of price expectations.

5. Rigidity of money wages and money prices introduces a new kind of unemployment associated with a too high money wage and money price level. It arises from a generalized notional excess supply on the real side of the economy coupled with notional excess demand in the money market. Like the case of profit-pessimism, in

equilibrium households are employment constrained and firms are sales constrained.

6. The case above is sometimes referred to as Keynesian unemployment, but this is not strictly correct. Keynes assumed that money prices were flexible; only the money wage is rigid and then only in a downward direction. Keynesian equilibrium is the consequence of a notional excess demand for money and a notional excess supply of labour, both generated by a too-high money wage. In Keynesian equilibrium households are quantity-constrained but firms are not. The two types of equilibrium do not necessarily conflict with each other. If money wages are stickier than money prices then in the short run both money wages and money prices may be fixed, while in the long run money prices may be flexible and only money wages fixed. This would be the case if money wage rigidity was due to different factors than was money price rigidity. This is quite probably correct, as explained under (10) below. Thus unemployment associated with money price rigidity may be regarded as a short-run phenomenon, and Keynesian unemployment as a longer-run phenomenon.

7. Transactors experience quantity constraints when trading takes place at disequilibrium prices. This phenomenon has been attributed to the absence of a Walrasian auctioneer or equivalently, to a lack of recontracting. The absence of a Walrasian auctioneer is certainly a necessary condition for disequilibrium. Macroeconomic models customarily assume, however, that the bond market is maintained in equilibrium, even without an auctioneer. This is because the bond price adjusts almost instantaneously to any realized excess demand. In practice therefore disequilibrium is more a problem of the lack of price adjustment than the absence of an auctioneer. Failure to adjust price may be a consequence of external constraints on transactors — such as government regulation — or self-imposed constraints. It can be argued that self-imposed constraints are most important, and that the most important motive for them is the desire to maintain goodwill. The goodwill motive applies to firms rather than to households, because it is firms that specialize in quoting prices, and in bearing

the risks that go with a commitment to trade at these prices. If firms are committed to supplying as much product as households demand at the quoted price then firms will always be demand-constrained except at the equilibrium price. Output will be set, not at the short end of the market, as is often suggested, but on the household demand curve. The only exception is where firms experience a supply constraint in the labour market, and carry no inventory of finished product.

8. When there is excess supply in the product market the goodwill motive will not affect the supply of output to consumers or governments. Its main effect on output will be channelled through investment demand. Investment demand is determined by stock adjustment. Firms' target inventory will be determined by their desire to accommodate unexpected changes in demand without losing goodwill. Firms' target fixed capital stock will be determined by a desire to meet all available demand next period without having to drawn on inventory.

9. The goodwill motive also applies to the labour market, but more selectively. It is easier for firms to discriminate between employees than it is between customers. Thus firms build up goodwill principally among skilled employees, for whom turnover costs are greatest. By offering wage stability and employment guarantees they effectively turn skilled labour into a fixed factor.

10. The goodwill motive cannot explain why unskilled workers stipulate for a basic money wage without employment guarantees. The most likely explanation is that differentials in basic money wages have a cultural rather than an economic origin; they are supposed to reflect the relative importance that society attaches to different occupations. The basic wage is normally set at the national level, and is a lower bound on the actual wage paid at the plant level. Trade unions will not accept a reduction in the basic wage, as this would be an admission that the status of the occupation concerned has been reduced.

11. Unemployment occurs when the equilibrium money wage is below the basic money wage. Unskilled workers are made redundant, and cannot find new work because employers will not hire them at below the basic wage.

Skilled workers not covered by employment guarantees may also be made redundant, but they can find reemployment by trading down to unskilled work. It is the unskilled workers they displace that become unemployed.

12. The dynamics of unemployment are governed by two main factors: the technical characteristics of production and investment, and the way in which expectations are revised. The most important technical characteristics are the decision lag for output adjustment, the gestation lag for the installation of new producer durables, and the rate of depreciation. These factors determine the lag structure of the productive sector of the economy, and also determine the extent to which fluctuations in aggregate demand are amplified within the productive sector through the feedback from output to investment.

13. Expectations are a major source of exogenous disturbance in the macroeconomy. Changes in expectation arise from changes in the climate of opinion, which is influenced by the news items selected by the media. Changes in expectations occur so frequently that it is unrealistic to expect wages and prices always to adjust in order to maintain full employment equilibrium.

12.2 ALTERNATIVE EXPLANATIONS OF REGISTERED UNEMPLOYMENT

In Chapter 1 a distinction was drawn between the neoclassical and disequilibrium approaches to unemployment. The disequilibrium approach, summarized above, regards unemployment as a consequence of market failures whose repercussions spread throughout the economy. The neoclassical approach on the other hand regards the determinants of unemployment as being specific to the labour market. Particular emphasis is placed on the role of unemployment benefit, and on the tendency for mistaken expectations to prolong job search.[2]

It is argued by neoclassical economists that unemployment benefit creates a direct incentive to register as unemployed because:

1. it encourages registration by those who would not normally participate in work, and also by people in the 'black economy' — that is uninsured workers who do not report their earnings, such as many of the part-time self-employed;

    2. it encourages those who previously worked to give up, or to work only intermittently. This effect is reinforced if the unemployment benefit is financed by an increase in the marginal rate of tax on wage income;

    3. it encourages the unemployed who are seeking jobs to prolong their search, and to be more choosy about the kind of work they accept.

Neoclassical job search theory is based on the fact that labour services are heterogeneous, and that information about the characteristics of workers and jobs is costly to acquire. Information costs tend to segment the labour market. Two firms may have identical jobs on offer, but because no-one recognizes that they are identical, the vacancies may be offered and filled at very different wages. Thus there is a dispersion of wages for similar types of work. Workers who recognize this may attempt to switch jobs in order to increase their wages.

A worker contemplating a move has two decisions to make: whether to initiate search, and how to carry out the search. The second decision is logically prior to the first. Job search may be carried on either as a full-time activity or as a spare-time activity. It has been argued that many workers will prefer full-time search because the loss of earnings involved is more than compensated for by the increased probability of finding a job. Search is initiated if the expectation of the increase in the present value of earnings exceeds the cost associated with the best search strategy.

If expectations of wages in other segments of the market are mistakenly high then workers will initiate search but be unable to find jobs. If they are pursuing full-time search then they will remain unemployed until their expectations become more realistic. The duration of unemployment will depend upon how quickly they revise their expectations in the light of the job offers that they have sampled. If wage expectations are inelastic then unemployment may persist for some time.

The combined effect of unemployment benefit and job search is illustrated in Figure 12.1. Money wage is measured vertically, employment horizontally, and the schedules are drawn conditional upon the money price level. The demand for labour is represented by DD' and the supply curve, in the absence of unemployment benefit, and with perfect information, is represented by $S_0 S_0'$. Full employment equilibrium is at E, where the money wage is W^e and employment is n^e.

The introduction of unemployment benefit shifts the supply curve

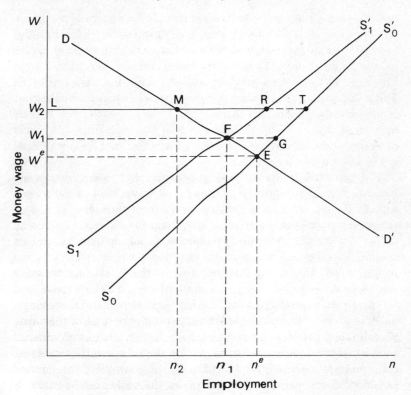

Figure 12.1. The neoclassical approach to unemployment

to the left, to $S_1 S_1'$. The reduction in labour supply shifts up the money wage to $W_1 > W^e$ and employment falls to $n_1 < n^e$. At the money wage W_1 there are FG workers who would previously have offered employment but who now prefer to register as unemployed.

Suppose that in addition each worker has a mistaken expectation of the money wage other workers are receiving. As a result he decides to quit in order to undertake full-time search unless his own wage is raised to $W_2 > W_1$. This means that labour supply becomes infinitely elastic at the money wage W_2. The supply curve is now LRS$_1'$, which intersects the demand curve DD$'$ at M. The withdrawal of workers from employment into search bids up the money wage to W_2, and employment falls to n_2. MR workers are involved in fruitless job search, the RT workers continue to register for benefit in preference to seeking work. The higher money wage will encourage some of those who previously withdrew from work to actively seek work again, so that RT < FG.

It is apparent that in the neoclassical approach workers are always on their supply curve. Changes in unemployment benefit and wage expectations change the supply curve, but do not force workers off it. This is in contrast to the disequilibrium approach, where unemployment is due to demand-constraints in the labour market which force workers off their supply curve. This difference is chiefly a reflection of differences in methodology, however; it cannot be made the basis for an empirical test of the two theories.

The predictive power of the neoclassical and disequilibrium approaches may be compared in a number of ways. Most of the alleged support for the neoclassical theory comes from time-series studies of aggregate unemployment. It has been claimed that the neoclassical theory can explain the time-dependence of unemployment, and its relation to other macroeconomic variables such as changes in the money supply. One of the original aims of the neoclassical approach was to provide microeconomic foundations for the Phillips curve, and for other postulates relating to it.[3] It has even been claimed that changes in levels of unemployment benefit can explain almost all of the unemployment in the Great Depression of the 1930s.[4] It is extremely difficult to discriminate between theories by the use of aggregate time-series data, however, because of the difficulty of controlling for omitted variables.[5] Quite apart from this, many of the studies can be criticized for not using the best available econometric techniques. On the other hand, the disequilibrium approach, as exemplified by Keynesian theory, has not performed very well in this respect either. The estimation problems encountered in the time series analysis, and the deficiencies of aggregate data, suggest that it may be easier and more reliable to test the theories using other kinds of evidence.

The dynamics of unemployment are best understood by concentrating on flows of people through the labour market, rather than on changes in the stocks of unemployed over time. The neoclassical theory suggests that most workers become unemployed as a result of quits: an increase in unemployment benefit causes workers to quit because the opportunity cost of leisure is reduced, while an increase in wage expectations encourages workers to search full-time for better-paid jobs. The disequilibrium approach on the other hand suggests that workers become unemployed through redundancy, as a result of the downward rigidity of the basic money wage. The evidence suggests that quits are important when the demand for labour is buoyant, but that as the economy enters recession the quit rate falls sharply.[6] At the onset of a recession the burden of unemployment is borne chiefly by redundant workers and by new entrants to the labour force. The evidence confirms the intuition that as a recession gathers momentum those who have jobs do their best to retain them; the idea that the recession is brought on by workers quitting receives no support from the evidence.

Job search theory suggests that workers perceive significant gains from full-time search, and that as a result many job changes are accompanied by spells of unemployment. The advantages of full-time search appear to be very small, however, while the disadvantages are potentially great.[7] For example many job vacancies are advertised in the press or handled by employment agencies (both public and private) and all of these can be monitored easily by people in work. Also employers may discriminate against quitters when hiring simply because, in the absence of better information, the employee's past record is the best guide to his future behaviour, and no-one wants to hire a worker who is liable to quit. The empirical evidence confirms that relatively few people find it necessary to become unemployed in order to find a job: a high proportion of all job changes are made without any intervening spell of unemployment.[8]

The neoclassical approach also suggests that the unemployed remain unemployed because they refuse the job offers made to them. They prefer a combination of benefit income and leisure to wage income combined with work. Alternatively they remain unemployed because they expect that the next wage offer will be much better than the present one.

The first argument ignores the fact that in most countries unemployment benefit is withdrawn if job offers are persistently refused. It is true that the unemployed may be eligible for other benefits, but these are usually not so great, particularly if the claimant has few dependants.

If the argument is reformulated in terms of social security benefit then it implies that workers with large numbers of dependants will be most resistant to re-employment. Because the money wage is independent of the worker's family commitments, while the social security benefit is not, workers with large families will be most likely to reject employment, and so they will come to predominate among the long-term unemployed. No empirical support has yet been forthcoming for this prediction.

The argument about unrealistic expectations is difficult to test empirically, though the evidence is that if expectations are unrealistic then they adjust fairly quickly in the light of experience gained in job search. The evidence supports the view that in a recession many redundant workers move down the occupational ladder, by trading down to lower-paid jobs. The concentration of unemployment is at the bottom of the occupational ladder, among the uneducated and the unskilled, who have no lower-paid jobs to go to.[9]

The neoclassical approach does not offer much help in explaining the composition of the unemployed. Because money wages are assumed to be flexible, the different characteristics of workers will be reflected in the relative wages they command, rather than in the relative incidence of unemployment among them.

The disequilibrium approach on the other hand assumes that relativities between basic wages are fixed, so that when market wages are forced down to basic wages, those groups of workers least in demand will become redundant. It follows that unemployment will tend to be highest in industries where the fall in demand is greatest. For reasons explained in Chapter 11, capital goods industries are prone to cycles in demand, and so it is here that cyclical unemployment is most likely to occur.

Because basic money wages are negotiated nationally, the wages prevailing in each location will not reflect the geographical variation in the cost of other inputs, such as raw materials, or in the amount of these inputs required (for example transport services for delivery of the finished product). Because of the downward rigidity of the basic money wage, labour in high-cost plants is particularly vulnerable to unemployment when demand contracts. If high-cost plants tend to be concentrated in particular regions then these regions will be especially vulnerable to unemployment in a recession. Taken together with the previous argument, this suggests that the cyclical sensitivity of unemployment will be greatest in regions where there is a preponderance of high-cost plants producing capital goods.

The labour force contains many people who are disadvantaged by age, sex, race, lack of qualifications, a criminal record, physical handicap, and so on. Given a choice of job applicants, employers will discriminate in favour of others. Basic wage differentials take account of these characteristics only to a limited extent. This means that the disadvantaged cannot obtain jobs through wage competition. When there is a shortage of vacancies, they are forced into unemployment because recruitment is based on non-wage criteria, and others are given priority.

This line of reasoning can be extended to many other characteristics of unemployment. The principle is simply that when money wages are low, relativities are fixed by basic wages. The allocation of labour is then governed not by wage competition but by quantity adjustment, using where appropriate some simple system of priorities in rationing employment.

On the whole the predictions of the theory seem to be borne out well in practice. The cyclical sensitivity of employment appears to be greatest in capital goods industries, in high-cost regions – particularly those remote from the main concentrations of demand – and for the very young, the very old, the unqualified, and so on. It may be possible to derive similar predictions from the neoclassical theory, but only indirectly, by relatively complex arguments. As most advocates of the neoclassical approach would be the first to agree, a simple explanation of the phenomena is preferable to a complicated one. On these grounds, the evidence on the incidence of unemployment supports the disequilibrium approach, and not the neoclassical one.

12.3 CURING UNEMPLOYMENT

Consider an employment equilibrium of the kind described by Keynes. The money wage is equal to the basic wage and unions are unwilling to negotiate a cut in this wage. Each group of workers fears a deterioration in its differentials if this occurred. Even if the unemployed are willing to bid down money wages, employers may fear sanctions if they take on labour at below the negotiated wage. There is no way in which the economy can adjust itself to full employment. To achieve full employment some kind of intervention is required.

An increase in government expenditure can stimulate employment through its effect on aggregate demand. The increase in demand results in the product price being bid up, the real wage falls, and firms' demand for labour increases. The higher level of employment generates both higher wage income and higher profit, and this feeds back onto aggregate demand through increased household consumption.

It is not necessary for the government to run a budget deficit. If taxes are increased by the same amount as government expenditure then, so long as the marginal propensity to consume is less than unity, the reduction in current consumption on account of higher taxes will be less than the increase in government expenditure, so on balance aggregate demand will increase, and employment will increase too.

It should be noted that the increase in government expenditure only works by increasing the product price and so inducing a mild inflation. The inflationary consequences are independent of how the government expenditure is financed; this follows immediately from the uniqueness of the full employment real wage. The financing of the expenditure affects only the money rate of interest. If the expenditure is financed by an increase in taxation, or by the issue of bonds, then the money supply will remain fixed, and the money interest rate will rise on account of the increase in the transactions demand induced by the higher money price level. If on the other hand the expenditure is financed by an increase in the money supply then the rise in the interest rate will be much smaller.

An increase in the money rate of interest will tend to reduce the reflationary impact of government expenditure. In particular it will reduce both consumer demand and investment demand. In this sense the additional government expenditure may at least partially 'crowd out' private expenditure. On these grounds it is preferable to finance additional government expenditure by increasing the money supply rather than by increasing taxation or issuing new bonds.

Recommendations of this kind — higher government expenditure backed by increases in the money supply — have received a very bad press in recent years. Since the analysis itself is quite sound, it must be the assumptions that are debateable. There is one particular assumption that is crucial: that wage bargaining is concerned with setting a money wage and not a real wage.

This assumption was made explicit by Keynes, and was certainly quite reasonable at the time that he wrote. In Britain in the 1930s the real wage was relatively high because trade unions had refused cuts in basic money wages, even though money prices had fallen quite sharply. Such behaviour can be rationalized on the grounds that it maintains a stable structure of money wage differentials. Keynes argued that if the money price level increased then trade unions would not stipulate for higher money wages until full employment had been obtained, and the experience of the late thirties appears to have borne this out.

In the postwar period, however, there seems to have been a move away from money wage bargaining to real wage bargaining. Consequently any attempt to reflate the economy by increasing money prices has elicited matching money wage demands from trade unions.[10] Thus the initial expansionary effect of government expenditure has been vitiated by increased production costs due to higher money wages. To put it another way, the increase in aggregate money demand has been matched by an upward shift in the aggregate supply curve induced by higher money wages.

Under such conditions, the long-run effect of reflating the economy will be higher money wages and higher money prices with employment and output unchanged. Moneyinterest rates may rise too, depending on the extent to which the government runs budget deficits financed by increases in the money supply. If the money supply increases in line with the increase in prices then money interest rates will remain fairly stable, while if a restrictive monetary policy is followed then money interest rates may rise quite steeply.

The situation is essentially one of classical unemployment – that is unemployment due to a too-high real wage, as described in Chapter 3. With classical unemployment government expenditure is ineffective in restoring full employment. Its only effect is to displace private expenditure by raising money interest rates and/or reducing the real value of money and bonds through inflation. A combination of classical unemployment and Keynesian policies of fiscal expansion generates all the symptoms of stagflation: persistent unemployment, inflation, and high money rates of interest.

12.4 CURING STAGFLATION: PRICES AND INCOMES POLICIES

The basic idea underlying a prices and incomes policy is to permit aggregate demand to be increased and maintained at a high level without inflationary consequences.

Consider first a pure prices policy, which limits the rate at which producers can increase their administered prices. The simplest case is that of a 'price freeze'. Assume that initially firms are producing on their supply curve, with output set so that the marginal product of labour equals the real wage. As government expenditure is increased to reflate the economy producers are faced with a dilemma: whether to continue producing at the existing level, and to ration the output among customers, or to increase output in order to satisfy all the demands. The goodwill motive suggests that in the short run at least they may prefer to do the latter, foregoing short-run profits in order to retain their major customers. They therefore produce at a point where the marginal product of labour is less than the real wage. Output increases, but income is redistributed to wages from profit.

This situation cannot persist for long, however. If firms expect the policy to continue for some time then they will perceive the cost of maintaining goodwill not as a short-run loss of profit but as a long-run loss. Consequently they will sacrifice goodwill by reducing output, and both the private and public sector will experience rationing. Rationing of the public sector will make it difficult for the government to achieve its planned appropriations, and underspending will result. Rationing of consumer goods will encourage households to reduce labour supply, since the marginal utility of income is reduced if it cannot be consumed but has to be saved. This may indirectly reduce unemployment by reducing labour supply – though in a manner which reduces household welfare, rather than increases it. It is possible though that consumption rationing may actually increase unemployment. Rationing may be tighter for some goods than others, and this may lead to some consumers being affected more than others. If these consumers happen to be key workers who are in demand even in a recession, then a reduction in their labour supply may put the jobs of complementary ancillary workers at risk. The problem cannot be avoided by a selective increase in money wages because income alone cannot guarantee consumption – only priority in rationing can do so. On these grounds a price freeze is unsatisfactory as an adjunct to a reflationary fiscal policy.

An alternative to a prices policy is a pure incomes policy. There are many different forms of incomes policy. The simplest is a wages policy which keeps down money wages during reflation. This ensures that as firms respond to increased aggregate demand by increasing their output, the real wage diminishes in line with the marginal product of labour. The simplicity of the policy means, of course, that it encounters political opposition from those who perceive it, quite correctly, as an attack on the living standards of the employed. But on the other hand by increasing employment it increases the living standards of those who were previously unemployed; and in many cases total real wage income is increased too, so that the gains of the unemployed outweigh the losses of the employed.

Wages policies are also criticized for reducing incentives in the labour market. These incentives are of many different kinds. A wages policy may prevent workers who are in demand from being encouraged to work longer hours by being offered higher pay. Alternatively it may prevent workers being encouraged to switch to jobs in which their marginal value product is higher, because the employer with the vacancy cannot quote a high enough real wage.

The importance of such constraints depends upon whether the wages policy controls basic wage rates or the actual wages paid. Most national wage bargaining is concerned with the basic wage. It is this wage that is most relevant to unemployment: most workers are unemployed because employers cannot offer them employment at the basic wage, irrespective of whether they offer higher wages to other workers whose services are in greater demand. A wages policy which controlled only the basic wage would still allow government expenditure to increase employment because the real wage of the marginal worker would fall as employment increased. Workers who were in demand would remain free to accept offers of higher money wages from firms who could afford them; so long as the firms' perception of the situation was correct there would be no increase in unemployment as a result. Nor would there be any increase of prices, for the higher wages of the workers producing commodities in excess demand would be paid for by a higher real output. All that would happen is that more work would be offered to marginal workers at the basic wage.

In principle, workers who were already in employment at above the basic wage might be able to maintain their real wage, even though the basic real wage had fallen. The main condition is that they are immune to competition from the workers who have just entered employment. The ability of such a non-competing group to sustain its real wage has no effect on employment or output – all that is affected is the distribution between wages and profit of the quasi-rent earned by the firm employing them.

The main problem would arise with workers who bargained at the plant level, or individual level, for an unrealistic real wage. This refers to workers who are not immune to competition but who act as if they are. Such workers would become redundant, but because their stipulated wage was above the basic wage, they could be replaced by other workers at the basic wage. The replacement workers might work for the same firm, or for a competing firm which had superseded it. Thus aggregate employment would not be affected. The only difference would be in the composition of the unemployed, who would be newly redundant workers, instead of those who were previously unemployed.

Another criticism of wages policy is that it builds up pressures that it ultimately cannot contain. Some of these pressures are market pressures which, as we have seen, may largely be avoided by confining the policy to basic wage rates. But there are also social and political pressures, and it is usually these which are crucial in terminating wages policies fairly abruptly. Once the pent-up forces are unleashed, they rapidly undermine all the achievements of the policy. The economy adjusts to a situation very like that which would have been expected to prevail had the policy never been applied.[11]

It can be argued that this problem is largely a consequence of the arbitrary way in which wages policies are imposed in the first place. They are often a hurried measure introduced when the rate of inflation is believed to be getting out of hand. Typically they have a fairly limited objective: to freeze the situation while the government attempts to find a longer-term solution to the problem. The success of the policy in controlling inflation, however, and also in breaking inflationary expectations, encourages the government to continue the policy, and it is here that the difficulties arise.

Many of these difficulties could be avoided if the policy were designed at the outset as a long-term measure. It is obviously inequitable to freeze a situation in which some workers have settled wages for the forthcoming year while others have not. It is also likely that some workers will have reached informal understandings with employers about future wages which will be breached by the imposition of a wage freeze.

A wages policy which involved a long-term commitment to establish and maintain a socially acceptable set of wage differentials would largely avoid these difficulties. Wages would not be frozen: they would adjust over time to achieve an agreed set of differentials in basic rates of pay. The adjustment would be controlled so that the average level of money wages increased only very slowly. It must be recognized however that if the adjustment were organized so that no-one's money wages actually fell, the process would be mildly inflationary. To the extent that the adjustment was a once-for-all event, however, the inflation would not be too serious from a long-run perspective.

It would of course be impossible to achieve a complete consensus on what the differentials between basic rates should be. This situation is hardly unusual in the social and economic sphere: true consensus can almost never be achieved. In practice people have to consent to being overruled by others when they are in a minority. What is important is that the process by which differentials are determined should command the respect of individuals on the grounds of the efficiency and fairness of its principles and the impartiality of its administration. It was argued in Chapter 9 that the process of unfettered competition in the labour market does not command widespread allegiance. While it may be efficient under certain ideal conditions, it is widely regarded as unfair. Collective bargaining, in which workers and employers exploit their monopoly power and monopsony power, is less efficient, and certainly no fairer. Its performance is even worse when frequent recourse is had to strikes and lock-outs as part of the bargaining process.

Both pure competition and collective bargaining involve using the market, in one form or another, to determine relativities. But there are alternatives to the market, and the most attractive of these is the political system. The political system could be used to establish the criteria that should govern differentials between basic rates of pay. Wages policy is of course already at the centre of political debate, but the debate so far, in Britain at least, has largely been concerned with whether the government should adopt an interventionist policy, rather than the form that the intervention should take. If instead different political parties proposed different criteria for a wages policy, then the criteria to be used could be established by the voting mechanism. Once the criteria had been established a National Wages Board could be set up to implement them.

It should be emphasized that the Wages Board would be concerned only with differentials between basic rates of pay. The emphasis on differentials means that it would not be concerned with arguments for higher pay based on increases in the cost of living. The emphasis on basic rates means that workers would remain free to bargain at the plant level for higher rates. Thus workers in temporary demand would receive temporarily higher wages, but once the demand fell away their wages would be liable to fall. This contrasts favourably with the situation in which a temporary demand is exploited to gain an increase in basic rates, so that when the demand is reduced workers have to be made redundant. If there were attempts by individual groups of workers to improve substantially upon the basic rates then competitive constraints would soon come into force. Either the employer would recruit cheaper labour at the basic wage, or he would go out of business due to competition from other employers whose workers demanded less.

The restriction of the policy to basic rates of pay would also reduce the force of the argument that profits and dividends should be controlled as well. To begin with, profits and dividends have no basic rate — firms can make losses as well as profits, and dividends can fall as low as zero. The main reason for confining the policy to wages, however, is that profits and dividends vary considerably between firms, so that if workers wish to appropriate profits it is best for them to do so at the plant or firm level rather than at the national level.

It must be admitted that these proposals are unlikely to prove popular with trade union leaders, not least because it appears to make their job superfluous. The setting of basic wages by the Wages Board would supersede national collective bargaining. The union leader would no longer be in regular confrontation with the leaders of employers' associations. His role would be transformed into that of an advocate. His role would be partially political, persuading people to vote for criteria which would favour his own members, and partly that of a witness presenting relevant information to the Wages Board.

Trade union opposition might be taken to the extent of making strike threats designed to influence the decisions of the Wages Board. It would then have to be considered whether the legal immunities of the trade unions should extend to threats of this kind. Assuming that the Wages Board were constituted as a judicial body, so that its decisions had the force of law, it would be almost without precedent to allow threats designed to influence judicial decisions of this kind. Once the setting of basic wages is removed from the sphere of voluntary bargaining between private individuals or groups into the sphere of judicial decision-making, threats cease to be acceptable as a method of influencing the outcome. By establishing that basic wages are to be determined by social criteria rather than unconstrained competitive forces a major objective of the democratic trade-union movement would have been achieved. It would be necessary to insist that in return for this concession, unions forego the use of tactics which, though justifiable in the market place, are not justifiable outside it.

12.5 CURING STAGFLATION THROUGH HIGHER PRODUCTIVITY

Another way of curing stagflation is through higher productivity. Suppose that initially a Keynesian unemployment equilibrium prevails, and that new working practices are then introduced which increase productivity. Normally both average and marginal productivity will be increased, though it is marginal productivity which is crucial for employment. An increase in marginal productivity encourages firms to hire more labour at the prevailing real wage.

Superficially a productivity increase is far superior to any other method of curing stagflation. Compared with a combination of wages policy and reflationary government expenditure, it seems preferable on at least three grounds. First, it not only generates full employment, but it permits a higher level of output, and so a higher level of welfare, once full employment is achieved. Secondly it does not call for any increase in government expenditure; private expenditure increases, but government expenditure does not. This obviates the need to maintain government expenditure at an artificially high level merely as a counter-recessionary policy. Finally it does not constrain wage relativities in the way that a wages policy does, and it is therefore compatible with greater efficiency in the allocation of labour.

In practice matters may not be quite so straightforward as this. It was implicitly assumed above that higher productivity generates its own increase in aggregate demand. The increase in aggregate demand stems from an increase in wage income due to higher employment and an increase in profit income due to the higher output generated by the higher employment. But aggregate demand will not increase immediately unless households expect wage and profit incomes to rise. The increase in wage incomes depends upon firms taking on more labour, and since productivity is increasing, this implies that firms plan to produce more output. But firms will produce more output only if they think they can sell it, and they will generate higher profits only if they are right. They will only be right if households demand more, and they will do this only if each household thinks that the others are going to demand more, and the firms are going to supply more, so that it expects its own income to increase.

In an idealized economy plans would be harmonized through trading in futures markets. The absence of futures markets is a form of market failure which, in the present instance, can be resolved most easily by government intervention. If the government decides to 'underwrite' aggregate demand by committing itself to a full employment policy then firms can be confident of having higher incomes. In fact the expectation that the government will intervene if necessary should be sufficient to ensure that it does not need to intervene. The prospect of intervention is sufficient to give firms and households the confidence to raise their expectations as soon as productivity improvements are introduced. The government may need to intervene just once to demonstrate the reality of its commitment, and the effectiveness of the policy; thereafter intervention will become unnecessary.

Another difficulty stems from the fact that the scope for productivity increases differs considerably between industries. Differential rates of productivity growth exert pressure on wage relativities. Demand for certain types of labour increases while demand for other types falls. Demand pressures pull up money wages in some sectors, and this leads to money wage demands in other sectors, motivated by a desire to maintain relativities. Thus the general level of money wages rises.[12]

If on average the money wage increases are matched by the increases in productivity then prices will not rise. But if money wage aspirations are based on the highest money wage increase initially attained in the high-demand sectors then it is almost certain that the resulting money wage increases will be inflationary. In this case differential productivity increase creates the kind of problems with relativities that a prices and incomes policy is needed to cure.

12.6 LIMITATIONS OF DEMAND MANAGEMENT

Keynesian economists argue that it is both undesirable and impractical for money wages to adjust in order to maintain the labour market in equilibrium. This establishes a *prima facie* case for the government to intervene in order to maintain a stable full employment level of aggregate demand.

It needs to be established, however, that the government is capable of fulfilling this role. Government efforts at demand management have been criticized on a number of grounds.

Government may not have up-to-date information on the state of the economy, so that it only responds to each situation with a lag. A demand management policy, which would be successful if it were timely, may well be unsuccessful if it is untimely. In fact the lags in government response may mean that fiscal changes occur at inopportune moments in the trade cycle, and so exacerbate the problem they were designed to solve.

To avoid this problem the government needs to forecast the state of the economy by applying a predictive model to past data. Such predictions are bound to have some degree of error because of unforeseen shocks which occur during the prediction interval. Moreover predictive models usually assume that the behavioural parameters of the economy are stable. Such an assumption may not be justified, for reasons explained below. These qualifications could mean that the government's predictive ability is so small that it would be better not to intervene at all. Intervention will simply add further shocks to those already experienced, and tend, if anything, to destabilize the economy.

The government's difficulties are compounded because at the same time that it is trying to predict the behaviour of the private sector, the private sector is trying to predict government behaviour. The more government intervenes, the more the private sector will attempt to anticipate what the government will do. Successful anticipation allows the private sector to adjust more fully to government policies. In certain circumstances the private sector may compensate fully for changes in the public sector, and as a result of this the impact of demand management policies may be nullified.

On this view government intervention creates a game in which the government and the private sector attempt to 'outguess' each other. In the long-run the most successful party is likely to be the one which learns most quickly about the other's behaviour. When one party learns about the other he will adjust his own pattern of behaviour accordingly, so that if the other party predicts his behaviour on a no-change assumption the prediction will be seriously wrong. From the government's point of view this means that as the private sector learns about government policy the behavioural pattern of the private sector will change. This is the problem of non-stable parameters alluded to above.

For similar reasons the government will modify its policy as it learns about private-sector behaviour. Governments are not necessarily so alert as the private sector, however. The individual rewards to successful forecasting are so great in the private sector compared with the public sector that expert forecasters are most likely to operate privately. The profit motive provides a powerful incentive for them to continually revise their expectations of government behaviour in the light of recent evidence. If the private sector learns more about the government than the government does about the private sector then over time the ability of the government to intervene intelligently in the economy may be seriously impaired.

These objections to Keynesian-style demand management are primarily methodological. In practice the force with which they apply depends on the particular policies involved, and the circumstances in which it is sought to implement them. Most critics of Keynesian policies have elaborated their criticisms in the context of an economy at, or close to, full employment. A favourite theme is to examine the response of the private sector to policies designed to force unemployment below its 'natural' rate. In this context Keynesian policies are, almost by definition, inappropriate and it is not surprising that the more sophisticated is the private sector, the quicker unemployment returns to its natural rate.[13]

Once it is conceded that some unemployment at least is of a classical or Keynesian type — rather than a purely neoclassical type — it can be shown that the anticipation of government action by the private sector may increase rather than diminish the stability of the economy. The chief problem is to ensure that the timing of interventionist policy is correct, so that the private sector in turn believes that the timing will be correct, and reacts accordingly. The simplest way for the government to ensure that timing is correct is for it to rely on automatic stabilization policies. For example a policy which offered employment on public works to anyone who was unemployed would automatically stimulate public sector demand at a time when private sector demand was falling off.

In the past public works programmes have usually been of a discretionary nature, and have been implemented on a large scale only when unemployment has reached what is believed to be a critical level (in Britain the Job-Creation Programme is a recent example of this). The most important example of an automatic stabilizer has been unemployment benefit. Because the rate of benefit is fixed, and not the overall budget for benefit payments, expenditure on benefit varies directly with the level of unemployment. The payment of benefit tends to reflate consumer demand and so move the economy toward full employment.

Nowadays, however, the differential between the wages paid on public works programmes and the level of unemployment benefit has become very low — particularly the net differential to the worker once travel and the other incidental expenses of work are taken into account. If it is felt that, for both economic and social reasons, the 'work ethic' should be encouraged, then it might be more appropriate to use public works rather than unemployment benefit as the major automatic stabilizer. The unemployed would be offered employment on local public works as of right, and only those medically (or otherwise) unfit would be offered unemployment benefit instead.[14]

This would have the advantage of reducing the incentive to register as unemployed by those not seriously seeking work. It would ensure that those seriously seeking work would be able to continue in a working environment while seeking new employment. It would also mean that some useful product (whether marketed or not) would be generated by these workers in their spell between conventional jobs.

The main difficulty would be to ensure that workers were not attracted to remain on the public works programmes instead of seeking work in the private sector. If this occurred the supply of workers to the private sector would be reduced, and the cost of privately-produced goods would be increased. As a result there would be a misallocation of resources between sectors, with consumers forced to consume fewer privately-produced goods and more publicly-produced goods than they would wish.

To encourage workers to move into private employment as soon as possible it would be essential to fix the wage on public works below the basic wage for unskilled work in the private sector. It would also be important to allow workers to take time off for job search. For example one day a week could be allowed off with full pay, additional days being taken when required, but without pay.

The effect of such a policy would be to make the government 'the employer of last resort'. The administrative difficulties should not be underestimated. An important advantage of the policy, however, is that public awareness of its existence would itself contribute to the stability of the economy. The expectation that employment and output would remain close to their full employment levels would stabilize household expectations of wage and profit income, and the resulting stability of consumption would stabilize firms' expectations of demand. It might be necessary for the policy to be implemented once, to convince people that it would work, but thereafter the private sector's anticipation that the policy will become effective automatically should stabilize expectations at a level compatible with full employment.

A number of variants of this policy are possible. A detailed evaluation of them is outside the scope of this book. The important thing is that in each case the automatic nature of the policy means that its effectiveness does not depend on the government's forecasting skill, and that the anticipation of the policy by the private sector contributes to, rather than detracts from, its success.

12.7 IMPLICATIONS FOR FUTURE POLICY

The preceding discussion has established that a combination of wages policy and reflationary fiscal policy would be perfectly feasible as a short-run policy for curing the current stagflation. It has also established that the long-run success of such policies depends on them being organized very differently from before.

The first requirement is that wages policy should set maximum levels for basic rates of pay rather than for the actual rates paid at the plant level. It is the downward rigidity of the basic money wage that keeps the marginal worker in unemployment by preventing him, or his potential employer, from bidding down the money wage. Workers who are receiving above the basic wage are in a position to renegotiate the wage in the light of competitive conditions. If they are in demand then there is no reason to prevent their wage being bid up: it is not inflationary, since it actually increases the supply of a product that is in demand, and so tends to reduce the price of that product relative to others.

The second requirement is that arguments over relativities in basic pay should be taken into the open, and become the subject of political debate. The intention would be that through persuasion, different groups would be able to win the sympathy of others, so that the area of conflict would be reduced. The mere existence of open debate might have some beneficial effects. It would make it possible for groups of workers to publicize their case without having to resort to industrial disruption to attract publicity. The fact that the importance of their job was the subject of discussion might enhance morale at work, and so lead to higher productivity.

The final requirement is that fiscal policy should be organized as an automatic stabilizer by obliging the government to act as employer of last resort. By replacing unemployment benefit payments with guarantees of employment on public works the government would at once avoid the forecasting problems associated with discretionary fiscal policy, and also eliminate many of the potential abuses of the unemployment benefit system.

These proposals are immune to many of the criticisms that have been levelled against wages policies and against discretionary fiscal policies in the past. They are designed to improve efficiency at the macroeconomic level without significantly impairing efficiency at the microeconomic level. They are less restrictive than many of the conventional Keynesian macroeconomic policies. Some Keynesians may object that they concede too much to the opponents of Keynesian theory, and this may well be correct. But on the other hand the policies described here form the basis for an initiative on stagflation which could attract support from a broad spectrum of opinion — excluding of course the more doctrinaire socialist and neoclassical economists.

12.8 IMPLICATIONS FOR FUTURE RESEARCH

Much of the contemporary literature on disequilibrium theory is concerned with the taxonomy of the different regimes which can occur when arbitrary wages and prices are imposed on an economic system. In applications of the theory most attention has been given to predicting the way that the economy may switch between regimes when transactors move off their notional demand and supply schedules and onto their effective demand and supply schedules.

This book has taken a rather different approach, and has focused on a very limited number of regimes. In part this reflects the subject matter of the book, which confines attention to regimes where there is a realized excess supply of labour. But it also reflects a view that there are certain regimes which are endemic in the real world, while other regimes are largely of hypothetical interest.[15]

To establish which regimes are endemic it is necessary to have a theory of the way that wages and prices are set, and the limitations that exist on their adjustment. Many writers seem to be content with the view that wages and prices are arbitrary because there is no Walrasian auctioneer. This suggests that wages and prices may be set indifferently either above or below their equilibrium values, depending simply upon the nature of the disturbance which has occurred since they were fixed.

This is a very superficial view of the nature of market failure in the macroeconomy. This book has outlined a theory of the product market based on firms' goodwill motive, and a theory of the labour market based on the social and cultural dimensions of the wage bargain. The theory of the product market asserts that firms administer prices in response to the previous period's forecast error, and that once the price is set they do their best to supply all that is demanded at this price. The theory of the labour market asserts that unions stipulate money wages which are designed firstly to maintain differentials and secondly to achieve where possible improvements in the real wage. There is a natural disposition to set a too-high money wage, and this creates unemployment associated with demand deficiency in the product market. In the short run the usual regime is one of excess supply in both labour and product markets, with households employment-constrained and firms sales-constrained. In the longer run, however, firms can adjust their prices to eliminate the sales constraint, creating Keynesian unemployment in which only the households are constrained.

This approach suggests that much macroeconomic behaviour can still be explained by quantity adjustments within the Keynesian regime. Switching of regimes is possible, but unlikely until the economy approaches full employment. Not only the Great Depression, but also contemporary stagflation, can be explained well in terms of the Keynesian regime.

On this view, future developments of the theory should concentrate on the mechanics of firms and household behaviour in an economy with administered wages and prices. The transaction costs, which the goodwill motive aims to minimize, need to be analysed in greater detail, as do the social and cultural attitudes which underlie the preference for quantity-adjustments rather than wage-adjustments in the labour market. Such a programme of research would be microeconomic as much as macroeconomic. Its aim would be to rationalize the implicit codes of conduct which govern behaviour in both labour and product markets. It would seek to show why certain types of market institution are superior to others in harmonizing the interests of individual transactors. In doing so it would attach due weight to the social and cultural dimensions of transactors' preferences, as well as to their purely egotistical aspect.

There would still be plenty of scope for taxonomy, but the taxonomy would be linked with behavioural postulates, derived from choice-theoretic foundations, predicting which parts of the taxonomy were of greatest practical interest.

BIBLIOGRAPHICAL REVIEW

Disequilibrium theory is essentially dynamic. It is concerned with the transmission of quantity constraints and information across markets. Two issues must be distinguished: the conditions which must prevail if the transmission process is to be complete, and the nature of the transmission process itself.

The first issue has received the most attention. Using the fix-price method of Hicks (1946, 1965) it is assumed that prices, though they may vary exogenously over time, do not always adjust to eliminate excess demands. If prices do not adjust then quantity is set at the short end of the market. Malinvaud (1977) describes the conditions: (a) demand and supply are equal *ex post*, (b) no-one is forced to trade a greater quantity than he would prefer, and (c) it is impossible to arrange additional mutually advantageous trades at the given price.

The second issue has been rather neglected, as Grandmont, Laroque and Younès (1978) point out. The fix-price method generates a disequilibrium which, if uncompensated, will be passed on to the next period. Decisions taken in one period cannot be regarded as independent of those taken in another period. If quantity-constrained individuals experience an excess or shortfall of stocks of some commodity, then their desire to restore stock equilibrium will affect their demands and supplies next period. The equilibria of fix-price models are only maintainable because it is presumed that there is a tatonnement during which stocks adjust, expectations are modified and the feedback responses from the quantity rationing are completely incorporated into plans.

This second issue is very important when analysing interactions within a multimarket economy. Constraints experienced within one market will cause agents to modify their trading decisions on this and all other markets, that is, they will express effective demands and supplies instead of notional demands and supplies. There are several formulations of effective demand.

231

The first formulation is that of Drèze (1975). Drèze demands are arrived at when individuals maximize utility taking full account of all quantity constraints which may arise in the course of trading. These constraints are known with certainty and so can be fully incorporated into the individual's optimizing decision, with the result that in equilibrium the Drèze demand and the actual trade are equal. Excess effective demand is zero so there is no further response by individuals to disequilibrium. The assumption of certainty dispenses with the need for a description of the adjustment process.

There is no measure of disequilibrium in the Drèze model, nor is the equilibrium unique. It corresponds to a given distribution of shortages but cannot be pinpointed unless the method of rationing is specified. To overcome these objections a second definition of effective demand has been formulated. This concept, the Clower demand, is to be found in Benassy (1975), Barro and Grossman (1971) and Clower (1965).

The Clower demand applies when individuals are uncertain about the operation of a general rationing scheme. Agents hold point expectations of the constraints they will face which may prove incorrect. The Clower demand for a commodity is derived by ignoring any constraint which may limit purchases of that commodity, but taking all others into account. Since the operation of the rationing scheme is uncertain, expectations may not be fulfilled and the Clower demand and the actual trade will differ, giving a measure of disequilibrium and a positive excess effective demand. Final equilibrium is reached by a tatonnement on quantities during which agents revise expectations, adjust stock imbalances and modify effective demands. There is no explicit adjustment to excess effective demand in the model; expectations, if they change in response to anything at all, respond to perceptions of past quantity constraints. Here, there is scope for the adjustment process to be modelled but the attempt is not made.

Variations on the Benassy model have since been developed independently by Heller and Starr (1979) and Böhm and Levine (1979). They use a Nash concept of equilibrium to derive effective demands which are conditional on the actions of other individuals. The final trade is determined both by attempts to evade a constraint and by the behaviour of other agents. The information requirements imposed, however, are rather strong. The former model supposes that effective demands are formulated by agents who are certain about the outcome of their own actions but whose expectations that the actions of other agents will not change may not be correct. Böhm and Levine discuss the situation with the certainty assumption reversed. Such strategic behaviour gives rise to excess effective demands and a measure of disequilibrium, but once again the models do not encompass any action on the part of agents which would constitute a response.

An alternative and possibly more fruitful approach is taken by Svensson (1980). He constructs a simplified version of the Benassy model in which there are probabilities associated with the constraints on all markets. Agents are assumed to have realized their effective demands on the first market they visit and then to attempt to trade on a second. Taking the probability of constraint into account, the agent then maximizes expected utility to derive an effective demand for that good. The effective demand for the first good is then determined by maximizing expected utility, given the effective demand for the second, and taking the probability of constraint on the first market into consideration. The effective demand expressed for the first good could be the Walrasian demand, the Clower demand or any level greater than or equal to that determined by the constraint, depending on the probability of constraint. The actual trade will also depend on the given probabilities and on whether the goods concerned are complements or substitutes. In this framework, the order in which markets are visited is crucial and, not surprisingly, it turns out to be optimal to visit first the market with the smallest ration or the highest probability of constraint.

The model is similar to Benassy's and defective on the same criterion: the question of market adjustment is left open. It is, however, more instructive because decisions are taken sequentially and explicit attention is paid to spillovers between markets in the derivation of effective demands. Unfortunately the complexity of the model makes the specification of the adjustment process a difficult task. It involves the revision of many expectations and it is necessary to take account of the type of good, the order of market visits and the probability of constraint.

A rather different way of looking at disequilibrium behaviour was suggested by Grandmont and Laroque (1976a) and Hahn (1977, 1978a). Here prices are temporarily fixed during the period, but are set by firms in order to evade quantity constraints. There is disequilibrium because expectations of demand are found to be incorrect. Hahn, for example, has agents form conjectures of how a given perceived constraint might be altered if a different price were offered. This conjecture shows, for a given price, the price vector at which an agent believes he must trade as a function of the excess of his current trade over the amount indicated by the quantity signals. There will be disequilibrium if the conjectured relationship is false.

The objections to this approach are, first, that the conjectures themselves are arbitrary, second, that for a large class of conjectures equilibrium cannot be shown to exist and, third, that agents' expectations may be fulfilled although they are based on false conjectures. Falsity of conjectures would only be discovered by experiment over time and then it would be difficult to assess whether the conjecture was, in fact, incorrect or some exogenous change had occurred. Some notion of correctness of conjectures would have to be appended to close the model. This line of development has some appeal because individuals do indeed respond to disequilibrium, but the analytical difficulties to be overcome may render progress in this direction very slow.

We now turn to a quite different class of models. Grandmont (1977a), Grandmont, Laroque and Younès (1978) and Green (1980) all recognize that for the constrained equilibrium of fix-price models to be realized in a single period, time must have been assumed away and the spillover effects, stock adjustments and revisions of plans and expectations which would take place in response to excess effective demand must be subsumed within the implicit tatonnement process. These models differ from all those discussed above in that they relinquish the requirement that actual trades will be set at the short end of the market.

One contribution in this direction is that of Grandmont, Laroque and Younès. They abandon the assumption that quantities transacted are determined by the short side of the market and use a game theoretic approach to prove that the only disequilibrium result which is stable in the sense that it cannot be improved upon is the one prescribed by the short-side rule. They assume that bargaining takes place among coalitions of traders who, when trying to improve on a proposed allocation, take into account the possible reactions of traders who are left out of the coalition. Admissable recontracting processes are restricted to those which take place on one market at a time.

The authors conjecture that a more satisfactory theory would be to design bargaining processes taking place without any price limitation which would yield endogenously determined price systems and corresponding fix-price allocations as stable outcomes. It would be interesting to speculate whether there exists an admissible recontracting process whose stable outcome would allow the long side of the market to decide actual transactions, thus providing a possible link between disequilibrium theory and the theory of implicit labour contracts first formulated by Baily (1974) and Azariadis (1975).

Green (1980) also considers a model in which the short side of the market does not dictate actual trades. The actual trade reflects an incomplete or imperfect matching process as a result of which there may be some unsatisfied demand co-existing with unsatisfied supply. The second characteristic of the process is that from the individual agent's point of view it is stochastic. The precise network of trading proposals may be unknown to the agent even if his information about the state of aggregate demands and supplies is very good. Green supposes that the actual trade of an agent is a random function of his own effective demand and the aggregate effective demand and supply on the market.

The particular manipulable rationing scheme proposed produces a theory of effective demand in which effective demands arise from the solution to agents' actual maximization problems, effective excess demand is typically non-zero in a short-run equilibrium, and in a large economy, the actual trades are feasible in the sense that their expected values are zero in every market and the discrepancy from true feasibility is negligible on a per capita basis.

In this model, the quantities perceived as màrket aggregates need not be correct in order for agents to compute their trial optimal actions. The rule which prescribes the actual outcome could produce a feasible result for any vector of effective demands. This is in contrast to the short-side trading rule which produces an outcome in which trades are consistent with perceived quantity constraints.

This theory of the resolution of incompatible effective demands does admit the possibility of a description of how equilibrium might be attained through a series of disequilibrium quantity adjustments, although Green assumes it is attained without delay. The suggestion is that agents modify their perception of aggregate effective demand in the light of the difference between effective and actual aggregates in the previous period.

What is interesting is that the rationing mechanism depends on the nature of the underlying matching process. Only some matching processes allow rationing mechanisms which depend on aggregates. Thus the matching process, the rationing mechanism, the signals used by an agent to estimate his constraints and the actual outcome are all interdependent. If the dynamic process underlying this model were spelled out more fully then it would be possible to derive an equilibrium of effective quantities which is determined by the dynamic process.

NOTES

CHAPTER 1   UNEMPLOYMENT, CONCEPTS AND DEFINITIONS

1. Keynes' terminology confuses matters, for this school is known to historians of economic thought as 'neoclassical'. This school did not recognize macroeconomics as a separate branch of analysis (quite rightly so, according to some contemporary opinion). Their views on macroeconomic issues must be inferred from their writings on such diverse issues as money, the trade cycle, and the distribution of income; see Cannan (1931, 1933); Clark (1899); Jevons (1875, 1909); Marshall (1923); Pigou (1927, 1933); Robbins (1934).

2. For a simple presentation of neoclassical macroeconomics see Miller and Upton (1974). A more advanced treatment, emphasizing the monetary aspects of the theory, is Sargent (1979). The neoclassical view of the labour market is presented in Addison and Siebert (1979). A critique of the neoclassical approach to unemployment is given in section 12.2; see also Buiter (1980).

3. This interpretation of Keynes is the one emphasized by some leading post-Keynesians; see for example Minsky (1976).

4. Methods of collecting unemployment data vary between countries. UK statistics are based on those registering as unemployed; as a result, those eligible for unemployment benefit may be overrepresented in the statistics, while those not eligible for benefit are probably underrepresented. On the other hand, US statistics are based upon household surveys and so are free from the registration bias present in the UK statistics.

5. The classic analysis of aggregation problems is Green (1964). On the

conditions for consistent aggregation see Deaton and Muellbauer (1980).
6. See Flemming (1973).
7. See for example Ehrenberg (1971); Fair (1969); Feldstein (1967);
Leslie (1980); Nadiri and Rosen (1969).
8. Keynes (1936), p. 15.
9. Keynes (1936), p. 267.

CHAPTER 2   THE MULTI-MARKET ECONOMY

1. See Hansen (1953) and Klein (1966).
2. See for example Green (1976) and Simpson (1975).
3. For the problems involved in specifying the technology of a multi-product firm see Ferguson (1969), chap. 10.
4. These results are presented very succinctly in Allingham (1975).
For a more discursive treatment see Simpson (1975). The definitive work is Arrow and Hahn (1971).
5. The notation indicates a partial derivative. In general $\partial y/\partial x$ measures the rate of change of the variable y with respect to the variable x when all other variables on which y depends, apart from x, are held constant. If y depends only on x then the derivative is written dy/dx, and is known as an ordinary derivative. For the explanation of this and the other mathematical notation used in this book see for example Casson (1973).
6. For a fuller discussion of these results see Deaton and Muellbauer (1980).

CHAPTER 3   ELEMENTS OF DISEQUILIBRIUM THEORY

1. See Clower (1965).
2. The seminal works are Walras (1874) and Edgeworth (1881). For a simple exposition of the Edgeworth approach see Bacharach (1976), chap. 6. As the number of transactors increases the two theories become, loosely speaking, asymptotically equivalent, see for example Hildenbrand and Kirman (1976).
3. The seminal work in this respect is Coase (1937); see also Williamson (1975).
4. See Marshall (1961).
5. There are several useful reviews of the literature, the most readable being Moses (1977). The most up-to-date is Drazen (1980), while the

most comprehensive is Weintraub (1979); see also Grandmont (1977a).
The macroeconomic implications are emphasized by Muellbauer and
Portes (1978). The pure disequilibrium approach has been developed
alongside the 'temporary equilibrium' approach. The key papers in
this area are Benassy (1975, 1977a, 1977b), Böhm and Levine (1979),
Clower (1967), Drèze (1975), Fisher (1978), Futia (1977), Grandmont
(1977b), Grandmont and Laroque (1976a, 1976b), Grandmont, Laroque
and Younès (1978), Grandmont and Younès (1972, 1973), Green (1973),
Grossman (1969, 1974), Hahn (1973a, 1977, 1978a), Heller and Starr
(1979), Korliras (1977), Kornai (1971), Latham (1980), Svensson
(1980), Varian (1975, 1977a), and Younès (1975). For further details
see the Bibliographical Review.

6. Consider for example the case of a consumer signalling his demands
for two substitute commodities, on both of which he anticipates a
binding quantity constraint. In each case he is 99 per cent sure that the
constraint will be operative, independently of the other constraint. In
each case there is a one per cent chance that there will be no constraint,
so that he can buy as much of the commodity as he likes.

If he formulates his Drèze demands on the assumption that both
constraints will be binding then in each market he will signal a demand
for the constrained amount. His Clower demand for each commodity
will be considerably larger than this, for since the two commodities are
substitutes, the expected rationing of each increases the effective
demand for the other. The laws of probability indicate that there is a
98 per cent chance that both constraints will be operative, in which
case the outcome is the same whether he expresses his Drèze demands
or his Clower demands. Of the remaining 2 per cent, there is a 1.99
per cent probability that just one of the constraints will be slack, and a
0.01 per cent chance that both will be slack.

If just one of the constraints is slack the consumer will achieve his
Clower demand for the commodity concerned, and will be better off
than if he had expressed his Drèze demand. The only problem arises
when both constraints are slack. In this case both the Clower demands
and Drèze demands are less than ideal. The Drèze demands result in too
little consumption of each commodity, the Clower demands in too
much. If the two commodities are very close substitutes than it is
possible that the Clower demands may result in a significant overcon-
sumption of both, affording consumer welfare considerably lower than
could have been achieved using the more conservative Drèze demands.

Against this it must be recognized that the probability of this event occurring is very slim indeed. The probability is a mere one hundredth of the probability that just one of the constraints is binding, and in this case, as we have seen, the Clower demand is clearly superior to the Drèze demand.

A thorough analysis of this subject calls for a much more general approach than the one developed here. It could be argued that the example has been chosen to show the Clower demand in a favourable light. In particular it could be objected that if the transactor is at all uncertain of his constraints then he will adopt a probabilistic approach to the determination of the Drèze demands, instead of the deterministic approach used here. The interested reader should consult the references cited in note 5.

7. See for example Bowen and Finegan (1969), Ch. 15–17.

CHAPTER 4   MONEY

1. Standard texts on money include Coghlan (1980) and Newlyn and Bootle (1978). The approach taken in this chapter is rather similar to that of Goodhart (1975), chap. 1.

2. This differs from the definition used by other writers, who define a medium of exchange as anything which allows a transaction to proceed, even though settlement occurs later. A claim which is accepted on the basis that it will be settled as soon as possible is defined here, not as a medium of exchange, but as a quasi-spot claim – see section 4.4.

3. See for example Hoel (1971).

4. On the role of information and transaction costs in the theory of money see Brunner and Meltzer (1971); Galeottis and Gori (1979); Grandmont and Laroque (1973); Hahn (1973b, 1973c); Honkapohja (1978); Laidler (1974); Madden (1975, 1976); Niehans (1978); Ostroy (1973); Ostroy and Starr (1974); Starrett (1973).

5. The central role of liquidity in the demand for money is emphasized in Hicks' lectures on the *Two Triads*, see Hicks (1967).

6. See Friedman (1956).

7. This is true only for small rates of interest. For the exact definition see chapter 6 of this volume.

8. For a model of user services see Baumol (1952) and Whalen (1966).

9. See Tobin (1958) and Markovitz (1959).

10. See for example Davidson (1978) and Minsky (1976).

CHAPTER 5   DEMAND-DEFICIENCY IN MONETARY ECONOMY

1. See Barro and Grossman (1971, 1976); also Buiter and Lorie (1977).
2. See Clower (1965) and Patinkin (1965). A similar approach has been developed by Malinvaud (1977, 1980); see also Honkapohja (1979); Korliras (1975, 1980); Lorie (1977); Varian (1977b). For a critique of the policy implications usually deduced from the theory see Hildenbrand and Hildenbrand (1978). The extension of the model to an open economy is considered by Dixit (1978).
3. See Barro and Grossman (1974).

CHAPTER 6   THE ROLE OF INTEREST RATES

1. There has been continuing controversy over the appropriate measure of household wealth when households hold government debt; see for example Barro (1974) and Ferguson (1964). See also Chapter 7, note 8 of this volume.
2. See for example Branson (1979). The classic reference is Hicks (1937).
3. See Leijonhufvud (1967, 1968). For an appraisal of the Keynesian reappraisal see Bliss (1975).
4. By interpreting Keynes in this way we are conceding that money wage rigidity is crucial to involuntary unemployment; see Lange (1944) and Modigliani (1944). For a review of the structure of the Keynesian model see Chakrabarti (1979) and Froyen (1976).
5. The fact that firms produce on their supply curve is emphasized by Weintraub (1958) and Wells (1969, 1974).

CHAPTER 7   INVESTMENT

1. This objective is the intertemporal equivalent of profit-maximization, see for example Hirschleifer (1970).
2. In fact the same result holds under much weaker conditions, see Modigliani and Miller (1958).
3. For a comprehensive treatment of the 'capital stock adjustment' principle see Lund (1971).
4. The user motive for holding inventory is discussed in Whitin (1957).
5. On the speculative demand for inventory see Brennan (1958).
6. For the significance of these assumptions see Ferguson (1969).
7. This is equivalent to the condition for investment equilibrium derived by Jorgenson (1963, 1967).

8. It is necessary to consider whether any additional restrictions should be imposed on (7.28). Since this is by assumption the final period within the household's planning horizon, should it be assumed that the government will redeem all outstanding liabilities held by the households at the end of this period? Suppose that the government not only issued no bonds during the future period but also reduced the fiducial stock of money to zero at the end of the period. This would imply that all future government expenditure and all repayment of bonds would be financed out of future taxation.

'Boundary conditions' of this kind would have important implications not only for the government but also for household behaviour. It has been argued by David and Scadding (1974) that households regard the government simply as an extension of themselves, and so effectively consolidate the government's accounts with their own when estimating their future budget constraints. This implies that government debt is no longer perceived as net wealth in the way described by the Mark III model. An increase in the supply of bonds in the current period will raise expectations of future taxation and so nullify any wealth effect. All that happens is that the government directs purchasing power away from the households; the households are not fooled by the fact that the government initially finances its expenditures through bond issues because they realise that ultimately the bonds must be repaid out of taxation.

The argument for imposing boundary conditions can be criticised on three grounds. First, there is ample evidence that government debt is used to transfer tax burdens from one generation to another, so that the reduction in anticipated post-tax income relates to another generation which may not yet be born; so far as each generation is concerned, no boundary conditions need to be imposed. Furthermore there are no historical examples of an organised repayment of national debt, while there are plenty of examples of governments repudiating debt; if an increase in the supply of bonds increases the risk of repudiation then this will show up in the price of bonds (i.e. in interest rates) rather than in the future tax burden. In this case the absence of a wealth effect has nothing to do with boundary conditions. Finally there are many other mechanisms which explain why wealth effects may be weak in a full-employment economy; for example a budget deficit financed by a bond issue may have inflationary consequences which will reduce the real value of bonds, and so offset the effects of the increase in the nominal supply.

CHAPTER 8   QUANTITY ADJUSTMENT VERSUS
PRICE ADJUSTMENT

1. See respectively Webb (1979) and Howard (1976, 1980). The lack of
a proper rationale for the fix-price assumption is considered in Barro
(1979); Calvo (1979); Grossman (1979); Hahn (1978b); Howitt (1979).
It has been suggested (Barro, 1972) that the costs of reviewing pricing
decisions and administering price changes may explain short-run price
stability. It is doubtful, however, if these costs are great enough to
account for the degree of price stability observed in practice. Administrative adjustment costs may explain why prices are not adjusted continuously but only at discrete intervals of time. Thus they may explain
why firms forego frequent small adjustments of price in favour of occasional larger adjustments of price. What they cannot explain is why firms
may prefer to operate with occasional small adjustments of price, i.e.
why they deliberately restrain the average rate of price adjustment over
time.
2. See in particular Negishi (1960, 1974, 1978, 1979) and Nikaido
(1975). A related study is Marschak and Selten (1974).
3. For a detailed treatment of oligopoly theory see Koutsoyiannis
(1979). The classical papers on the kinked demand curve are Hall and
Hitch (1939) and Sweezy (1939).
4. The classical statement of this view is Knight (1921). For a recent
restatement and development of the theory see Casson (1981).
5. The time–state–preference theory of contingent forward contracts
is developed in Arrow (1970); Debreu (1959), chap. 7; Hirschleifer
(1970), chap. 9. The limitations of the theory due to transactions costs
are considered by Hahn (1973b) and Radner (1968). In what follows
the terms 'futures contract' and 'forward contract' are used inter-
changeably.
6. A model of the labour market based on this approach is presented
by Mortensen (1971); for various developments see Pissarides (1976).
A microeconomic theory of search for non-price attributes is developed
by Wilde (1979). For a general survey of market behaviour under
imperfect information see Case (1979), Hey (1979) and Rothschild
(1973).
7. On the economics of repeat-trading see Ehrenburg (1972).
8. The concept of goodwill underlies the theory of implicit contracts as
developed by Azariadis (1975, 1976); Baily (1974); Gordon, D.F. (1976);
Grossman (1978); Mayers and Thaler (1979). For a critique of the
theory of implicit contracts see Akerlof and Miyazaki (1980) and
Gordon, R.J. (1976).

CHAPTER 9   WAGE RIGIDITY

1. See for example Mulvey (1978).
2. See for example Sells (1923).
3. For an evaluation of this point see section 12.2.
4. The role of cultural factors in the labour market is touched on by Akerlof (1980) and Solow (1980a, 1980b).
5. In other words, by a 'superfairness' criterion.
6. See Oi (1962),
7. See Reder (1964).

CHAPTER 10   PROFIT EXPECTATIONS

1. The economics of insider trading are considered by Manne (1966).
2. For a review of underconsumptionist arguments see Bleaney (1976). A critical perspective is given by Durbin (1933). One of the most influential underconsumptionist writers was Hobson (1922). A much more simplistic analysis was given by Douglas (1931) and was subsequently demolished by Nash (1935). For an influential analysis of demand-deficiency centred on profits see Foster and Catchings (1925).

CHAPTER 11   DYNAMICS OF EMPLOYMENT AND OUTPUT .

1. This assumption underlies most of the elementary dynamic Keynesian models, see for example Kurihara (1963).
2. The classic paper is Samuelson (1939). A disequilibrium view of the accelerator theory is given by Grossman (1972).
3. For estimates of the capital—output ratio in the UK see Beckerman *et al.* (1965), chap. 8.
4. This is established from the properties of the cubic equation (11.34).
5. A model similar in some respects to the present one has been developed by Green and Laffont (1980).

CHAPTER 12   SUMMARY AND POLICY IMPLICATIONS

1. An alternative definition of unemployment would involve comparing actual employment with the effective labour supply as defined by Clower. In the models we have discussed, however, the distinction is not an important one because households normally perceive a binding constraint only in the labour market, so that the Clower effective supply is normally equal to the notional supply.
2. On the neoclassical approach to unemployment see Alchian (1971);

Fisher (1976); Phelps (1971); Salop (1979). For a critique along the present lines see Hines (1976); see also Buiter (1980).

3. See for example Alchian (1971), and Lucas and Rapping (1971).

4. See for example Benjamin and Kochin (1979) and Lucas and Rapping (1972). There have been many studies of the contemporary effects of unemployment benefit, see for example Grubel, Maki and Sax (1975); Katz (1977); Maki and Spindler (1975, 1978).

5. Hatton (1980) has shown that Benjamin and Kochin's results can be explained by the fact that they have detrended all their explanatory variables except the benefit—wage ratio, so that the upward trend in unemployment during the period appears to be due to the trend-inclusive variable. Once this specification error is rectified Benjamin and Kochin's results become statistically insignificant.

6. See Parsons (1973, 1977).

7. See Classen (1977) and Ehrenberg and Oaxaca (1976).

8. See for example Mattila (1974).

9. See for example Casson (1979) and Smyth and Lowe (1970).

10. See Maynard (1978).

11. For a critical appraisal of incomes policies see Parkin and Summer (1975).

12. See for example Paunio and Halttunen (1976).

13. See for example Sargent (1979) and Sargent and Wallace (1976). For a non-technical discussion see Modigliani (1977).

14. See Musgrave (1980). Similar proposals were announced by President Carter in 1977.

REFERENCES

Addison, J.T. and Siebert, W.S. (1979) *The Market for Labour: An Analytical Treatment*, Santa Monica: Goodyear.

Akerlof, G. (1980) 'The Case Against Conservative Macroeconomics: An Inaugural Lecture', *Economica* N.S. vol. 46, pp. 219–37.

Akerlof, G. and Miyazaki, H. (1980) 'The Implicit Contract Theory of Unemployment meets the Wage Bill Argument', *Review of Economic Studies* vol. 47, pp. 321–38.

Alchian, A.A. (1971) 'Information Costs, Pricing and Resource Unemployment'. In E.S. Phelps *et al. Microeconomic Foundations of Employment and Inflation Theory*, London: Macmillan.

Allingham, M. (1975) *General Equilibrium*, London: Macmillan.

Arrow, K.J. (1970) *Essays in the Theory of Risk-Bearing*, Amsterdam: North-Holland.

Arrow, K.J. and Hahn, F.H. (1971) *General Competitive Analysis*, Edinburgh: Oliver and Boyd; republished Amsterdam: North-Holland, 1979.

Azariadis, C. (1975) 'Implicit Contracts and Underemployment Equilibria', *Journal of Political Economy* vol. 83, pp. 1183–201.

Azariadis, C. (1976) 'On the Incidence of Unemployment', *Review of Economic Studies* vol. 43, pp. 115–25.

Bacharach, M. (1976) *Economics and the Theory of Games*, London: Macmillan.

Baily, M.N. (1974) 'Wages and Employment under Uncertain Demand', *Review of Economic Studies* vol. 41, pp. 37–50.

Barro, R.J. (1972) 'A Theory of Monopolistic Price Adjustment', *Review of Economic Studies* vol. 39, pp. 17–26.

Barro, R.J. (1974) 'Are Government Bonds Net Wealth?', *Journal of Political Economy* vol. 82, pp. 1095–117.

Barro, R.J. (1979) 'Second Thoughts on Keynesian Economics', *American Economic Review, Papers and Proceedings* vol. 69, pp. 54–9.

245

Barro, R.J. and Grossman, H.I. (1971) A General Disequilibrium Model of Income and Employment, *American Economic Review* vol. 61, pp. 82—93.

Barro, R.J. and Grossman, H.I. (1974) 'Suppressed Inflation and the Supply Multiplier, *Review of Economic Studies* vol. 41, pp. 87—104.

Barro, R.J. and Grossman, H.I. (1976) *Money, Employment and Inflation*, Cambridge: Cambridge University Press.

Baumol, W.J. (1952) 'The Transactions Demand for Cash: An Inventory-Theoretic Approach, *Quarterly Journal of Economics* vol. 66, pp. 545—56.

Beckerman, W. *et al.* (1965), *The British Economy in 1975*, Cambridge: Cambridge University Press for NIESR.

Benassy, J.P. (1975) 'Neo-Keynesian Disequilibrium Theory in a Monetary Economy', *Review of Economic Studies* vol. 42, pp. 503—23.

Benassy, J.P. (1977a) 'On Quantity Signals and the Foundations of Effective Demand Theory', *Scandinavian Journal of Economics* vol. 79, pp. 147—68.

Benassy, J.P. (1977b) 'A Neo-Keynesian Model of Price and Quantity Determination in Disequilibrium'. In G. Schwodiauer (ed.), *Equilibrium and Disequilibrium in Economic Theory*, Dordrecht: Reidel.

Benjamin, D.K. and Kochin, L.A. (1979) 'Searching for an Explanation of Unemployment in Interwar Britain', *Journal of Political Economy* vol. 87, pp. 441—78.

Bleaney, M. (1976) *Underconsumption Theories*, London: Lawrence & Wishart.

Bliss, C.J. (1975) 'The Reappraisal of Keynes' Economics: An Appraisal'. In M. Parkin and A.R. Nobay (eds.), *Current Economic Problems*, Cambridge: Cambridge University Press.

Böhm, V. and Levine, P. (1979) 'Temporary Equilibrium with Quantity Rationing', *Review of Economic Studies* vol. 46, pp. 361—77.

Bowen, W.G. and Finegan, T.A. (1969) *Economics of Labour Force Participation*, Princeton, N.J.: Princeton University Press.

Branson, W.H. (1979) *Macroeconomic Theory and Policy* 2nd ed., London: Harper & Row.

Brennan, M.J. (1958) 'The Supply of Storage', *American Economic Review* vol. 48, pp. 50—72. Excerpt reprinted in B.A. Goss and B.S. Yamey (eds.) (1976) *The Economics of Futures Trading*, London: Macmillan.

Brunner, K. and Meltzer, A.H. (1971) 'The Uses of Money: Money in the Theory of an Exchange Economy, *American Economic Review* vol. 61, pp. 784—805.

Buiter, W.H. (1980) 'The Macroeconomics of Dr. Pangloss: A Critical Survey of the New Classical Macroeconomics', *Economic Journal* vol. 90, pp. 34—50.

Buiter, W. and Lorie, H. (1977) 'Some Unfamiliar Properties of a Familiar Macroeconomic Model', *Economic Journal* vol. 87, pp. 743—54.

Calvo, G. (1979) 'Quasi-Walrasian Theories of Unemployment', *American Economic Review, Papers and Proceedings* vol. 69, pp. 102—7.

Cannan, E. (1931) *Modern Currency and the Regulation of Its Value*, London: P.S. King.

Cannan, E. (1933) *Economic Scares*, London: P.S. King.

Case, J.H. (1979) *Economics and the Competitive Process*, New York: New York University Press.

Casson, M.C. (1973) *Introduction to Mathematical Economics*, London: Nelson.

Casson, M.C. (1979) *Youth Unemployment*, London: Macmillan.

Casson, M.C. (1981) *The Entrepreneur: An Economic Theory*, Oxford: Martin Robertson.

Chakrabarti, S.K. (1979) *The Two-Sector General Theory Model*, London: Macmillan.

Clark, J.B. (1899) *The Distribution of Wealth*, New York: Macmillan.

Classen, K.P. (1977) 'The Effect of Unemployment Insurance on the Duration of Unemployment and Subsequent Earnings', *Industrial and Labour Relations Review* vol. 30, pp. 438—44.

Clower, R.W. (1965) 'The Keynesian Counterrevolution: A Theoretical Appraisal'. In F.H. Hahn and F. Brechling (eds.), *The Theory of Interest Rates*, London: Macmillan. Reprinted in P.G. Korliras and R.S. Thorn (eds.) (1979) *Modern Macroeconomics*, London: Harper & Row.

Clower, R.W. (1967) 'A Reconsideration of the Microfoundations of Monetary Theory', *Western Economic Journal* vol. 6, pp. 1—9.

Coase, R.H. (1937) 'The Nature of the Firm', *Economica, N.S.* vol. 4, pp. 386—405.

Coghlan, R. (1980) *The Theory of Money and Finance*, London: Macmillan.

David, P.A. and Scadding, J.L. (1974) Private Savings, Ultrarationality, Aggregation and 'Denison's Law', *Journal of Political Economy* vol. 82, pp. 225—49.

Davidson, P. (1978) *Money and the Real World* 2nd ed., London: Macmillan.

Deaton, A. and Muellbauer, J. (1980) *Economics and Consumer Behaviour*, Cambridge: Cambridge University Press.

Debreu, G. (1959) *Theory of Value*, New Haven: Yale University Press.

Dixit, A. (1978) 'The Balance of Trade in a Model of Temporary Keynesian Equilibrium', *Review of Economic Studies* vol. 45, pp. 393–404.

Douglas, C.H. (1931) *The Monopoly of Credit*, London: Chapman & Hall.

Drazen, A. (1980) 'Recent Developments in Macroeconomic Disequilibrium Theory', *Econometrica* vol. 48, pp. 283–305.

Drèze, J.H. (1975) Existence of an Exchange Equilibrium under Price Rigidities, *International Economic Review* vol. 16, pp. 301–20.

Durbin, E.F.M. (1933) *Purchasing Power and Trade Depression*, London: Jonathan Cape.

Edgeworth, F.Y. (1881) *Mathematical Psychics*, London: Kegan Paul.

Ehrenberg, R.G. (1971) 'Heterogeneous Labour, the Internal Labour Market, and the Dynamics of the Employment – Hours Decision', *Journal of Economic Theory* vol. 3, pp. 85–104.

Ehrenberg, R.G. and Oaxaca, R.L. (1976) 'Unemployment Insurance, Duration of Unemployment and Subsequent Wage Gain', *American Economic Review* vol. 66, pp. 745–66.

Ehrenburg, A.S.C. (1972) *Repeat Buying: Theory and Applications*, Amsterdam: North-Holland.

Fair, R.C. (1969) *The Short-run Demand for Workers and Hours*, Amsterdam: North-Holland.

Feldstein, M. (1967) 'Specification of the Labour Input in the Aggregate Production Function', *Review of Economic Studies* vol. 34, pp. 375–86.

Ferguson, C.E. (1969) *The Neoclassical Theory of Production and Distribution*, Cambridge: Cambridge University Press.

Ferguson, J.M. (ed.) (1964) *Public Debt and Future Generations*, Chapel Hill: University of North Carolina Press.

Fisher, F.M. (1978) 'Quantity Constraints, Spillovers and the Hahn Process', *Review of Economic Studies* vol. 45, pp. 19–31.

Fisher, M.R. (1976) 'The New Microeconomics of Unemployment'. In G.D.N. Worswick (ed.) *The Concept and Measurement of Involuntary Unemployment*, London: Allen & Unwin, pp. 83–94.

Flemming, J.S. (1973) 'The Consumption Function when Capital Markets are Imperfect: The Permanent Income Hypothesis Reconsidered', *Oxford Economic Papers* vol. 25, pp. 160—72.

Foster, W.T. and Catchings, W. (1925) *Profits*, Boston: Houghton Mifflin.

Friedman, M. (1956) 'The Quantity Theory of Money – A Restatement'. In M. Friedman (ed.) *Studies in the Quantity Theory of Money*, Chicago: University of Chicago Press, No. 1—21.

Froyen, R. T. (1976) 'The Aggregative Structure of Keynes' General Theory', *Quarterly Journal of Economics* vol. 90, pp. 369—87.

Futia, C. A. (1977) 'Excess Supply Equilibria', *Journal of Economic Theory* vol. 14, pp. 200—20.

Galeotti, M. and Gori, F. (1979) 'Some Notes on a Dynamical Approach to Money-Mediated Exchange'. In M. Aoki and A. Marzollo (eds.) *New Trends in Dynamic System Theory and Economics*, London: Academic Press, pp. 391—403.

Goodhart, C. A. E. (1975) *Money, Information and Uncertainty*, London: Macmillan.

Gordon, D. F. (1976) 'A Neo-Classical Theory of Keynesian Unemployment'. In K. Brunner and A. H. Meltzer (eds.) *The Phillips Curve and Labour Markets*, Amsterdam: North-Holland.

Gordon, R. J. (1976) 'Aspects of the Theory of Involuntary Unemployment, – A Comment'. In K. Brunner and A. H. Meltzer (eds.) *The Phillips Curve and Labour Markets*, Amsterdam: North-Holland.

Grandmont, J. M. (1977a) 'The Logic of the Fix-Price Method', *Scandinavian Journal of Economics* vol. 79, 167—86.

Grandmont, J. M. (1977b) 'Temporary General Equilibrium Theory', *Econometrica* vol. 75, 535—72.

Grandmont, J. M. and Laroque, G. (1973) Money in a Pure Consumption Loan Model, *Journal of Economic Theory* vol. 6, 382—95.

Grandmont, J. M. and Laroque, G. (1976a) 'On Temporary Keynesian Equilibria', *Review of Economic Studies* vol. 43, 53—67.

Grandmont, J. M. and Laroque, G. (1976b) 'On the Liquidity Trap', *Econometrica* vol. 44, pp. 129—35.

Grandmont, J.M., Laroque, G. and Younès, Y. (1978) 'Equilibrium with Quantity Rationing and Recontracting', *Journal of Economic Theory* vol. 19, pp. 84—102.

Grandmont, J.M. and Younès, Y. (1972) 'On the Role of Money and the Existence of a Monetary Equilibrium', *Review of Economic Studies* vol. 39, pp. 355—72.

Grandmont, J.M. and Younès, Y. (1973) 'On the Efficiency of Monetary

Equilibrium', *Review of Economic Studies* vol. 40, pp. 149–66.

Green, H. A. J. (1964) *Aggregation in Economic Analysis,* Princeton, N.J.: Princeton University Press.

Green, H. A. J. (1976) *Consumer Theory* revised ed., London: Macmillan.

Green, J. R. (1973) 'Temporary General Equilibrium in a Sequential Trading Model with Spot and Future Transactions', *Econometrica* vol. 41, pp. 1103–24.

Green, J. R. (1980) 'On the Theory of Effective Demand', *Economic Journal* vol. 90, pp. 341–52.

Green, J.R. and Laffont, J.-J. (1980) 'Disequilibrium Dynamics with Inventories and Anticipatory Price-Setting', NBER Working Paper No. 453.

Grossman, H. I. (1969) 'Theories of Markets without Recontracting', *Journal of Economic Theory* vol. 4, pp. 476–9.

Grossman, H. I. (1972) 'A Choice-Theoretic Model of an Income-Investment Accelerator', *American Economic Review* vol. 62, pp. 630–41.

Grossman, H. I. (1974) 'The Nature of Quantities in Market Disequilibrium', *American Economic Review* vol. 64, 509–14.

Grossman, H. I. (1978) 'Risk-Shifting, Layoffs and Seniority', *Journal of Monetary Economics* vol. 4, 661–86.

Grossman, H. I. (1979) 'Why Does Aggregate Employment Fluctuate?', *American Economic Review, Papers and Proceedings* vol. 69, 64–9.

Grubel, H. G., Maki, D. and Sax, S. (1975) 'Real and Insurance-induced Unemployment in Canada, *Canadian Journal of Economics* vol. 8, pp. 174–91.

Hahn, F. H. (1973a) *On the Notion of Equilibrium in Economics,* Cambridge: Cambridge University Press.

Hahn, F. H. (1973b) 'On Transaction Costs, Inessential Sequence Economies and Money', *Review of Economic Studies* vol. 40, pp. 449–62.

Hahn, F. H. (1973c) 'On the Foundations of Monetary Theory'. In M. Parkin (ed.) *Essays in Modern Economics,* London: Longman.

Hahn, F. H. (1977) 'Exercises in Conjectural Equilibria', *Scandinavian Journal of Economics* vol. 79, 210–26.

Hahn, F. H. (1978a) 'On Non-Walrasian Equilibria', *Review of Economic Studies* vol. 45, pp. 1–17.

Hahn, F. H. (1978b) 'Keynesian Economics and General Equilibrium Theory: Reflections on Some Current Debates'. In G. C. Harcourt (ed.), *The Microeconomic Foundations of Macroeconomics,* London:

Macmillan.

Hall, R. L. and Hitch, C. J. (1939) 'Price Theory and Business Behaviour', *Oxford Economic Papers* vol. 2, pp. 12–45. Reprinted in T. Wilson and P. W. S. Andrews (eds.) (1951) *Oxford Studies in the Price Mechanism*, Oxford: Clarendon Press.

Hansen, A. H. (1953) *A Guide to Keynes*, New York: McGraw-Hill.

Hatton, T. J. (1980) 'Unemployment in Britain between the World Wars: A Role for the Dole?', University of Essex, Department of Economics, Discussion Paper No. 139.

Heller, W. P. and Starr, R. (1979) 'Unemployment Equilibrium with Myopic Complete Information', *Review of Economic Studies* vol. 46, pp. 339–59.

Hey, J. D. (1979) *Uncertainty in Microeconomics*, Oxford: Martin Robertson.

Hicks, J. R. (1937) 'Mr. Keynes and the 'Classics': A Suggested Interpretation', *Econometrica* vol. 5, pp. 147–59.

Hicks, J. R. (1946) *Value and Capital* 2nd ed., Oxford: Clarendon Press.

Hicks, J. R. (1965) *Capital and Growth*, Oxford: Oxford University Press.

Hicks, J. R. (1967) *Critical Essays in Monetary Theory*, Oxford: Clarendon Press.

Hildenbrand, K. and Hildenbrand, W. (1978) 'On Keynesian Equilibria with Unemployment and Quantity Rationing', *Journal of Economic Theory* vol. 18, pp. 255–77.

Hildenbrand, W. and Kirman, A.P. (1976) *Introduction to Equilibrium Analysis*, Amsterdam: North-Holland.

Hines, A. G. (1976) 'The Microeconomic Foundations of Employment and Inflation Theory: Bad Old Wine in Elegant New Bottles'. In G. D. N. Worswick (ed.) *The Concept and Measurement of Involuntary Unemployment*, London: Allen & Unwin.

Hirschleifer, J. (1970) *Investment, Interest and Capital*, Englewood Cliffs, N.J.: Prentice-Hall.

Hobson, J. A. (1922) *The Economics of Unemployment*, London: Allen & Unwin.

Hoel, P. G. (1971) *Introduction to Mathematical Statistics* 4th ed., Chichester, Sussex: Wiley.

Honkapohja, S. (1978) 'On the Efficiency of a Competitive Monetary Equilibrium with Transaction Costs', *Review of Economic Studies* vol. 45, pp. 405–15.

Honkapohja, S. (1979) 'On the Dynamics of Disequilibria in a Macro

Model with Flexible Wages and Prices'. In M. Aoki and A. Marzollo (eds.) *New Trends in Dynamic System Theory and Economics*, London: Academic Press.

Howard, D. (1976) 'The Disequilibrium Model in a Controlled Economy', *American Economic Review* vol. 66, pp. 871–9.

Howard, D. H. (1980) *Disequilibrium Model in a Controlled Economy*, Farnborough; Hants: Lexington Books.

Howitt, P. (1979) 'Evaluating the Non-Market-Clearing Approach', *American Economic Review, Papers and Proceedings* vol. 69, pp. 60–9.

Jevons, W. S. (1875) *Money and the Mechanism of Exchange*, London: H. S. King.

Jevons, W. S. (1909) *Investigations in Currency and Finance*, (ed. H. S. Foxwell), New edition, London: Macmillan.

Jorgenson, D. W. (1963) 'Capital Theory and Investment Behaviour', *American Economic Review* vol. 53, pp. 247–59.

Jorgenson, D. W. (1967) 'The Theory of Investment Behaviour'. In R. Ferber (ed.), *Determinants of Investment Behaviour*, New York: NBER.

Katz, A. (ed.) (1977) 'The Economics of Unemployment Insurance', *Industrial and Labour Relations Review* vol. 30, pp. 431–526.

Keynes, J. M. (1936) *The General Theory of Employment, Interest and Money*, London: Macmillan. Republished (1973) *The Collected Writings of John Maynard Keynes, Volume VII*, London: Macmillan, for the Royal Economic Society.

Klein, L. R. (1966) *The Keynesian Revolution* 2nd ed., London: Macmillan.

Knight, F. H. (1921) *Risk, Uncertainty and Profit*, Boston: Houghton Mifflin. Republished Chicago: University of Chicago Press, 1971.

Korliras, P. G. (1975) 'A Disequilibrium Macroeconomic Model', *Quarterly Journal of Economics* vol. 89, 56–80. Reprinted in P. G. Korliras and R. S. Thorn (eds.) (1979) *Modern Macroeconomics*, London: Harper & Row.

Korliras, P. G. (1977) 'Non-Tatonnement and Disequilibrium Adjustments in Macroeconomic Models'. In G. Schwödiauer (ed.), *Equilibrium and Disequilibrium in Economic Theory*, Dordrecht: Reidel.

Korliras, P. G. (1980) 'Disequilibrium Theories and their Policy Implications: Towards a Synthetic Disequilibrium Approach', *Kyklos* vol. 33, pp. 449–74.

Kornai, J. (1971) *Anti-Equilibrium*, Amsterdam: North-Holland.

Koutsoyiannis, A. (1979) *Modern Microeconomics* 2nd ed., London: Macmillan.

Kurihara, K. K. (1963) *Applied Dynamic Economics*, London: Allen & Unwin.

Laidler, D. E. W. (1974) 'Information, Money and the Macroeconomics of Inflation', *Swedish Journal of Economics* vol. 76, pp. 26–41. Reprinted in D. E. W. Laidler, (1975) *Essays on Money and Inflation*, Manchester: Manchester University Press.

Lange, O. (1944) *Price Flexibility and Full Employment*, Bloomington: Principia Press.

Latham, R. (1980) 'Quantity-Constrained Demand Functions', *Econometrica* vol. 48, pp. 307–13.

Leijonhufvud, A. (1967) 'Keynes and the Keynesians: A Suggested Interpretation', *American Economic Review* vol. 57, 401–10. Reprinted in P. G. Korliras and R. S. Thorn (eds.) (1979) *Modern Macroeconomics*, London: Harper & Row.

Leijonhufvud, A. (1968) *On Keynesian Economics and the Economics of Keynes*, London: Oxford University Press.

Leslie, D. G. (1980) 'A Supply and Demand Analysis of Hours of Work'. In D. Currie and W. Peters (eds.), *Contemporary Economic Analysis, Volume 2*, London: Croom Helm.

Lorie, H. (1977) 'A Model of Keynesian Dynamics', *Oxford Economic Papers* vol. 29, pp. 30–47.

Lucas, R. E. and Rapping, L. A. (1971) 'Real Wages, Employment and Inflation', in E. S. Phelps *et al.* (eds.), *Microeconomic Foundations of Employment and Inflation Theory*, London: Macmillan.

Lucas, R. E. and Rapping, L. A. (1972) 'Unemployment in the Great Depression: Is there a Full Explanation?', *Journal of Political Economy* vol. 80, pp. 186–91.

Lund, P.J. (1971) *Investment : the Study of an Economic Aggregate*, Edinburgh: Oliver & Boyd; republished Amsterdam: North-Holland, 1979.

Madden, P. J. (1975) 'Efficient Sequences of Non-monetary Exchange', *Review of Economic Studies* vol. 42, pp. 581–96.

Madden, P. J. (1976) 'A Theorem on Decentralised Exchange', *Econometrica* vol. 44, pp. 787–92.

Maki, D. R. and Spindler, Z. A. (1975) The Effect of Unemployment Compensation on the Rate of Unemployment in Great Britain, *Oxford Economic Papers* vol. 27, pp. 440–54.

Maki, D. R. and Spindler, Z. A. (1978) 'More on the Effects of Unemployment Compensation on the Rate of Unemployment in Great Britain', *Oxford Economic Papers* vol. 30, pp. 147–64.

Malinvaud, E. (1977) *The Theory of Unemployment Reconsidered*, Oxford: Basil Blackwell.

Malinvaud, E. (1980) *Profitability and Unemployment*, Cambridge: Cambridge University Press.

Manne, H. G. (1966) *Insider Trading and the Stock Market*, New York: Free Press.

Markovitz, H. M. (1959) *Portfolio Selection*, New Haven: Yale University Press.

Marschak, T. and Selten, R. (1974) *General Equilibrium with Price-Making Firms*, Berlin: Springer.

Marshall, A. (1923) *Money, Credit and Commerce*, London: Macmillan.

Marshall, A. (1961) *Principles of Economics*, 9th edition (ed. C. W. Guillebaud), London: Macmillan for the Royal Economic Society.

Mattila, J. P. (1974) 'Job Quitting and Frictional Unemployment', *American Economic Review* vol. 64, pp. 235–9.

Mayers, D. and Thaler, R. (1979) 'Sticky Wages and Implicit Contracts: A Transactional Approach', *Economic Inquiry* vol. 17, pp. 559–73.

Maynard, G. W. (1978) 'Keynes and Unemployment Today', *Three Banks Review*, No. 120.

Miller, M. H. and Upton, C. W. (1974) *Macroeconomics: A Neoclassical Introduction*, Homewood, Illinois: Irwin.

Minsky, H. P. (1976) *John Maynard Keynes*, London: Macmillan.

Modigliani, F. (1944) 'Liquidity Preference and the Theory of Interest and Money', *Econometrica* vol. 12, pp. 45–88. Reprinted in F. A. Lutz and L.W. Mints (eds.) (1951) *Readings in Monetary Theory*, Philadelphia: Blakiston for the American Economic Association.

Modigliani, F. (1977) 'The Monetarist Controversy or, Should we Forsake Stabilisation Policies?', *American Economic Review* vol. 69, pp. 1–19. Reprinted in P. G. Korliras and R. S. Thorn (eds.) (1979) *Modern Macroeconomics*, London: Harper & Row.

Modigliani, F. and Miller, M. H. (1958) Cost of Capital, Corporation Finance and the Theory of Investment, *American Economic Review* vol. 48, pp. 261–97.

Mortensen, D. T. (1971) 'A Theory of Wage and Employment Dynamics'. In E. S. Phelps *et al.*, *Microeconomic Foundations of Employment and Inflation Theory*, London: Macmillan.

Moses, E. (1977) *Sunday: A Problem in Equilibrium and Dynamics*, M. A. Dissertation, University of Essex, Colchester, Essex.

Muellbauer, J. and Portes, R. (1978) 'Macroeconomic Models with Quantity Rationing', *Economic Journal* vol. 88, pp. 788–821. Revised version in W. H. Branson, (1979) *Macroeconomic Theory and Policy* 2nd ed., London: Harper & Row.

Mulvey, C. (1978) *The Economic Analysis of Trade Unions*, Oxford: Martin Robertson.

Musgrave, R. S. (1980) *Abolishing Unemployment*, London: Economic Research Council.

Nadiri, M. I. and Rosen, S. (1969) Interrelated Factor Demand Functions, *American Economic Review* vol. 59, pp. 457–71.

Nash, E. F. (1935) *Machines and Purchasing Power*, London: Routledge.

Negishi, T. (1960) 'Monopolistic Competition and General Equilibrium', *Review of Economic Studies* vol. 28, pp. 196–201.

Negishi, T. (1974) 'Involuntary Unemployment and Market Imperfection', *Economic Studies Quarterly* vol. 25, pp. 32–41.

Negishi, T. (1978) 'Existence of an Under-Employment Equilibrium'. In G. Schwödiauer (ed.) *Equilibrium and Disequilibrium in Economic Theory*, Dordrecht: Reidel.

Negishi, T. (1979) *Microeconomic Foundations of Keynesian Macroeconomics*, Amsterdam: North-Holland.

Newlyn, W. T. and Bootle, R. P. (1978) *Theory of Money* 3rd ed., London: Oxford University Press.

Niehans, J. (1978) *Theory of Money*, Baltimore: Johns Hopkins University Press.

Nikaido, H. (1975) *Monopolistic Competition and Effective Demand*, Princeton: Princeton University Press.

Oi, W. Y. (1962) 'Labour as a Quasi-Fixed Factor', *Journal of Political Economy* vol. 70, pp. 538–55.

Ostroy, J. M. (1973) The Informational Efficiency of Monetary Exchange, *American Economic Review* vol. 63, 597–610.

Ostroy, J. M. and Starr, R. M. (1974) 'Money and the Decentralisation of Exchange', *Econometrica* vol. 42, pp. 1093–114.

Parkin, M. and Sumner, M. T. (eds.) (1975) *Incomes Policy and Inflation*, Manchester: Manchester University Press.

Parsons, D. O. (1973) 'Quit Rates over Time: A Search and Information Approach', *American Economic Review* vol. 63, pp. 390–401.

Parsons, D. O. (1977) 'Models of Labour Market Turnover: A Theoretical and Empirical Survey'. In R. G. Ehrenberg (ed.) *Research in Labour Economics, Volume 1*, Greenwich, Conn.: Jai Press.

Patinkin, D. (1965), *Money, Interest and Prices* 2nd ed., London: Harper & Row.

Paunio, J. J. and Halttunen, H. (1976) 'The 'Nordic' Approach to Inflation: Interpretation and Comments'. In M. Parkin and G. Zis (eds.) *Inflation in the World Economy*, Manchester: Manchester University Press.

Phelps, E. S. (1971) 'The New Microeconomics in Employment and Inflation Theory'. In E. S. Phelps *et al.*, *Microeconomic Foundations of Employment and Inflation Theory*, London: Macmillan.

Pigou, A. C. (1927) *Industrial Fluctuations*, London: Macmillan.

Pigou, A. C. (1933) *The Theory of Unemployment*, London: Macmillan.

Pissarides, C. A. (1976) *Labour Market Adjustment*, Cambridge: Cambridge University Press.

Radner, R. (1968) 'Competitive Equilibrium under Uncertainty', *Econometrica* vol. 36, pp. 31–58. Reprinted in P. Diamond and M. Rothschild (eds.) (1978) *Uncertainty in Economics*, London: Academic Press.

Reder, W. (1964) 'Wage Structure and Structural Unemployment', *Review of Economic Studies* vol. 31, pp. 309–22.

Robbins, L. (1934) *The Great Depression*, London: Macmillan.

Rothschild, M. (1973) 'Models of Market Organisation with Imperfect Information: A Survey, *Journal of Political Economy* vol. 81, pp. 1283–308. Reprinted in P. Diamond and M. Rothschild (eds.) (1978) *Uncertainty in Economics*, London: Academic Press.

Salop, S. C. (1979) A Model of the Natural Rate of Unemployment', *American Economic Review* vol. 69, pp. 117–25.

Samuelson, P. A. (1939) 'Interaction between the Multiplier Analysis and the Principle of Acceleration', *Review of Economic Statistics* vol. 21, pp. 75–8.

Sargent, T. J. (1979) *Macroeconomic Theory*, London: Academic Press.

Sargent, T. J. and Wallace, N. (1976) 'Rational Expectations and the Theory of Economic Policy', *Journal of Monetary Economics* vol. 2, pp. 169–83. Reprinted in P. G. Korliras and R. S. Thorn (eds.) (1979) *Modern Macroeconomics*, London: Harper & Row.

Sells, D. (1923) *The British Trade Boards System*, London: P. S. King.

Simpson, D. (1975) *General Equilibrium Analysis*, Oxford: Basil Blackwell.

Smyth, D. J. and Lowe, P. D. (1970) 'The Vestibule to the Occupational Ladder and Unemployment: Some Econometric Evidence on United

Kingdom Structural Unemployment', *Industrial and Labour Relations Review* vol. 23, pp. 561–5.

Solow, R. M. (1980a) 'On Theories of Unemployment', *American Economic Review*, vol. 70, pp. 1–9.

Solow, R. M. (1980b) 'Alternative Approaches to Macroeconomic Theory: A Partial View', *Canadian Journal of Economics* vol. 12, pp. 339–54.

Starrett, D. A. (1973) 'Inefficiency and the Demand for "Money" in a Sequence Economy', *Review of Economic Studies* vol. 40, pp. 437–48.

Svensson, L. E. O. (1980) 'Effective Demand and Stochastic Rationing', *Review of Economic Studies* vol. 48, pp. 339–55.

Sweezy, P. M. (1939) 'Demand under Conditions of Oligopoly', *Journal of Political Economy* vol. 47, pp. 568–73.

Tobin, J. (1958) 'Liquidity Preference as Behaviour Toward Risk', *Review of Economic Studies* vol. 25, pp. 65–86.

Varian, H. R. (1975) 'On Persistent Disequilibrium', *Journal of Economic Theory* vol. 10, pp. 218–28.

Varian, H. R. (1977a) 'Non-Walrasian Equilibria', *Econometrica* vol. 45, pp. 573–90.

Varian, H. R. (1977b) 'The Stability of a Disequilibrium IS-LM Model', *Scandinavian Journal of Economics* vol. 79, pp. 260–70.

Walras, L. (1874) *Elements of Pure Economics*, W. Jaffe (ed.) (1954) English edition, London: Allen & Unwin for Royal Economic Society.

Webb, R. H. (1979) 'Wage-Price Restraint and Macroeconomic Disequilibrium', *Federal Reserve Bank of Richmond Economic Review* vol. 65, no. 3, pp. 14–25.

Weintraub, E. R. (1979) *Microfoundations*, Cambridge: Cambridge University Press.

Weintraub, S. (1958) *An Approach to the Theory of Income Distribution*, Philadelphia: Chilton.

Wells, P. (1960) 'Keynes' Aggregate Supply Function: A Suggested Interpretation', *Economic Journal* vol. 70, pp. 536–42.

Wells, P. (1974) 'Keynes' Employment Function', *History of Political Economy* vol. 6, pp. 158–62.

Whalen, E. L. (1966) 'A Rationalisation of the Precautionary Demand for Cash', *Quarterly Journal of Economics* vol. 80, pp. 314–24.

Whitin, T. M. (1957) *The Theory of Inventory Management* 2nd ed., Princeton, N.J.: Princeton University Press.

Wilde, L. L. (1979) 'An Information-theoretic Approach to Job Quits'. In S. A. Lippman and J. J. McCall (eds.), *Studies in the Economics of Search*, Amsterdam: North-Holland.

Williamson, O. E. (1975) *Markets and Hierarchies*, New York: Free Press.

Younès, Y. (1975) 'On the Role of Money in the Process of Exchange and the Existence of a Non-Walrasian Equilibrium', *Review of Economic Studies* vol. 52, pp. 489–502.

INDEX

accelerator, investment   190–2, 195–8
adaptive expectations   188–93
addi-log utility   29–31, 112–22
aggregation   1, 7, 19
auctioneer   35–40, 207, 229

banks   57–59
bankruptcy   52–3
Barro and Grossman model   76–95
barter, parable of   59–64
benefits, effect on unemployment   3, 159, 209–15
bonds, *see* indexation of bonds; *see also* interest rates, portfolio choice
budget constraints   20

capital stock   123–33, 190–5, 197–8
classical economics   2–3, 43–45, 98, 205–6, 217
Clower demands   48–51, 232–3
competition   2, 33–43
confidence, business   4, 71–2
consumption function   17, 34, 84–6
contingent contracts   143, 148–9

demand, *see* Clower demand; *see also* excess demand and supply

demand management   215, 224–8
depreciation   56, 70, 123, 128–31
disequilibrium
    principle of   33–4, 141–2
    literature of   231–5
dividends   124–5, 184
divorce of ownership and control   5
Drèze demand   48–51, 232–3

Edgeworth process   35–7
equilibrium
    existence and uniqueness   23
    general   21–4, 27–8, 79–82, 134–5
    partial   4
    social efficiency of   23
equity, valuation of   99, 124, 129, 172–4, 184–5
excess demand and supply
    effective   43, 83, 91–5, 231–5
    net   20
    notional   37–8, 91–5
    realized   9–12, 37–40
excess employment   16
expectations   3, 21–4, 27–8, 49, 79–82, 99–100, 134–8, 170–95,
        209–15, 224–7, 231–5

forward contracts, *see* futures contracts
frictional unemployment   2
futures contracts   5, 97, 136–8, 223

Great Depression   71, 212, 229
goodwill   126, 143–4, 147–57, 207–8
government
    behaviour   78
    budget constraint   78, 101, 136–8

homotheticity   30

IS curve   105–22, 138
implicit contracts   147–57, 234
income effect   24, 29–31, 42–3
incomes policy, *see* wages policy; *see also* prices policy
indexation of bonds   184–5
inflation   88–91, 97–100, 217–24
information, cost of   38–40, 56, 203—4, 210
insider trading   172–4
interest rates   3, 7, 96–122, 129–35
intertemporal substitution, *see* substitution, intertemporal
inventories   126–7, 192–5, 198–202
investment   123–40, 184, 190–202

Job Creation Programme   226

Keynesian economics   4, 16–8, 34, 54–5, 73–4, 84–7, 94–5, 98,
      108–11, 120–2, 138–40, 207, 212, 215–7, 224–5, 228–30

LM curve   105–22, 138
layoffs, *see* redundancies
leisure   3, 9–12, 25
liquidity   51–3, 67–70, 74

monetary policy   6
money
   excess demand for   4, 83, 87—8, 181–3, 206
   in macro models   76–122
   theory of   54–75
money illusion   12
multiplier
   income   85, 195–9
   supply   90–1

natural rate of unemployment   3
neoclassical economics   3, 209—15

oligopoly theory   142–6
overemployment   16

preferences of households   25, 76, 99
portfolio choice   67–72, 100–5
price
    adjustment of   24, 33–40, 141–55, 200–2
    properties of   20, 22, 35–7, 40–1
    and interest rates   99–122
prices policy   217–8
productivity, promotion of   222–4
profit
    definition of   20
    expectations of   23, 100, 170–87, 190
    retention of   124, 133, 184

quantity adjustment   91–5, 141–55, 169
quantity constraint   41–8, 82–91, 189–90, 207, 231–5
quantity theory of money   65, 115–6
quits   144, 149–51, 212–3

rationing schemes   65, 232–5
recontracting   37–40, 141–2
redundancies   13–4, 212–3
repressed inflation   88–91

saving   100–22, 134–5, 137–40
search   3, 62–4, 144, 149–52, 209–15
separations, *see* quits; *see also* redundancies
short-side rule for quantities   41–3, 153, 231
short-time working   7–9
speculative premium   68–70, 75
stabilizer, automatic   224–8
stability conditions   197–202
stagflation   6, 91, 217–24, 229

statics, comparative 43
statistics of unemployment 6
stock-adjustment 51–3
substitution effect 29–31, 42–3
    intertemporal 96–122, 129–33
supply, *see* excess demand and supply

trade unions 3, 157–64, 221–2
transaction costs 39–40, 64–5

underemployment 9, 45–7
unemployment
    definition of 9–12
    dimension of 6–9
    involuntary 12–4
    voluntary 12–4
See also classical economics, Keynesian economics, neoclassical economics
utility, *see* addi-log utility; *see also* preferences of households

wage rates 12–3, 150–2, 154–69, 215–7
wages policy 178–80, 205, 217–22, 224
Walras' Law 17, 20–2, 26, 78, 125, 170, 182
Walrasian auctioneer, *see* auctioneer